Divine Accordance

Holly Burger

Divine Accordance, First Edition, Paperback

Lightworkers Alliance®, Art-a-Fire®

Holly Burger, Longmont, Colorado

ISBN: 978-0-9838551-2-5

Cover art and design, text layout and design, publishing by Holly Burger.
Published via CreateSpace.com, Amazon.com.

Editors:

Alli Brook

Michelle LeJeune

Elizabeth Jackson

For more information:

www.LightworkersAlliance.com

holly@lightworkersalliance.com

This book is dedicated to my family. To my husband, Bobby, who somehow saw my Light beyond the craziness; you are the love of my life. To my daughter, Jennifer, born working magic as a grounding mark and stabilizing force for me. And to Beck and Nick, my incredible stepsons, the boys God gave me.

Table of Contents

Chapter One

An Introduction to Lightwork

I want to begin by telling you what is possible to glean from this book. Communication: A path is set forth here, in detail, for you to open your personal channels of communication to your guides and Angels. Clarity: This book offers the journey that I took to become a clear channel of information that is from ethereal pure Light Beings.

This book explains a simple meditation technique that I use and teach. I can't emphasize enough what meditation has done for me, how it has changed my life and enhanced my ability to receive spiritual guidance. As a person who hears and sees beings that do not have bodies (ethereal beings) I consider myself a channel. I am not a trance channel; I am present and conscious for all communication. I am an antenna for frequencies that are available to everyone and I use my ability to relay messages in my work as an intuitive consultant, or as I call it a *conscious channel*. If you are interested in learning more about your own abilities and gifts, please read and do the exercises in these pages.

The backbone of *Divine Accordance* is prayer. These prayers were written by me, I typed them or scribbled them on paper, but I am not the true author; that credit goes to my spiritual guides. The prayers came to me during my meditations and while working with clients. For years, I have shared these prayers and witnessed their many successes. *Divine Accordance* is the result of thousands of readings and healings. It deals with healing a vast range of emotional pollution, physical stagnation and ego struggles. Each prayer and idea in this book is structured for you to release negativity and heal so that you can be an amazing Lightworker. Or an amazing mom. Or crossing guard. Or structural engineer, lawyer, advocate, healer; these prayers are not directed at who you are as much as what you are. Inherently, you are Light.

However, my Lightworking story doesn't start off pretty. As a young child I heard strange voices and sensed that I was being watched by someone or something. I grew up feeling different, distracted and confused. I thought I might be crazy, but was never able to talk about it. Although my parents were not religious, many of my friends and extended family were. I attended a range churches and began to study the differences noticing many judgments portrayed in religion. At the age of twelve, I told a religious friend who was not allowed to wear pants that I didn't think God wanted my legs to freeze. In my way, I felt that the Almighty was caring and nurturing, not restrictive or cruel. But that small knowing didn't help with my sense of abandonment. For years, I felt alone, very, very alone, as if I had been somehow accidentally dropped on Earth.

From an early age I was known as "sensitive". There were times I felt intuitive, but never psychic. Sensitivity was something I felt ashamed of; it came with vulnerability and emotional pain. As a child, I suffered on the inside because of these sensitivities. I became a people pleaser, putting others before myself. This resulted in co-dependent relationships.

Can you see in your mind's eye an innately intuitive, scared, likely stifled, young girl? That was me. I was born Sagittarius, ready to have fun and willing to organize it, but the psychic baggage I carried around drained me. By the time I was in my early twenties I felt like the world was too heavy for me. In fact, I was under the impression that I had to carry it.

I can thread an interest in psychic phenomena throughout my life. However, it was not until 2002 that I understood what being psychic actually meant. I saw the Light. I met my guides and spiritual teachers as if they were in the same room introducing themselves. It wasn't like meeting a human being and smiling, offering a hand; it was pure Light showing me that I was of much higher consciousness than I realized. The details of that story come in a later chapter.

I am sharing the foundation of my work with the hope that you, too, will come to view yourself as Divine, true, pure Light. In *Divine Accordance* you will read how I learned from my spiritual guides and numerous living teachers to become a clear and open channel for receiving sacred messages and guidance.

Books, these paper things full of printed words, can be mystical, magical tools. Stop and think for a moment of all the pictures your mind conjures up when you read words. Now take that a step further: What do you think the subconscious mind does with words and stories? This book is not simply a reader; it is full of keys that unlock the many hidden jewels buried deep in your being. In *Divine Accordance* you will discover the tools to find your lost keys of awareness. Please, read at your own pace and be ready for transformation. It can be life changing. It certainly was for me.

This book is available for two reasons. Well, maybe three. It began with a prayer. The first prayer I wrote was *Discord Prayer*, which is in Chapter Eight. I was struggling with a friendship, and as I typed at my computer (journaling about my complaints) poetic words came through. The *Discord Prayer* poured out of me with such unconditional love that I knew it came from somewhere else. It felt like a gift and it healed me. I deeply needed guidance the day I heard the *Discord Prayer* and the words became a treasure. When I shared the prayer with a friend, the feedback was positive. Remember my sensitivity from the past; I would never have continued writing or channeling without positive feedback. I crave the type of personality that sweeps rejection aside and plows through adversity. I unfortunately have not found it... yet.

At that time I was beginning to do intuitive readings for people. I had a rough start doing consultations; my low self-confidence was mirrored back to me often. My education was on the job; as I had little training. I would begin each reading by setting *sacred space* (a technique you will learn) and requesting only *Christ Consciousness Light Beings* to bring information and healing for my client. (Christ Consciousness refers to the term "Christos" of Greek origin. It represents the highest title of ascension which is why it was given to Jesus of Nazareth. However, it is an adopted Christian term, it predates Christianity.)

In sacred space, when someone asked a question, the answer often sounded like a prayer. Later, I would write the information and ask my guides for clarification. The prayers formed organically in sessions or meditations.

They kept coming. I gave them to clients who came for sessions or small classes I held; and people passed them on to their friends. Wonderful stories came back of success, healing, clearing and spiritual growth; I felt encouraged and happy. I was told of healed relationships, deeply desired sleep, houses selling, relationships forming, physical healings, careers improving, the release of habits, clearings of all kinds, people hearing their own guides, and much more. People were excited and this excitement, enhanced my confidence.

Requests kept coming in for the prayers. I seemed to be printing and passing prayers out all the time. People were asking me questions like, "Where did this prayer come from?" They wanted to know more about the birth of the prayers, what they could do, how each prayer was meant to heal. So I put together a small booklet and added a paragraph of explanation to each prayer or technique. One of my favorite prayers, *Divine Accordance Prayer*, seemed to hold the energy for my writing. I was guided to use that name for my little, stapled, black and white, home printed book.

People would buy a copy, and then came back and buy two or three more. It was astonishing. I kept fixing typos and reprinting.

At one point, I went in and took out everything that I thought was from ego. It was an ironic move to take ego out, since the only thing that can judge ego is... ego. Essentially, I removed the descriptive writing that I had added as a prelude to each prayer. That left the prayers, all alone, to be absorbed by hearts and minds, without an appetizer. Channeled messages have a certain frequency. Sometimes it is difficult to absorb them without a bridge. It was Becky Robbins, I mention her in my acknowledgements, who helped me see that people wanted more and that I could create the connection they needed for the prayers to sift into their subconscious minds.

So I wrote a "shitty first draft" (Thank you Anne LaMott, *Bird by Bird*[1]!) of *this* book. You now hold an expansion of what was a 48-page booklet, called *Divine Accordance*. When the expansion (this book) took on a life of its own I renamed the former *Pocket Prayer Book: Excerpts from Divine Accordance*. It turns out that when we experience threads of dimensional transitions together, a book gets lengthy. And that is how the flower opened. It was organic; I occasionally resisted, but embraced the guidance with gratitude.

The second reason this book is available is personal: I needed a reference, a resource for teaching psychic development classes and channeling lessons. This reference holds prayers, exercises (or exorcises, if need be) and practical ways to apply the study of metaphysics to everyday life. I needed a daily guidebook—one I wish I had read twenty or so years ago.

The third reason, which may or may not be the main reason I was inspired to write, is that I was spiritually guided to.

Divine Accordance is a compilation of multi-dimensional advice. You will find continual mention of clients, friends and their sessions. Most people opted to remain anonymous; there are many pseudonyms, please don't confuse these with someone by the same name. Confidentiality is essential to me, no one is mentioned without their permission. There are constant references to my guides. Who are these guides? What are their names? It's not as important as you might think. What is crucial is my ability, and yours, to ascertain pure Light. It's also crucial that you understand that you will work with *your guides*; we each have our own hierarchy of helpers between us and the Divine.

Be prepared to shift and clear energy. I have seen many beings, alive and passed over, of this life and beyond, heal with the powerful energy that comes from working with guides, Angels, Archangels, Ascended Masters and Christ Consciousness Light.

But you will discover that for yourself. I encourage you to find your own relationship with this book. Personalize the information; rework the words, scribble and underline, make margin notes. You are the conductor of this journey. You have guides and Angels working with you. I trust that you know what is most important for you.

While you read this book, I hope you embrace the showers of gratitude, blankets of comfort and immeasurable amounts of unconditional love from the spiritual realms.

How has this work helped me personally? A long time ago, I didn't like this planet much. It seemed to me that leaving was a good idea; I felt a little crazy, hearing voices in my head, and life seemed to have little purpose. I was depressed and felt tortured. Was all this because my psychic gifts made me empath everything to an extreme? Maybe, or perhaps it was these sensitivities that led me to this line of work which opened my psychic abilities? Luckily for me, it doesn't matter. Now, I am happy to live on Earth; I love my life and my people. I am satisfied and open. I can honestly say that my spirituality has led me to give and accept move love.

In these pages, you will encounter my attempt to honor all belief systems. I begin prayers with "Father, Mother, God, Goddess, Creator, Source of All That Is". Can you find your beliefs about a higher force somewhere in these words? I hope so, but if not, please substitute a more appropriate word. You will find my words for Source capitalized, including the word Light. Capitalization denotes reference to Spirit, or energies that are, to me, nouns with names.

Relationship to Source is personal and labels for The Divine are many. Once, during a class I was hosting, we had a discussion about the names for God. Someone threw out one I have never forgotten: the Great Cosmic Brother/Sisterhood of Creation. Now, that's a mouthful. A wonderful mouthful!

It is my experience that the thought form held about one's connection to Source is often more significant than the name. How many rungs would an imaginary ladder have if it extended all the way to heaven? When you were five, what would you have answered? And when you are ten, twenty or thirty years smarter what will you say? Our concept of the *Great Mystery* is ever evolving.

Because it is simple, I use the term "God", and I see it as genderless, or *Father/Mother/God.* At times, I will say Source with the same intent. During that same class (I kept my list) someone said, *The Cosmic Birther of all Radiance and Vibration.* I completely resonate with *Creator, Source of All That Is*, which I learned during a workshop with Vianna Stibel[2]. But I have also heard, *The Creative Source of All That Is.*

Whether it is God, Innate Intelligence, Elohim, Yahweh, Universal Power, ONE, Jehovah, Lord, Adonai, Ancient of Days, Messiah, El-Shaddai, The Almighty, Holy Spirit, Abba/Father or any name; we speak of our source—the energy from which we beget—as our ultimate vibration. It is upon that place, or space, that I call when I communicate with the ethers. It is my intention to work with the highest frequency of Light, consistently, and to create a safe and protected place for my clients.

Each name for Source represents a personal relationship to *The Divine Spark of Creation.* Please substitute how I address *The Absolute* with what comes from your heart. Exemplify your connection, your channeled experience.

The title of this book, and accompanying prayer of the same name, is about setting *sacred space* for healing and communication with Source. It is my intention to work with Divine Will. To put aside my desires and let God be the guide. My mantra is: *I am in surrender; God's will be done. Thy will is my will, we are one.*

May each of us be guided, guarded, protected and loved on our journey to learn and live in Divine Light.

Chapter Two

Getting Vertical

Before I considered myself a Lightworker, I struggled with my concepts of spirituality and religion. There were momentary glimpses of Divinity, little crumbs along my jagged, rough, potholed spiritual path; but crumbs weren't enough. I was starving for happiness, lost in my life and depressed.

The life I was lost in looked roughly like this: At twenty-three, a divorced single mother meets a wonderful man. Let's call him Bobby Burger (his real and true name). They unite as a family, Bobby, with his two boys, and Holly, with her daughter. Holly relocates to Colorado and the family weaves together. Years go by and then Bobby's ex-wife is diagnosed with cancer and dies, leaving her then fourteen and sixteen-year-old sons devastated. Timewise, these events lead to just a few years before I met my guides and work as I do now.

As you will learn later, near this time I also lost two best friends. Somehow, I managed to develop psychic abilities, albeit poorly, while learning things the hard way. That has changed, and you will find how as you continue reading. I want to help you as much as I can. So imagine someone struggling and desperate, barely coping with her life. We each have four main bodies; physical, mental, emotional and spiritual. I felt bombarded from every angle.

Meanwhile, the outside reality didn't look bad. We purchased an old farmhouse with room for everyone and a barn/studio for my artistic endeavors. The kids got along great; Bobby and I were stable. Yet inside, I felt the chaos of psychic challenges and constant empathy, I could hardly tell my feelings from someone else's. Bobby's ex-wife lived with lung cancer for two and a half years before leaving this world. It was a difficult time for everyone and I became depressed, not only for her, but for the boys, and lastly, for me. I was overwhelmed with family management, psychic influx and over-feeling. Many times I was told that I was too sensitive and emotional. If anyone has accused you of being too sensitive, know that sensitivity is the first step of awareness. It is a sign that you are opening psychically.

After three traumatic funerals, our family was in a daze. My young stepsons coped with the loss of their mother by being typical teenagers. This, of course, meant bending, breaking or destroying things; things like rules, cars, themselves... Luckily, no permanent physical harm came to anyone, but the emotional and mental struggles were daily.

At that time, I felt a strong spiritual connection to birds, animals, my *Medicine Cards*[3] and Native American teachings. I hobbled along the weirdest spiritual path. Sometimes, I would receive messages and if I spoke them people would appreciate the information and want more. Yet if I tried to consciously locate a message, I would spout ego-derived ideas that did not carry the frequency of the spontaneous communication. It was difficult because I could not trust myself to deliver accurate information. My belief system was shaky, I didn't have a clue where I found the good connections. My self-esteem suffered because I felt drawn to something greater, but I couldn't figure out exactly what that was. I was lost in the craziness in my head. My depression deepened.

After moving to Colorado, my body changed. I suffered fatigue (which I had never felt), migraines, chronic PMS and abdominal pain. My doctor found no reason for the pain. But my guides were on it, I *heard* the word "endometriosis" several times and I actually listened, which was rare at that time. I researched the symptoms, and found mine to be the same. This was pre-internet, I did actual library research! After an ultrasound, my doctor reported that I did not have endometriosis. I was still early on my spiritual path, but natural medicine appealed to me. From library books I learned what herbs to take for endometriosis and started a strict regimen. I also did acupuncture three times per week.

But abdominal pain persisted. After two emergency room visits, another doctor insisted that exploratory surgery was necessary. The surgery told a different story. There was quite a bit of endometriosis and scar tissue as well. Scar tissue is strong and resilient; when it adheres parts of your body together, if you move in a certain way it pulls, hence my pain.

The exploratory surgery gave me relief from pain for a few months, and then everything came back. Migraines, heavy menstrual cycles, PMS for twenty-eight out of thirty days (my poor husband!) and, my favorite, weight gain. Two years later, I had a hysterectomy. This concluded my female problems and my lease on life was renewed. Or so I thought.

All of this was simultaneous with Bobby's ex-wife's cancer struggle and with the sudden death of two friends. My mental body was vying for control; my physical body was trying to recover; my emotional body was overwhelmed, and my spiritual body was in revolt! So, guess what happened next? I landed at a spiritual group. That's where my Lightworking story took a turn.

Once, I visited a metaphysical store. On the counter was a basket of rocks with writing on them. Have you seen something similar? One said "love", another "peace", and so on. I picked up one and it said, "Make your blocks stepping stones." Oh right. Just wake up and the hardest thing in your life comes into your mind and you leap out of bed and gloriously look to the blue sky singing, "Today, la-la-la, is the day, la-la-la, that my heartbreaking misery turns into the building, la-la-la, blocks, la-la-la, and foundation, la, la, la, of my life... LA-LA-LA." Uh-huh, yeah.

To me, that little rock was not speaking about the future; it was speaking about the past. Old blocks are your stepping stones. Because now, years later, I see that I am the master weaver of my complicated story. Those major issues are now bricks in my foundation. It may seem strange, but I am grateful. All the trials and experiences are how I compassionately developed my sense of self. Those experiences are the blocks or bricks on my path to my Lightwork.

My bumpy road is here, for you, in organized pages. Use this map to open yourself to unconditional love without drama, blame, projection, guilt, denial or depression. I offer my personal story as an example. I hope it helps you see that we are all in this together; your spiritual enlightenment is as important to me as mine.

Post hysterectomy, I thought my life would be perfect. But challenges kept coming. My hormones settled, but what I didn't understand is that surgically induced menopause would be the gateway to a spiritual alignment like nothing I had ever known. Or heard of.

Well into my thirties, I learned the cure for depression. And it wasn't from a bottle. This cure taught my heart to open and gave me the will to live. I received this miracle through spiritual connection. It begins with deeply connecting to Gaia, which is the mythological name for Mother Earth, and discerning your Divine connection to Source. I call this *vertical alignment*. I see it as a *pillar of Light*, vastly stretching from the core of the Earth to high above me.

To begin, we must learn about vertical alignment, the connection we each have to Earth and to Source. Creating vertical alignment describes grounding and connecting to the I Am Presence/Source/God. It is imperative for Lightworkers to maintain *vertical energy*. Are you wondering if you are a Lightworker? Well, let's see if you pass the test to qualify. Do you act kindly to other people? Do you love? Do you feel connected to something that seems whole and pure and true? Does your conscious mind crave knowledge about mysticism, the beyond, God/Goddess, Source, Light, the ethers? I assume I heard a yes in there somewhere, and you might think that those are normal attributes of any good human. They are, but I want to ask a favor. Feel into your heart for a moment and read those questions again. Do you love, I mean do you feel a love that can bring you to tears? Love that makes you want to adopt every dog at the pound or give your lunch to a homeless person? Do you ever wonder why you are here and why it's so hard? Or how could you get dumped on this planet of atrocities by some higher power? Do you find yourself wanting kindness, craving it like your starving for someone to open a door for you? Do you ever hate God? Hate the power that made life and love but also rape and murder? That's a sign. Truly, compassion and emotion run high in Lightworkers. We tend to vote for underdogs and get passionate about anything that hurts what we love. Also, we change our minds. A lot. It's part of the speed-of-light learning curve. Or remembering curve. We will get into that later

If you can relate, I dare say you are a Lightworker. A note on that word: Lightworker. Some people don't like it. I have heard people say things like, it's not work. I beg to differ; seriously, this is work. But I love it. I love the success of a communication that brings awareness. I love the light in a client's eyes after a session. I love the release. The freedom. It is work, my work. And it's done with Light.

As you read this book, you will open spiritual avenues for your personal guidance. Anticipate integrations and healings at every level. Assume you are ready to hear, see, feel and know your own personal Divine guidance and prepare for Divine messages. Prepare for releasing. This work, spiritual work, cleanses you. Purging, the cathartic experience of healing spiritually, may take time. Read this book at your own pace; open it when you are drawn to its messages, prayers, affirmations and the exercises given within. Allow your being to expand into the space realized when you cleanse, clear and heal.

You have many gifts and abilities. Do you know where you are strongest psychically? Below are the four main categories of psychic ability, sometimes called *the clairs.*

> *Clairaudient: clear hearing, the sense of hearing something that is not received by your physical ears.*
>
> *Clairvoyant: clear sight, the sense of seeing either with an inner seeing (often called third-eye vision) or seeing what others don't see, like ghosts.*
>
> *Claircognizant: clear knowing, the sense of knowing something without being told, related to intuition.*
>
> *Clairsentient: clear feeling, the ability to sense and understand someone's feelings or emotions; empathy.*

These are the most common abilities, but there are more clairs. It's possible to have psychic reactions to spiritual messages that are personal and unique, such as a sense of smell or the twitching of an eye. As you read, pay particular attention to any repetitive reaction you experience; this may be one of your psychic abilities at work.

The definition of Lightwork mentioned at the beginning of this chapter, may be slightly cryptic. The funny thing about Lightwork is you don't have to know you are a Lightworker to be one. Lightwork, quite simply, is working with Light; not lightbulbs type of light, I am talking about ethereal Light. Anyone motivated to do something that makes the world a better place works with Light. Lightworkers are not specific to healing or psychic work. They are often covert or unusual. I have encountered Lightwork in small ways at grocery stores, gas stations and bank lines. Once, I was in a grocery line behind a young man and woman. When the couple received their total they began chatting with the clerk, and putting items back because they had spent too much. The woman in front of them, still collecting her bags, insisted on helping. She gave them forty dollars. Nice Lightwork, yes?

You may know of famous Lightworkers like Mother Teresa, Maya Angelou, Gandhi and the Dalai Lama. However, covert Lightworkers fill our schools, hospitals, prisons, churches, mosques and synagogues. Do you remember certain teachers from your past? I remember Mr. Brown, my high school English teacher. God bless him! Tenth grade was the first time I felt confidence as a writer. Thanks for the Lightwork, Mr. Brown!

Most of us have experienced animals doing incredible Lightwork (I love a good dog story), but what about parents or even children?

In Berthoud, Colorado, there is an old train depot which I have used for spiritual classes. It has a big parking lot and endearing outdated décor. Because various groups meet at the Depot, I would take time to pray to clear negative energy before our gatherings. For me, clearing involves quiet meditating. Emphasis on quiet.

Before one particular group session, my sister happened to be passing through Berthoud with three young children, ages four to seven (my grandson and her two kids). They stopped in to say hello. The kids began running around the large room playing games. While my sister and I chatted, they got louder and louder. Meanwhile, I had one eye on the clock. When would they leave so I could work on setting space for tonight's class? As time ticked by, I became nervous, and the kids got rowdier. Little voices were now big echoes. I didn't want to chase them off, but it was getting close to class time. In my mind I said, "God, when are they going to leave so I can clear this space?"

I distinctly heard, "You don't have to clear it, they are." In a second, I realized these carefree children were running, laughing, yelling, screaming and doing my work! Their joy was clearing the room! Little Lightworkers!

I am certain we all know Lightworkers; it is my belief that we all can be Lightworkers. You might recognize Lightworking attributes within yourself or in someone small, like the overjoyed children. It doesn't matter whether or not you can hear your guides; you can choose Lightwork as your conscious path. You can upgrade your existence, if you are a covert Lightworker, to the life of a conscious Lightworker.

We can all expand our comfort levels by getting to know our personal energy issues and creating opportunities for healing and self-expansion. You can pave the way for your path of Lightworking to open. The clearer we are, the more capable we are of doing our work, first for ourselves and ultimately for everyone and everything. I like the idea that peace begins with me, or... start in your own backyard.

What exactly is in my backyard?

Have you ever noticed how easy it is to see what other people need to do? I, for example, can overlook the fourteen dirty dishes that I left on the counter and tell you exactly which one someone else left for me to clean.

We tend to notice what other people do, or don't do. We form thoughts to go with our judgments: they need to do this; he should do this; she had better try that. I have found that spirituality does not eradicate criticism. If a mind thinks critically, we must address that tendency. Criticism is harsh; it hurts the giver and receiver. If you catch yourself monitoring the neighbor's metaphorical backyard with judgment, try to stop. Take a moment to go within and examine your space, know what you are truly feeling. Try the Feeling Exercise.

Feeling Exercise

Find a place to sit. If you enjoy taking notes, grab some paper and a pen. You can sit anywhere: at home, in a restaurant or park, or even in your car. Close your eyes and take a moment to breathe. When you are comfortable, sense your physical body. Feel everything you can. If you want, jot a note about your feelings.

Breathe again, close your eyes and now feel your emotional body. What would it say if you asked, "How are you doing?" Sad, happy, excited, nervous? Maybe jot another note. Do this with your mental body, also taking notes. Next, with your spiritual body and more notes. Keep your eyes closed when you are feeling. Practice utilizing your extra senses.

Use your imagination if nothing comes to mind. When you are ready, bring your awareness back to your physical location and ask yourself these questions:

Do I feel safe?

In this exact moment, how do I feel?

Am I grounded, do I feel connected to the Earth/to Gaia, supported by my planet?

Do I feel connected to my Source?

Explore your answers. As you sense these subtle energies, note any messages you receive; they are important to read later. You might find a new voice of compassion or helpful ideas. Many times, I have jotted a note while enjoying the energy around me and assumed it to be nothing, only to read it later and find a spiritual voice in my own writing. What a gift and surprise. This is a good start to meditating, which we will discuss soon.

You can expand this exercise by exploring beyond your four main bodies. Feel into your room or space. Remember not to trespass, this is not about how others are doing; please don't use your psychic abilities to spy. Empower yourself with confidence and clarity by becoming aware of you. You may discover masked emotion, instead of what you perceive to be your feelings. Open to the integrity of your being; trust yourself.

The *Feeling Exercise* can help you discover what is in your own backyard, possibly what you are blind to that others can see. When we are aware, we feel more confident, less vulnerable. Your ability to sense becomes an inner gauge. Every hunch, inkling, instinct, notion, idea and gut feeling has an origin. Do you know what that is? Could it be your psychic ability? Or possibly spiritual guidance?

We all have special ways of communicating with ourselves psychically. But do we know when it is happening? Recently, I sensed that hurrying to an appointment was unnecessary, even though it would make me late. Nervously, I forced myself to drive the speed limit and follow my intuition. When I arrived, about five minutes late, I had to wait ten more. In hindsight, I wish that I had taken the time to sense where the information was coming from; I assumed it was a hunch. During my extra ten minutes of waiting, I thanked my guides and Angels for their help, hoping that next time I would tune in to the information and use my senses to feel comfortable.

It's possible you already have an inner voice that is so familiar you don't realize that it is your spiritual guidance. Practice exploring your own energy, and then notice how you perceive the energy of others. Locate the gifts and talents (your clairs) that are essential for personal growth. Explore any messages that come forth. Please don't worry it should be more or wonder if it's good. Let it be exactly as it is. It's your awareness, your sense, your interpretation. No matter where it is, on whatever scale you can dream up, it is perfect. Perfect for you, perfect for now.

If you consider the energy fields around you as your yard, it makes sense to explore your backyard, and your front yard, maybe the side yard, and don't forget the... well, that's in a later chapter!

What is spirit anyway?

So that you can understand my references to spirit, I will explain what my guides have taught me. Briefly, a Soul incarnates and goes to a body; the spirit is what holds the body and Soul together, sort of like ethereal glue.

The word spirit can refer to ghosts, boogie monsters, dis-embodied beings, your dead aunt, etc. For example, "The spirits kept me up all night!" All that we cannot see can be referred to as spirit. To avoid confusion, I will refrain from using spirit as a general word. If I mention Spirit, I am speaking of the part of us that exists and is named and I will use a capital "S".

When I ask my guides about the origin of Spirits, Souls and why I am here, I get stories. This is one I've paraphrased. Let's pretend there's a Soul named Super-Spectacular, nicknamed Sue. Consider Sue descending a ladder from high above (metaphor alert). As Sue descends, she begins to forget not only where she came from, but also where she is going and why. Obviously, she is moving toward something, so she continues her descent. At the point of forgetting everything, Sue the Soul, finds herself without form. Luckily, Sue has spiritual guides who gently direct her to a womb where she joins a physical body already in the progress of developing. Being a Soul, Sue has no resistance, only flow and purity of consciousness. While Sue is falling asleep, forgetting more and more (even her own awareness of being a Soul) something begins to form between her and the body; an ethereal sticky substance, attaching the Soul to the body so it doesn't vacate, it is her *Spirit*.

Now the Soul has committed to the body and can stay. When the body is born, it receives a name. Mothers don't know the Soul name of their babies, and the Spirit is new so it has no name. The mother chooses a name she likes. Let's say Sue the Soul is renamed Suzanne, due to the highly intuitive nature of her mother. Suzanne is now equipped with a Soul, Spirit and body. When Suzanne is finished experiencing life on Earth, she will die. Her body will return to Earth through cremation or burial; her Soul will go back up the ladder to Source, and the Spirit will change. Without the physical body, the Spirit moves into an essence; it becomes part of the archive of the Soul. Each Soul contains the history of every Spirit it has become; these are your past lives.

On some death occasions, or shall we say opportunities, the Light that comes forth to gather a Spirit is refused. In this case, the Spirit can stay attached to Earth without a body. It can get stuck in the astral field, a type of in-between place in the fourth dimension around our planet. (More dimension talk soon...)

In Chapter One, I mentioned *Christ Conscious Light*. I can't remember when I first heard it, but it stuck. Patricia Cota-Robles[4] uses it, and I have heard it from others, as well. When a Jewish client told me that she didn't sit well with this term, I did my own research. That is how I learned that Christ is Greek for 'Christos', a title meaning 'anointed one'. Jesus of Nazareth was given the title. But being Christed is not synonymous with Jesus. Christ Consciousness is the term describing enlightenment, or to be in one's God Self. It is the most advanced description that can be given to a human or Light Being. As you can imagine, that is who I want to work with in my Lightwork.

One other term I want to discuss is the *High-Self*. Between each being and Source is a light that is called the *Oversoul*, *Higher Self* or *High-Self*. This is a place of residence for your High-Self Committee, see it as a combination of you and Source/Creator. When I came into contact with my High-Self, I saw many Light Beings. Since then I have seen others with committees, or groups of pure Light Beings at the High-Self level that hold one's best interests and greatest intent. When you do the *Feeling Exercise*, you can work with your high-self. Now, let's talk about those questions.

Question #1: Do I feel safe?

Ask yourself, "Do I feel safe?" Then write about anything that comes to mind and look for clues. For a million reasons, we may not feel safe or secure. Bad childhood, fired from a job, yelled at by a teacher, hurt in a past life, abandoned by a lover, etc. There is, however, good news. It's all energy! Energy can shift and change. If you don't feel safe, there is hope; you can change that feeling. If you feel depressed, shamed, stagnant, angry, sad or ungrateful—remember *any* feeling can change.

> *A client, I'll call Brenda, had significant improvement in creative projects and overall communication after we worked on a childhood experience. When Brenda was a shy six-year old, her parents occasionally hired a babysitter. Brenda remembers liking her babysitter and looking forward to their time together. It was a big surprise when*

the babysitter claimed Brenda scribbled crayon on her important homework. Brenda defended her innocence, having no memory of ruining anyone's homework

As an adult, Brenda began having flashbacks of this memory. Including the humiliation of being accused and punished. Although Brenda did not receive severe punishment, something imprinted itself on her young mind. She was no longer good; her reputation was damaged, along with her self-confidence. Afterward, Brenda felt it was unsafe to express herself, especially artistically.

When Brenda began searching for creative blocks, the incident surfaced. Initially, she ignored the memory because it did not seem relevant, but her guides offered reminders; it was time to heal. When she spoke of the memory in our session, we were led into prayer work; it was time to heal Brenda's memory and her subconscious mind's storage of humiliation, shame and punishment.

Brenda is now a successful artist, but does not use crayon! Born creative, I believe Brenda may have drawn a beautiful picture on an available piece of paper, possibly as gift. Once occupied with something else, such as another toy, the memory of her artwork drifted. The accusation was of "scribbling on homework"; this would not make sense to the young aspiring artist.

I was honored to be of service in this situation. The fear and restriction ingrained in young Brenda's mind was healed by releasing the subconscious imprints of humiliation and punishment. During our session, in raised frequencies, Brenda was able to change her feelings about the childhood incident by revisiting it with the intention of healing. I used strong vertical energy and high frequencies to create *sacred space* for a healing session with her. I followed my spiritual guides' specific instructions for

Brenda's healing. There are ways to begin the process of healing, and to feel safe, without involving a psychic. You can use affirmations, for instance: "I feel safe" or "I am loved". You can talk about a memory: "I was once criticized by a teacher, but I realize that it was her opinion and she was having a bad day".

Feeling safe is essential, we need that space to heal. What would you tell a friend, or child, who does not feel safe? It's an important question. Why is it an important question, besides the fact that asking questions activates the part of your mind that answers *and* triggers your guides to offer help? (Did you catch all that?) Because we are all healers, innately. Sometimes, when we have something trapped within ourselves our inner-healers are switched off, like a television set. Asking can turn on that inner feed. Visualize a small child asking a grumpy old man something like, "What do you most want to know?" Most adults, grumpy or not, would take the time to answer with sincerity, consciousness and, most importantly, integrity. Try having a conversation with your inner child, or an actual small child. See what compassion and wisdom pours forth from you for your own healing. Sometimes, we feel safer by helping others to feel safe, even if the *other* is another part of ourselves.

When you ask yourself those four questions from the *Feeling Exercise*, intend to give the most open answers, even if you don't exactly know them in the moment. Remember, we overflow with traits that are actually *reactions* to times when we did not feel safe. You are a fundamental advertisement of your history. Is your life a series of protective moves or conscious decisions? Are you reacting or are you proactive? If you are not feeling safe, and find yourself consistently reacting to past danger, you may find it difficult to be your Lightworking self. We are consciously evolving, in other words *enlightening*. When you address subconscious fear and release restriction, you begin to feel safe. Lead the creative, safe, Lightworking life you were born to live.

Question # 2: In this exact moment, how do I feel?

You can use this book to energetically and spiritually heal yourself, and others, but remember—start with your own backyard. Let's imagine that you go to a movie, alone. Visualize yourself sitting in a large crowded theater. Before the movie begins, you listen as the people around you enter. There's activity and distraction all around you; and you start to pick up energy. While your physical ears are busy listening, consider... what else are you doing? Is one of your clairs working? Could you be using your awareness to check out the people sitting behind you? Could you sense something about another person while they are talking?

After you sense what is going on around you, examine yourself. Pay attention to your body language: Are your arms crossed for protection? Is your head tilted down in thought or up with an open and inviting expression? Now, a biggie: what feelings are you experiencing that weren't with you a few minutes earlier? Play this game at a restaurant or seminar, open up to inner feelings you may be overlooking. This is a careful expansion of the *Feeling Exercise*. Remember, just check what's around you, no psychic spying! Don't underestimate your clair-abilities.

Consciously aware people must be able to sense their feelings and those of others for one simple reason... to know the difference. Have you heard the term *empathic*? An empathic person senses the feelings or emotions of others, much like a clairsentient (one who psychically senses emotions). The problem with empathy arises when one cannot discern between another's emotions and their own. If you are empathic and clairsentient, it is essential to learn when you *choose* to feel. That may sound ominous, but you can do it. It does not serve a Lightworker when empathy is creating an unconscious vacuum that is turned on and sucking up emotion from every direction.

Unfortunately, empathy can afflict psychic people negatively. Empaths can sense so acutely that they get confused, not knowing which emotions are their own. The story I use to explain empathic ability goes like this: *I happily went to the grocery store. After I got home, I felt like my dog died, and I don't even have a dog!* There are times when I have stood where other people stand, like that grocery store line, and felt a new consciousness enter my thoughts. If you tune in, you can identify the emotions of people who passed through the exact same spot you occupy right now. Know what you are sensing personally, then you will realize when something strange/different/unusual comes into your thinking.

Why would we empathize? Why would we feel energies or emotions that aren't our own? In other words, why would we spend time examining the backyard of someone else? Maybe, possibly, because we are making sure we are safe. It's a radar system. Do you understand? When you ask yourself those questions about safety, take a close look at question number one: do I feel safe? And question number two: in this exact moment, how do I feel? Ask yourself, "Am I assessing *my* feelings or am I *empathizing* feelings?" The answer will tell you whether you are checking in with yourself personally, to see if you are safe, or if you are checking in with the feelings of people around you to see if you are safe. A person that spends time and energy empathizing will not be able to create safety. If we are sending our energy out, horizontally, we are not creating a vertical connection between Gaia, our physical bodies and Source.

And then... Creating Vertical Energy

Lightwork is sometimes covert. When you think of a Lightworker, you might consider someone famous like Oprah Winfrey. She's no more a Lightworker than you are. It's a term to describe people on a path of spiritual opening. Do you know the best part of being a Lightworker? There is no person to judge you, no contest, no grade, no rules. It's between you and Source. On the bright side, if you love—you spread light. On the even brighter side—if you are conscious, spiritually awake and aware, you spread light. We either are, or can choose to be Lightworkers. For the sake of the information offered here, let's make the call right here and now: you are a Lightworker. From now on, you can proudly claim your status and confidently move forth in your characteristically wonderful gestures, called Lightwork. (Cue: fireworks and music!)

As a Lightworker, you belong to a vast community of beings: *the other Lightworkers.* This is what my guides call an *alliance.* We connect to each other through the Divine. Imagine a stream of light, going from tiny points on Earth to Source. You will have to stretch your imagination to see the Oneness, but you can do it. Imagine you connect to every person, animal, Angel, guides, Ascended Master, Archangel and more. Just make sure you see that connection extending from you to Source and Source to the others, vertically. Any other way creates horizontal connections; those are the ones to avoid. The common term for that is *cording.* We are all connected through an intricate grid system, but for this lesson think of light, your Light, and reflect on the most Divine connection each of us can have. It is to Source, not to each other. Using our abilities to connect *horizontally,* person to person, is similar to a telephone line and it only impairs our ability to connect *vertically.* Beware, do not confuse connecting horizontally with feeling or sensing the energy around your body.

Your *vertical energy* is a *pillar of Light* and it offers you many opportunities, specifically: protection. In your *pillar of Light,* you can create raised frequencies for communication with ethereal guides of Light. It takes time and discipline to train your awareness to work inside a field of protection. The prayers and exercises in this book teach you how to do that. Also keep in mind that this is no new thing to you, Light is innately who and what you are. You might assume you are learning, but ultimately it is remembering. There is more detail on this in Chapter Three, where you will read an important prayer, *Choose to Remember.*

Next is the *Vertical Alignment Technique.* It is essential that you ground to the core of the Earth/connect with Mother Gaia, to be the sturdiest version or yourself. Think of a tree with shallow roots; we don't want any Lightworkers tipping over when a strong gust of wind flies by. The more Light you integrate, the stronger your grounding needs to be. This is true for me still, after years of this type of work one would think grounding would be complete, or at least automatic. However, I still go through integrations which need an avenue to the Earth's core. It's never done. I liken it to an outbreath, we don't just breathe in—we inhale, then release it.

You will see that *Vertical Alignment Technique* is written twice. First, as an exercise with directions to guide you, use this until you can manage grounding and connecting from memory. Later you can use the *Technique* without directions to enhance your vertical connection. Grounding and connecting with Source are part of my daily practice. I get vertical before doing any type of Lightwork with another person; it is essential for anyone dealing with spiritual energy.

Vertical Alignment Technique
(with directions)

Before meditation, it's helpful to create your venue. Plan ahead so that noise, phones or people don't distract you. Light a candle or incense, bring a spiritual feeling to your space; treat it as sacred. You might like a special shawl, soft instrumental music or your favorite journal. Sit in a comfortable chair with your spine straight and feet on the floor. Be conscious in your space, be calm.

Focus on your chest in the area of your heart; this is your heart chakra. Take a few centering breaths and close your eyes. Imagine a pure white flame in your heart chakra. Let it burn bright and true. Say the following:

> *Father/Mother/God/Goddess, Creator, Source of All That Is, I call forth to the highest frequencies of Light. Please help me access my internal flame.*

Imagine the white flame growing into a ball of Light. Let it expand into a small sun within your chest. Feel the warmth and glow. State:

> *I allow my internal Light to nourish and replenish me. I am blessed through Divine channels; I am loved.*

Now imagine a radiant beam from your ball of Light moving up through your body, slowly and carefully through throat, head, and out the crown chakra (the top of your head). Send this beam of Light straight up. This will follow your *crystalline cord of Light*. Continue your prayer by asking:

I call forth to my guides and Angels: please assist me; help me connect with my High-Self.

High above you, imagine another ball of Light, this is your High-Self. Watch or sense your *crystalline cord of Light* travel up and unite with your High-Self. Take a moment to feel or sense this connection.

Then, visualize a great sun above your High-Self; this represents the I Am Presence/Source/Creator. Send your *crystalline cord* to the center of this Light, asking:

I call forth to my guides and Angels: please assist me; help me connect with the I Am Presence.

After a moment of connecting and feeling, allow the I Am Presence/Source/Creator to return a Light back to you through your *crystalline cord*. Feel this Light enter your body through the crown chakra and join the pure white Light in your heart chakra. Say:

I am One with Divine Light.

When you are ready, send another beam of Light down through your body and into the Earth. You can send Light down both legs and see it meet again below your feet or as a single beam coming out the root chakra at the base of your spine. This is your grounding cord. Ask:

Angels and guides please assist me further; help me ground and connect with Gaia, the Soul of Earth, in the most appropriate way.

Send your Light deep into the Earth. Your guides will help you find the best way to anchor. Feel Gaia welcome your Light and your Divine Connection. Say:

I am one with my planet: Earth, Gaia.

When you are ready, allow the Light to travel up the grounding cord to your physical body. Feel the Light from Source and the Light from Earth/Gaia merge within you.

Let the Light Expand into a Pillar. Feel it surround you, wide enough for your arms to spread. Feel the nurturing warmth and support from Gaia. Feel the peace and love from Source. You are now a great conduit of Light between the Mother and the Father.

Continue your prayer:

As a physical conduit, in service of the Divine, I am a pillar of Light between Earth/Gaia and the I Am Presence.

Thank you and Amen.

When you are complete, take a moment to journal any thought or new awareness. Come back to your conscious mind; make sure you are still grounding.

You will remain in your *pillar of Light* as long as the level of energy you created for your connection is present. In truth, we are permanently connected to the Divine and with Earth/Gaia. The point isn't to create the connections, it is to maintain and enhance them. *Vertical Light* supports consciousness and opens you to receive communication. As humans we tend to reach out to each other with energy. If this energy is oriented by ego or a judging thought it can become draining, even unhealthy. Horizontal energy is like a pancake, open and flat. Vertical energy is strong and stable.

The *Vertical Alignment Technique* helps your mind understand connection to Earth and Source Light. Ultimately, we are one with everything. We incarnated on planet Earth leaving many of our tools packed away, safely, in an ethereal suitcase. Until we can understand limitless life without matter, it is helpful to nurture ourselves with techniques that are easy to understand, like *Vertical Alignment*.

Vertical Alignment Technique

(without directions)

Father/Mother/God/Goddess, Creator, Source of All That Is: I call forth to the highest frequencies of Light. Please help me access my internal flame.

I allow my internal Light to nourish and replenish me. I am blessed through Divine channels. I am loved.

I call forth to my guides and Angels: please assist me; help me connect with my High-Self.

I call forth to my guides and Angels: please assist me; help me connect with the I Am Presence.

I am One with Divine Light.

Angels and guides please assist me further, help me ground and connect with Gaia, the Soul of Earth, in the most appropriate way.

I am one with my planet, Earth, Gaia.

As a physical conduit, in service of the Divine, I am a pillar of Light between Gaia and the I Am Presence.

Thank you and Amen.

In addition to the *Vertical Alignment Technique*, there is a prayer which is also helpful with this integration.

Vertical Alignment Prayer

(different from exercise)

Father/Mother/God/Goddess, Creator, Source of All That Is; I call forth to the highest frequencies of Light. Please help me access my internal flame.

I allow my internal Light to nourish and replenish me. I am blessed through Divine channels, I am loved.

Please assist me, help me connect with my High-Self and the I Am Presence.

I am One with Divine Light.

Please assist me further, help me ground and connect with Gaia and Earth in the most appropriate way.

I am One with my planet, Earth, Gaia.

As a physical conduit, in service to the Divine, I am a pillar of Light between Earth and the I Am Presence.

Thank you and Amen.

Dimensions of Confusion

It would be helpful to be on the same page when it comes to dimensions. Whether you believe in nine, twelve, eighteen or some other number, we are all experiencing the dimensions of planet Earth. Recognize the first dimension as rocks and Earth, the second dimension as animals and plants and third as the human realm. The fourth dimension is often called the astral plane, dead people can get stuck there and it's full of psychic information. (Psychics can get stuck there, too.) The fourth dimension can also refer to our subconscious mind, but I like to leave that bit for advanced studies. For our purposes, we will carefully dodge the 4D for safety while learning. I love the fifth dimension; some call it the dimension of the Ascended Masters. It's like heaven; in fact, some regard it *as* heaven. The sixth and higher dimensions are where you can find guides, Angels and more. If you explore any dimension stay in your *pillar of Light*, remember that everything can come to you, every experience, every vision, every piece of information.

What is channeling?

Since the beginning of my work, I have thought of myself as a conduit. I go into a meditative state and allow my guides to speak through me while I am aware of everything. Working with etheric beings in this way is sometimes called channeling. There are degrees of channeling. One might surrender body and voice to be a trance channel (generally considered to be very dangerous) or work consciously, as I do.

Remember that when a person channels, the conduit is a human, emotional being. There will be a percentage of personality, thought, ego or experience from the channel. We are our four main bodies—physical, mental, emotional and spiritual. If you use your physical vehicle to channel spiritual aspects, it would be fair to assume the mental and emotional would be present. This is important to remember. A resonance of ego will likely be available in channeled teachings. In the past, I have judged messages from psychics because I felt they were not clear. However, when I sat with the information for a bit, I felt the message open and speak to me. Eventually, I was able to set aside my ego response of suspecting ego so that I could absorb the Light being offered. At times our human judgment impairs us, we spend more time looking for perfection than listening.

The beauty of working with Christ Consciousness Light is the pureness of God/Goddess/Source. We will talk about this more, as you develop or enhance your specific clair abilities. When it comes to messages and channeling, we can serve ourselves by looking for consistency over perfection. When I personally experience judgment, rather than berate myself for not being absolutely clear, I have learned to celebrate my being, my learning and whatever frequency I am encountering at the time. I look for the truth, even if it's a tiny seed, whether I am listening or talking. This takes practice. Through many years of working with ethereal beings I have learned to feel confident that I am working with Christ Consciousness Light and to accept the messages as simply that, messages. They are like envelopes; you open them and if you don't like the contents, look in the next envelope.

Channeling is a wonderful tool. As you continue reading, you will learn how to open yourself as a channel and conduit for your High-Self to receive clear Divine messages from Creator. We are all conduits for higher ways of being. Each one of us sat down at an ethereal table and chose the circumstances in which we incarnated. Why are we here? I trust we are here to elevate Light frequencies on our planet. Daily we are presented with circumstances that give us the chance to make decisions. We choose: light or dark, fear or joy, old pattern or healing. It is moment-by-moment, day-by-day, lifetime-by-lifetime. Now is the time to recognize that we are not cattle being poked by prods; we are individuals with histories and awareness. We can use our intelligence to gently remove the prods from the herders and walk them into a new way of thinking.

One of the ways I can tell if I am on the right track is by sensing if my guides are near me. My husband tells me that he can't win an argument because he has to fight with my guides *and* me, but that isn't true. When my ego flares up the guides move away. It's not a conscious choice on their part, they don't jive with ego frequencies; joy frequencies are much higher. I have imagined Angels and guides looking at their glowing white watches saying, "Here she goes again, let's take a break." I do admit, that's a mental illustration to make me wrong, one of my favorite genetically blessed tricks. Or, as my mom would say, "She comes by it honestly." That means that my sister, mother, grandmother, great grandmother, etc., all have a berating ability. I often worry that I am *wrong*. The funny thing is that when I worry I am wrong, I actually move about in the world trying to make others conclude that I am right. Hence my excellent arguing ability; and just so you know, I prefer the word debating, it sounds less *wrong*. From that, maybe you can glean a bit about our human tendency to question ourselves. Learning to recognize your guides involves an inner trust, something I am perpetually learning to enhance.

Debating and arguing whether with spouse or self, it's all the same thing. It's discordant energy and it is not conducive to spiritual communication. If you want your spiritual pure Light guides to channel through you, as often as possible, you must create space for them.

Who gets to channel?

I don't know at what age I began hearing my guides. I don't have a sweet spiritual history with cozy stories from my grandma. I drove a car and dragged myself behind it. I tortured, haunted and hated my favorite person: me. Somehow, I opened a door to the spiritual realms, but didn't know how to manage the entities, lost Souls, clingy ghosts and guidance all talking at once. The craziness was always with me. Maybe I was born psychic, but I had no references. From a young age, I was told to stop talking, stop pointing things out, stop interjecting when you aren't asked, stop, stop, stop. So that's how I thought: stop, stop, stop. Those negative thoughts had a great effect on my will to live; I wanted to leave. I was interested in death, which makes sense now, but back then, I thought it was because I shouldn't be here.

I was frustrated and depressed, trying to stifle the gift of actually *hearing* my spiritual guidance. But how do you turn off the thing that will actually heal you? It wasn't easy, but I tried. As a teenager, I wrote about my emotions. I had notebooks of poems and ramblings about depression and loss. I turned to music, commiserating with sad songs. But I had not lost, or suffered; I was living the life of an empath, feeling moments that were *not* happening to me. My sensitivities were acute; I felt emotional, lonely and unloved. I was often overwhelmed, not understanding that many of my feelings were from somewhere else. Then, I found that drugs and alcohol had a lovely numbing effect on my 'sensitivities'. Finally, I was relieved of the activity in my mind.

My drinking career was in full bloom by the time I was in High School. I was coping, but not hidden. My intuition was noticed, friends came to me with their problems and finally I felt like I had a group of people that I could trust. Then I met my first husband. We married young... that pause was for you to imagine that I got married at 15 or 16, that way you won't be appalled to learn that I was actually married at 18. Yes, I was pregnant. After all the years of hating myself, closing down my spiritual connection and wandering Earth via an arid Soul, I was in love. He was everything to me. He made me consider that I was possibly pretty. He not only loved me, he adored me and clung to me. I became his healer. Our marriage lasted 3 years.

The blessing was my daughter, Jennifer. As soon as I found out I was pregnant I stopped smoking (both kinds) and drinking. I became a model pre-mother. In hindsight, this pregnancy was a spiritual intervention. Suddenly I was the sacred vessel, and I took the care of my child very seriously. At first, it seemed perfect. I dedicated myself to Jennifer and my husband. Later, I would say that my husband kept forgetting he was married, which is not all that strange for an eighteen-year-old young man. But I never forgot, and I never strayed from my commitment to them.

During the following years, I moved physically and grew emotionally. I left my husband and continued on my journey of trying to fight depression and the strange voices. I met my current (and favorite) husband when I was twenty-three. He scooped up Jennifer, and me, and we created a new family with his two sons in Colorado. All the while, I enjoyed weekends of partying (that's what we called it) and struggled with my emotional stability. This gave only small and slight openings to my guides. I would receive little bits of guidance in heart-centered moments. If I intently listened to a friend's problems, I would hear or sense a resolution, which I shared. Often they would be grateful so I would try to find more guidance and share it and then share it again and maybe again if we didn't have time. My ego was starving, my mental body imbalanced and my heart was all over the place.

In agonizing slow motion, I found my way to be me. I learned to set *sacred space* for messages from ethereal guides, to wait for permission before sharing any messages and most importantly, I learned to love myself.

As my story unfolds, I will share tricks to living peacefully, easily and comfortably. The thing I want you to know is that you don't have to suffer. You don't have to put up with depression, insomnia, worry and doubt. A few years after moving to Colorado, I found a path of Light and followed it. It began bumpy and uncomfortable, yet somehow I stayed on it to discover that I, Holly Burger, have a gift. Who knew? Maybe you have a gift to discover. This book is my road map of spiritual discovery, made in hindsight.

It's intended to help you discover and grow your gifts. My path of sharing was affirmed recently when a client of many years told me she heard an Angel speak. Amazing! We don't usually know how to cultivate our spirituality, where to focus or when or why. I may not be on hand to ask your guides questions for you, but I have ethereal arrows. And they all point to the clearing and healing that we all need/want/desire to gain spiritual communication.

This is not a special gift bestowed upon the lucky, righteous or dedicated. It's simple organization; when we line up, we connect. It's all about *getting vertical.*

Chapter Three

Preparing for Your Guides

Would you like to have clear communication with your spiritual guidance? Wouldn't it be wonderful to sit in the morning, say a few prayers and listen to ethereal Beings of Light speak to you about your questions? This type of clarity is the direct result of taking Lightwork seriously and carefully setting *sacred space*. The following chapter provides systematic instructions on how to set *sacred space* for spiritual communication, you will learn to open your heart and stay energetically protected. This information is how I learned to receive clear, unencumbered messages while working with beings of Pure Light.

What guides need is your attention. If you want to have clarity, begin with *sacred space*. I use the following prayers before I do any type of Lightwork. These prayers are full of history and research and reflect my spiritual education; and I do mean *education via Spirit*. Although I have also learned from books and teachers/students, most of the information in this book is from my guidance. These prayers are the product of my multi-dimensional work. Woven into these words are ancient techniques and wisdom I can't explain. But if you want something to be different, change it. As you read the following three prayers, you will find some information repeated. When I set space for a session, I jumble ideas together and add words because I listen to my guides. After reading the prayers so many times, I have formed a relationship with the energy. This may happen to you, which is why I encourage you to tailor each prayer to suit your needs. You may want to ask about sealing windows, doorways, water pipes or some other area you sense is open to lesser energies. Stay tuned in to your feelings and needs. *Create* your *sacred space*. As my guides have encouraged me to use my voice, I encourage you: use *your* words to make these prayers *your* tools.

If you are going to invite company, create a place for them to arrive. I am talking about Light Beings, high frequency guides, Angels, Ascended Masters and more. How would you prefer to welcome them? Your *sacred space* may be an actual location with candles and cushions. You may have a meditation room or spot in your home. I encourage you to create altars and quietude for communication with your guides, but more importantly I want you to learn to access the appropriate energy through you. What I mean by that is we should be able to create *sacred space* anywhere; in a forest, in a hotel room, in an airport. *Sacred space* is about energy, not location. I have a meditation chair, and I love it. It's on the short side, and it fits me perfectly, but I don't limit myself to this chair. I want my meditation to be priority, not the place. That said, where we meditate does hold a higher frequency. I find people in my chair all the time! It's quite funny when someone tall sits there with their knees high, I laugh because I know the energy called to them.

These questions are two questions I hope you never forget:

How will I *welcome* my Light Beings?
How will I *recognize* my Light Beings?

The *Vertical Alignment Technique* from Chapter Two will establish a *pillar of Light* around you; we all need this for meditation and Lightwork, and I never skip this step. Often I wake in the night saying, "Connect me to the core of the Earth, align me with the I Am Presence". When my energy seems off, or I encounter any discordant energy, I *get vertical.* At the beginning of each reading, we *get vertical.* And, what may surprise you is—it's never redundant. After years of the *Vertical Alignment Prayer* and *Technique* I find that I am connecting with stronger energy, holding the old energy longer and learning to raise my frequency with new capacity for Light.

Since I first wrote these prayers, many clients have used them for their healing work, meditation, ceremony, counseling/hypnotherapy sessions and more. Some have been shy about telling me, worrying I might be upset. Yet never have I felt more grateful! My work, work that came from my guides is useful to someone else! What joy! Without exception I have advocated that the prayers, the words, are free. The printing, effort, time, well that's another story. The business end of what I do involves compensation, and we will talk more of that in later chapters. Thank you for understanding when I ask that you please honor the copyrights of this writing for publishing purposes.

Please remember: your guides are your biggest fans; they root for you and support your journey; they don't demand, command, order or project. Light Beings are never demeaning or sarcastic. In my experience guides point, suggest and gently direct or *guide.* They may ask you questions that open your mind and expand your awareness. They may be cryptic or inconclusive, likely they will be funny.

To set *sacred space*, arrange your body and your tools. Then open with these prayers. Please adjust the I/we factor to suit your circumstance.

Prayer for Setting Space

Father, Mother, God, Goddess, Creator, Source of All That Is; please assist us in setting sacred space by sealing this area off on the north, south, east, west, above, below and all areas in between.

We invite our guides, Angels, Ascended Masters and all appropriate Beings of Light sent to us by Source; allowing only those Beings that are one-hundred percent pure Christ Consciousness frequency or higher, the most advanced forms of truth and unconditional love to assist us.*

Please further assist us in grounding and connecting to Gaia in the most appropriate way for our work today. Please strengthen and repair our grounding cords if necessary. As we feel the connection to Gaia, we embrace our agreements and allow the energy to return to our physical bodies.

Via our crystalline cords of Light, help us connect to our High-Selves, and then the I Am Presence (Source). Please strengthen and repair the cord if necessary. As we align with Source we offer ourselves in service to the Divine, working with the highest and best good of all involved.

In this surrender and alignment with Source we allow guidance, protection and love from Source and those sent by Source.

Thank you and Amen.

**Christ Consciousness refers to the term "Christos" of Greek origin. It represents the highest title of ascension, which is why it was given to Jesus of Nazareth.*

Divine Accordance Prayer

Father, Mother, God, Goddess, Creator, Source of All That Is; I offer myself in surrender to the Divine will of God and ask that my work and communication be governed by this surrender. It is commanded by my client and me that our work be for the highest and best good of all involved.

We allow only those Beings that are one-hundred percent pure Christ Consciousness frequency or higher, the most advanced forms of truth and unconditional love to assist us.

We ask that all communication be Oversoul-to-Oversoul or higher. Please assist us in putting aside mind, ego and personality so that information can come through in a clear and concise manner, as accurately as possible.

In this surrender and alignment with Source, we allow guidance, protection and love from Source and those sent by Source.

Thank you and Amen.

Release Protocol

Father, Mother, God, Goddess, Creator, Source of All That Is; with gratitude, appreciation and love; we ask that all things released during this session (work, prayer, massage) be surrounded with Light and taken onto their own highest outworkings. Please heal and seal all exits and entrances used by any negative force or negative entity in any field, level or layer of existence.

Please help us to release any energies, frequencies or thoughts that have attracted negativity in any form. We ask for assistance in holding a vertical frequency of Light, or the most appropriate alignment as we heal, surrender and release.

Please teach us to hold the frequencies of Light available to us, as each of us align further with the truth of whom and what we are.

I clearly see: I Am Light.

Thank you and Amen.

Understanding the Prayers

In fourth grade, I learned that any good invitation should include who, what, when, where and why. Put your Emily Post[5] hat on and let's talk etiquette. If you are going to work with Divine Light Beings, you want to make sure to invite them, that's the *who. What* explains your intention. *When* is usually now. *Where* is in your *sacred space* and *why* gives your reason. I also like to add *how*. Let's consider the first three prayers an invitation:

> *Who: We start each prayer with Father, Mother, God, Goddess, Creator, Source of All That Is, this begins our connection. In Prayer for Setting Space, we ask for our guides, Angels, Ascended Masters and all appropriate Beings of Light sent to us by Source, and most importantly only those beings that are one-hundred percent pure Christ Consciousness.*
>
> *What: What is your intention? In Release Protocol the intention is to release any energies, frequencies or thoughts that have attracted negativity in any form and to seal all exits and entrances used by any negative force. Release Protocol also asks: please teach us to hold the frequencies of Light available to us, as each of us align further with the truth of whom and what we are.*
>
> *Why: With your intention stated, next include why. This is important so that the energy comes to you accurately. At times, we want something for a reason, but Spirit may see another "what" for your "why". Divine Accordance Prayer asks to put aside mind, ego and personality so that information can come through in a clear, concise and as accurate as possible.*
>
> *When & Where: It may seem obvious that you are where you are, but there is no time, space or dimension to ethereal beings. So let's*

> *make it clear, I ask for this area to be sealed off on the north, south, east, west, above, below and all areas in between with pure Light from Source, now, as in Prayer for Setting Sacred Space. Often I will mention where I am (at my desk, city, state, etc.) and where my client is located, if we are on the phone.*
>
> *How: In vertical energy with surrender and protection, via Source, with pure Light Beings. Divine Accordance Prayer says: I offer myself in surrender to the Divine will of God and ask that my work and communication be governed by this surrender. Release Protocol states with gratitude, appreciation and love.*

These three prayers came separately and they each hold strong, individual meaning. After reading them many times I developed a relationship with the energy that upholds each request. This led to a more prayerful opening where I organically speak, mixing the requests and prayers. As I do this, I look for what is needed, keeping the etiquette piece in mind. If something seems odd, I ask myself questions. Did I invite the Light Beings? Did I ask for *sacred space* to be sealed off? Did I set an intention? And so on. If I am setting intentions, I will set *sacred space* first. If I am writing, *sacred space*. When I was writing this, I set a lot of *sacred space*... and I did a lot of praying.

Remember those two questions: how will you *welcome* your Light Beings and how will you *recognize* your Light Beings? You know how to welcome them, later you will learn how to recognize pure Christ Consciousness Light Beings. Unfortunately, I didn't know how to do this when I began.

Bumpy Beginnings

My spirituality did not begin elegantly; I did not see Light or light or even a light.

It was rocky; picture me walking without looking at the path and falling, a lot. Fortunately, I was raised to be open religiously; I went to different churches with relatives and friends. I don't have spiritual dogma (at least not from this life); I am not as one friend says "a recovering catholic". Although, during a period of grieving, I hated God. That sounds so bad now, I wince as I write, but it's true.

From early on in life, I was suspicious, I felt as if I was being watched and constantly wanted to ask, "Did you hear that?!" When I listened to the craziness in my head, I felt crazier. I didn't talk about hearing voices or seeing things because I didn't want to end up in a padded room. Most of my life I ran between hate and fear. I walked a long and (like I said) rocky road to get to my centered self of today.

During my crazy time, I attracted two polarities: other crazy people and help. The other crazy people were a lot like me; lost, talented but chaotic, restless, unhappy, searching. Back then, my energy was bogged down with negativity and I was attracting more of it. I was encumbered with entities, ghosts and worse because I didn't know how to set *sacred space*. My psychic connections were random and unreliable. I would open ethereal doors, and forget to close them, which creates a most uncomfortable life. Then I would attract help, but most of the time my resistant was stronger than the desire to heal. I was a mess.

Often, when I met spiritual people they would *see* me, then I would get obsessed with what they were seeing. I looked under every rock, and I took some of them home. I collected books and divination cards and reached out horizontally until I was exhausted. My body suffered, I was overwhelmed. I share this part of my past in case you are lost. If my pain can comfort you, I will lay it down in detail, but I would rather talk about what helped me and how I centered and healed.

Learning to set space clears the bubble of craziness around you. It offers a nice quiet place for you to examine your thoughts and motivations. In *sacred space*, we are tender with our desires, and can release blocks that hinder. It is Source Light within that protects us from our own negativity. I learned that little by little, going through agonizing choices. There were years of struggle, but now I am clear. There are times when I need help, and times when I pick up negative energy, but for the most part I am free. Now I know that I was not abandoned; I am special and significant and worthy of all the effort. I am worthy of time and specific details. I am worthy of careful creations, consciousness and love. And so are you. You are worthy of all this and, you are worthy of safe, *sacred space.*

Why can't I be spiritual now?

I like to visualize my Soul in an ethereal room, sitting at a big round table with other members of my Soul family. Over friendly discussion about our next lifetime, one Soul says, "I need to experience this..." and another says, "I will help you, but can you lend a hand here?"

We work out the details and then incarnate, as volunteers. Some stay in the higher, non-physical realms and guide the incarnated. We're one big, friendly family of Light, right? You might be asking: What about those ethereal suitcases full of the gifts I hid from myself, when do I get those? Or, perhaps you are wondering: why would I plant triggers (aka: lessons, accidents/incidents) along the way to wake me up, why not a gentler road? These are frequent questions, and Creator gives the same answer every time; *because you chose.* My great idea is that we choose differently; better, smarter, more carefully. Unfortunately, my great idea usually turns up right after a problem appears.

Before we incarnate *veils* of protection are put in place to help us release our past and memories. We must arrive open and available for learning. That means our past lives are hidden; as well as any related worries, concerns or fears. Unless... we have access to our psychic vision. You might be glimpsing between the veils. You might be tapping into your past. Have you ever wanted to learn about something and find a book on the subject the next day? Or hear someone mention the subject you are curious about? That is your guides at work, you are creating what you want. Sometimes, we run into a Soul family member, have an experience and wake up a little. The person may seem familiar. These are not accidents. We attract what we are ready to recognize, and as that happens we grow, or remember. All of these shifts and recognitions help us learn to carry a higher frequency, memory barriers (veils) lift; and our ethereal suitcases open.

Why all the suffering? In one word: addictions. We are addicted to all kinds of useless impedimenta, but mostly we are addicted to doubt. We doubt our own consciousness; we doubt our own authority. For generations we have been restricted through religion or some governing force. There are laws that tell us we are bad and incapable of making our own decisions. How many people do you know that *feel* into their belief systems? Does God/Goddess/Creator/Source exist because a book told you, or because you sense a higher power and your own purpose through that power? We have been groomed to obey. We have been threatened, burned, beheaded, dismembered, raped, tortured and hung. Why don't we grow up smiling at God? Because we are empathizing old paradigms; the persecution, pain and agony. The regret.

Long, long ago humans needed reminding of what was good and what was bad. Maybe we needed discipline or guidelines, like a child. A few of us misbehaved for a century or two. Today we embrace spiritual adulthood. We no longer need layers of religious figures telling us about a potential relationship with God. Each generation births children that are considerably more spiritually conscious than the last. They are beacons of Light reminding us that our bond to God/Goddess is innate. How many old religious ideas can you think of that have been modified? Ideas about judgment are changing because more and more people no longer resonate with sin, punishment and hell. We know we have lived other lifetimes; we can feel the truth in stories about near death experiences. We see and hear about miracles and sense the power of Father, Mother, God/Goddess. We are remembering, right now, that God feels like love and acceptance, instead of guilt and criticism. Each day is an opportunity to awaken, to be fearless and explore what makes a spiritual moment. But it's a choice.

When you choose to remember your Source, your knowledge and your identity as the aspect of the Infinite that you are, you step into your truth. Choosing to remember is a strong decision. Making that decision is taking the first step, owning it... is walking. Let's walk that spiritual path together.

Choose to Remember

I choose to remember with grace and ease. I release judgment of all others and myself for putting the veils of incarnation in place. My life and experiences are guided by love. I design my learning openly with a heart full of Light.

I Am, I remember.

Thank you and Amen.

What does my spiritual walk look like?

Now you know how to welcome pure Light Beings; *sacred space* is your neighborhood. Next is learning how to recognize your guides, Angels and Beings of Light. But before we get excited and start looking for Archangels, let's talk about two key words in Lightwork: *clearing and protection.* It's quite easy to understand that you don't have to clean up if you don't make a mess. I see my work that way; I try to be careful first, instead of learning the hard way. Historically this was not my technique. In my past, I followed curiosity. Derailing curiosity can be challenging, after all, we are naturally inquisitive about what we wish to learn.

One of the most important objectives I have learned about working with others is to connect at the *Oversoul level. Oversoul* is another word for *High-Self.* It is a place between you and Creator that offers clear energy of Divine Light. Can you guess what dimension your Oversoul resides? The fifth. When I work with others I ask for "Oversoul to Oversoul connection" so that I don't work with anything lower or lesser. I also request access to the Akashic Records, the archive of everything. Past lives, words, happenings, places, *everything*. How is that possible? I have this idea about a giant library with massive shelves and storage. Of course we are talking about energy here; so it's not a material place.

When it comes to doing Lightwork with others, I wait for a *request*. Guidance activated by questions is the best way to go. Occasionally, I feel pushed by my guidance to work with someone spontaneously, so I will make an offer. Next is a story about breaking my own rule.

> *While at my daughter's work, I noticed someone's energy field. Before I could even register that I was peeking I asked my daughter, "What's wrong with Leanne, her energy looks terrible." Instantly, I thought of someone talking (me), and then both hands fly up to cover their mouth (mine). It was completely out of character for me to look, assess and make a statement about someone without a request.*
>
> *While I worried about invading privacy, my daughter explained that Leanne was not doing well. I felt a 'push' from my guides, and made the decision to follow their direction. Through my daughter, I offered to do a few minutes of energy and prayer work, Leanne accepted saying she felt terrible and could use support. As we walked to a back room for privacy, I prayed for guidance. I wish I could say that I sounded ethereal and remarkable, but the truth is I sounded desperate and afraid. My thoughts came out something like this, "Father, Mother, God, Goddess, Creator, Source of All That Is, please assist me in being of service to the Divine and to Leanne, this was your big idea so you better help me right now. Help me to be clear and put aside my mind, ego and personality to be a clear channel of Light because right*

now I feel pretty stupid because Leanne did not ask me anything and she is not even a client!"

My human side was feeling insecure. This was sudden and I felt scattered, what about my sacred space? I may have been unprepared; but guess what? I am not doing the work! Source is doing the work; I am simply a conduit for energy! It took about five minutes of prayer for me to calm and settle enough to be a clear channel. But I did it.

Offering myself in service to Source, I used the Vertical Alignment Technique to open to my High-Self so that I could be a clear channel of Light and not work from my ego. I felt the sweep of energy and the presence of Light, I felt guided. After asking her permission, I stood behind Leanne and placed my hands on her shoulders. I asked my daughter to place her hands on Leanne's feet for grounding. Aloud, I prayed for sacred space and requested Leanne's guides and Angels, along with mine, to assist all healing. I prayed for everyone's highest good, Christ Consciousness Light and Divine Will while I felt energy moving through me into Leanne. It was a simple energy flow. I did not take the time to assess the healing or ask Leanne questions. The healing happened in about ten minutes, and then we were done.

Leanne immediately sat down on a nearby stool; she was surprised to sense tingling energy moving through her body. I noticed more color in her face, brighter eyes and more energetic presence. She began talking with great emotion, explaining, "I have been feeling worse than I ever have in my life." Still listening to my guidance, I suggested that Leanne do something to take care of herself. I closed with gratitude, releasing the guidance that we had called in, asking that we be disconnected from each other completely.

At the time, I had no idea what took place. It was as if someone said,

"Do you want to be of service?" I agreed. The same someone said, "Now?" I agreed. Then it was over. Afterward Leanne, my daughter and I went back to our day. Later I peeked again—this time consciously, and Leanne's energy looked fine. When I asked, my guides explained that she needed healing and vertical alignment; Leanne was re-grounded and her connection to Source became reinforced. Leanne also received a chakra clearing and ethereal body balance, quite a healing for only a few minutes.

A few hours later Leanne told me she booked a massage for that evening. I was happy that she made a move to receive more care; breaking a downward spiral of depression.

Again, this was unusual because Leanne did not seek me out or ask me for help. But it's a good example of being a Lightworker on call, and using *sacred space* to get a clearer connection for asking what is requested. There were signs: the vision of Leanne's energy field, my daughter's knowledge of Leanne's state and the availability of quiet space. I inched forward, never asserting myself, so that Leanne made the choice. I embraced the event as Divine Timing and allowed myself to be in service. I was careful, if not resistant. I didn't offer anything extra. No advice, no healing ideas; only a little grounding and channeled energy for clearing (which the guides did).

Why be careful? Why only work when asked? The answer is simple: safety. For me Lightwork comes with two important requirements: *responsibility and protocol.* We need to learn responsibility because we are integris beings discovering how to navigate between our physical selves and our spiritual selves, and that area is primarily unknown; we navigate using a trust compass and faith. How do we act responsibly? With protocol.

A long time ago, someone taught you to look both ways before you cross the street, that's a protocol. If you are studious, and I predict you might be, you may have run across the idea that we are the Divine Creators of our reality. If, by chance, you were able to get something out of your ethereal suitcase of knowledge that you weren't quite ready for, well, that could lead to trouble. Our veils; the abilities, gifts and talents; the awareness, all of our ethereal assets, are policed by our guides for our own good. It's like keeping knives away from kids.

Regardless of what type of trouble Lightworkers can find, why don't we start by asking for complete protection? The *Prayer for Protection* will give you an idea of what to beware of when you are doing Lightwork. I use this prayer, or a version of it, before every session, it reinforces setting *sacred space*. More redundancy, more reminders.

Prayer for Protection

Father, Mother, God, Goddess, Creator, Source of All That Is; please surround me with a complete, safe and unfractured container of Light sealed off on the north, south, east, west, above and below. Please see that I am connected to Source and to Gaia/Earth so that I may know my own presence as I know yours, Father/Mother/God/Goddess.

Please see that I am not compromised at any level or at any frequency. I ask that an invincible barrier of protection, shielding and guidance be sent from my highest source of Light, where truth and only truth are allowed, I accept no other. Please help me to release negative energy, thought forms, entities, blocks, ideas or anything not serving my highest good and escort these out of my safe container of Light.

I ask for assistance in cutting all cords, around, above and below me. Please turn any negative energy I am responsible for into love and please turn any negative energy directed towards me into love. I know that as I say this it is true. I offer my most gracious thanks to all who work with me.

Thank you and Amen.

Prayer for Protection speaks about protection from Source for any level, known or unknown to us. It uses the highest spiritual resource for protection from all known and unknown dangers. But please remember, nothing protects us like Light. *Vertical Light* is your strongest and purest defense against negative energy.

Ask and It Is Given

When we make a request to our guides, often help arrives instantly. From the human/third-dimensional perspective, the help can be miraculous and instantly healing. I have seen this work! I have seen clients release old issues simply by asking and intending. The entire problem is visible and available, then it's gone. But many times, sadly, the client will talk about the *story* (and I have done this myself), which solidifies the problem keeping it in the forefront of your mind. It is as if we want to remember an issue, not release it. What we could ask ourselves is: *how do I receive what I want?* Are you open to healing? Is your heart ready to embrace the healing? Are you attached to what is in the way?

The heart can weigh heavy from trapped emotion. We are experts at hiding feelings, anger and frustration. If you worry that you have something pent up that is becoming a block, try *Heart Protection Prayer.* Expanding the heart center can seem daunting, even scary. Within the arms of God/Source all of our tasks become easier and feel safer. *Heart Protection Prayer* can assist the mind's addictive qualities, and open space for our mental bodies to heal and release. Or, as someone once said, *forget.* We all have the ability to access information and ideas for help; yet sometimes we are tired, overwhelmed or sad and we need a reminder of where Divine guidance is and how protected we are while we search for it. When you request something, make sure you are comfortable enough in your heart to surrender to a new way of being. Have you ever stopped talking about something mid-sentence? The words disappeared. If this happens, don't call the issue back. Use this prayer, give yourself support to clear fear and explore unconditional love.

Heart Protection Prayer

> *I allow Source energy to protect, guard and guide me through all experiences in my life. I surrender my ego to Divine Will and know that I am the Light and Love that I crave.*
>
> *I allow the Christ Consciousness flame to burn brightly within me and throughout all of my bodies. As my heart energy expands, and my love grows I know that I am protected.*
>
> *Thank you and Amen.*

As we make our requests and open our hearts to healing, we can use the next prayer, *Highest Source of Light,* to activate the conscious and unconscious mind to the omnipresence of Source energy. When we are children, we may see God greater than or older than us, like an adult. As we grow, it's imperative that we allow our idea of God to grow also.

During a session, "Amanda" talked to me about a book she read. This book taught how to connect with God. She said she was practicing the recommended work but her connection did not seem quite right. As Amanda spoke, I had a vision of a book with a bookmark in it, as if it were not fully read. So I asked her if she completed the book. No, she said, she had not. She asked, "Is not completing the book important?" It turned out to be very important. There was something else there for her that would complete the information/download that came from the book. How do you get a download from a book? There isn't a blanket answer, like read three quarters of it, then place it under your pillow. Each portal of information, whether it's a book, meditation, etc., offers something. It's up to you to intuit when you are complete. Amanda wasn't complete, and she knew it, that is why she asked the question.

I could see that Amanda's connection with God was inadequate; she was capable of a stronger link to her Divine Source. Gently and carefully, without challenging her, I shared my impression. Amanda knew that she needed a stronger version of God; it was what drew her to the book in the first place. We asked Amanda's High-Self for the missing information from the book. I watched as she resisted the idea, and then embraced it. Her energy shot up to a much higher dimensional connection.

I see connection to Source as an evolution, something we can improve and strengthen as we grow spiritually. When our hearts open to faith, we have a stronger sense of Source. For me Divinity is a sense of beauty, contentment, unconditional love and appreciation without thought. I also find my connection to Source to be a place of no questions, where peace is not a word but a feeling. That is today's description; I don't know what tomorrows will be. I am a work in progress when it comes to understanding God/Goddess/Source of All That Is and I believe we all are.

Source does not have a destination or home, but is omnipresent. Therefore, we can't send our prayers in a letter or email. When I ruminate on prayer, I visualize a chain of Angels. I offer my prayer in English; each Angel translates until the prayer is completely Light, then it is pure enough for Source to receive it. With Source, my words are Light that has the power of creation. If I am open enough, if I can receive, embrace, allow; my prayer will receive an answer. If I am blocked, angry or resistant my prayer may take a different turn. That creative force may develop into one of those dreaded learning experiences (you know, the ones they make bumper stickers about). If I am blocked my request may become a force designed to release an interfering memory or worry. Have you heard the phrase, *be thankful for unanswered prayers*? Maybe those are the prayers you can't receive without drama.

It is a challenge for us, the human race, to be open to receiving. We are learning every day to open and accept in new ways, to be amenable to new realms of consciousness. For now, as we heal and release any resistance to our requests, let's make sure that we work with the *Highest Source of Light* when we pray. And by the way, thank you for participating in the expansion of consciousness that opens all of us to receive.

Highest Source of Light

I command now, on behalf of myself, guidance from Father, Mother, God, Goddess, Creator, Source of all That Is. When I pray, let it be known that I am protected by the Highest Light Source and guided by the same. My communication in prayer and meditation is through the most advanced form of Light, from me to the Highest Source of Light known to me as God. My protection aligns me with the highest Light and unconditional love of the Divine I Am Presence.

Thank you and Amen.

Now you know how to create vertical energy and set *sacred space*. You work with your heart, establish protection and use protocol. You are accessing your highest connection to the Divine, what is next? Well, we are back to that responsibility piece. Setting and opening *sacred space* is like opening the door to your home, it's good to close it. When you are complete with your work or meditation, release the Beings of Light you have invoked and the *sacred space*. To separate from clients, I usually ask, "...to be disconnected from each other, the Akashic Records and Oversoul connection; each in our own *Pillars of Light*." *Closing Prayer* may be helpful, or use your own words. Just make sure you disconnect, release and get grounded. And, I know you won't forget to express gratitude!

Closing Prayer

We wish to thank all Beings of Light that have assisted us today as we release them back to their realms of choice. We ask that Source bless them with the highest frequencies of love, appreciation and gratitude on our behalf.

We disconnect from all those we have invoked through name or frequency and ask that they be blessed with light, love and appreciation through the light of God.

We release ourselves back to our third-dimensional expression, where we choose to be the forward expression of Light, and ask for assistance in grounding.

We disconnect from each other, the Akashic Records and the Oversoul; and release our sacred space. We ask that there be no transference and that all information be received through each person's own discernment.

Thank you and Amen.

Chapter Four

Lightworking Tools and Toolboxes

Generally speaking, everything and anything can be a tool for Lightwork. When I first saw quartz crystals, I wanted one. Then I wanted all of them! I learned that each facet and divot means something; each crystal is a healing tool. As I opened to listening and feeling, I wanted divination cards, pendulums, feathers, relics and pictures. I wanted massages, healing work, readings, Reiki and chakra clearings. When my heart finally opened to healing, I wanted information, education and books! Oh, how I wanted books.

As I cleared and healed, I worked with prayer, acupuncture, spinal alignment, massage, communication, dancing, singing, and more. I tried cranial sacral work, Tai Chi, activations and hypnotherapy. I paid attention to what worked; even slight messages like when my former dog Shelby would cling to me, never leaving my side, right before I became sick. After this happened thirty or forty times (or was it fifty?), I started taking immune builders if Shelby acted clingy. Animals in general send me running to *Animal-Speak* by Ted Andrews[6]. There are visuals that stop me in my tracks, for instance: birds. I am convinced that all birds are messengers. (I also recommend Steven Farmer's *Animal Spirit Guides*[7].)

If Lightworking tools were physical equipment, like a hammers or saws, we would need a new toolbox every month or so. Sometimes it's an odd thing, one client has a particular type of pen she uses to write her morning meditation. Many people read clouds or traffic. There are useful tools found in writing and songs, through advice from an elder or the clear voice of a child. I love to read my old journal notes for information or visit with a friend to see what topic comes up. Many of our tools aren't tangible, and they won't find their way into a toolbox. Have you ever caught the same episode of a TV show that you rarely watch? Or hear the same song twice in a day? I perk up for anything repeated, thinking it could be a spiritual message I might have missed. I pay close attention to details so that I don't miss spiritual messages.

Have you ever had an inkling about something? For instance, you put on a pair of flats (for guys, loafers) and they look good, but something nags you. Instead of stopping and asking yourself, "What?" you leave your house. Then it starts to rain, it pours and the temperature drops and your precious feet are hardly covered. You think, "Oh, that's what that feeling was about, wear warmer shoes!" An inkling is a spiritual tool. It's that little tap on the shoulder from your guides, or that inner part of you that sees the future. Have you ever ignored that spiritual tap until it becomes a push? And then resisted the push until it turns into a shove? I try to avoid harsh messages, but sometimes I'm not listening. Here's an example of a harsh message.

> *My husband and I decide to take a road trip to Cody, Wyoming over 4th of July weekend. The morning of, I was stressed, rushed and worried about everything. I had no focus, no time to meditate and I was running late. My stress level should have been low, at the time we were pet-free empty-nesters, but it wasn't. There was that tap-tap-tapping from my guides, and it was making me anxious. We chose to take my husband's classic car, a beautiful 1976 Mercedes. We stopped at the*

store and after, I couldn't breathe. My throat constricted, my chest hurt and I thought my heart was going to race out of my chest. It was an anxiety attack. Did I cancel the trip? No. Did I meditate? No. I calmed down and we continued.

Several hours into the trip, my husband got a speeding ticket. By this time I was feeling better and I queried, "Is this what my stress was all about? A ticket?" My guides didn't answer. Well, I thought, if that's all it was, then fine. Six hours passed, we arrived to our first hotel in Sheridan, Wyoming. Then we visited a beautiful canyon called Crazy Woman Creek. My husband and I made lots of jokes about the creek and me having so much in common. I loved the drive through this enchanting part of the Bighorn Mountains. The road was dirt, but fine for our workhorse Mercedes.

Near the end of the road we hit a little gully and heard a strange noise, but nothing happened so we drove back to our hotel. I was driving; and chose to back into the parking spot. Backing in was the only intuitive thing I did that day. The next morning, the car wouldn't start. I was beginning to get the picture. The panic, the worry and the heart pounding weren't about a speeding ticket. They were about being trapped in Wyoming with no vehicle. On a holiday weekend. The closest Mercedes dealership was four hours away, and it was Friday. We couldn't find a mechanic. We couldn't find a tow truck. We were stuck. After a fun day of local television, lots of phone calls and several walks around town, I finally said, "OK, guides, I didn't listen at first, and I learned my lesson. But now I need help. How does this get fixed?"

We ended up renting a sixteen foot U-Haul truck to pull a trailer that held my husband's Mercedes. For $600.00. Limited resources, fifty-mile limit on towing and, viola, this ridiculous big truck was our *new adventure. Everyone, because by now we had friends at the hotel, was happy that the car was nose out because it made it much easier to get on the trailer. I took full credit for backing in.*

What did I learn? Hindsight says: never leave the house in a panic. Sit, feel, meditate and ask what to do. I have since dubbed the Mercedes the zip-code car, it is supposed to stay in our zip code. I also had a talk with myself. Barring physical harm or death, anxiety attacks are a bit aggressive. And as far as car breakdowns, we were in decent circumstances. However, I promised to listen more and avoid letting a little tap become a push that turned into a shove. And/or the whisper that becomes a loud suggestion that turns into shouting. By opening ourselves to Divine communication we can avoid spiritual shoving and shouting.

Spiritual Reference Book

Have you heard the old saying, School of Hard Knocks? I have, in fact I have heard it so many times that I want to change it. What about School of Heart Knocks? Or Heavenly Knocks? My old way of learning was not pleasant, I did not enjoy it and to survive, something had to change. And so it did, at the speed of light... pun intended. Healing tools started popping up everywhere; I found healing books, friends were getting certified to heal, I was learning modalities and whoa, how could I keep it all organized?

Create a resource. If you are like me, you will need a notebook, instead of two hundred tiny slips of paper careening around your life. I call this a *Spiritual Reference Book*, or *SRB*. It's a perfect friend when you are sad, distracted or bogged down with negative energy. Maybe you're brilliant when you are struggling, and I hope you are, but most (including me) seem to forget even the simplest tools. So let's get organized. I recommend a binder with pockets and plastic dividers with tabs. An address book can become an *SRB*. The key to usefulness is how you arrange it. I go by category for instance: healings, readings, music, books. You can organize any way you like, but I do suggest an index or table of contents. When I get a reference for healing work, I write down the practitioner's name and number under a specific category, like massage or energy work. You can jot notes, like cost or your opinion. Regardless of the container (it can be shoebox) make sure that your toolbox is accessible. Because your *SRB* is a spiritual toolbox.

My *Spiritual Reference Book* includes a category called 'detox care' which came about after a series of events. When I cleanse, I get so spacey that I need a reference. Here's the story on that: it was a great cleanse. I was juicing and taking supplements and feeling clear. Then I used my debit card a few times. As I spent money, it never occurred to me that I should check the balance of my account. When I discovered that my checking account was empty, I made a deposit. It was easy, I simply grabbed the checks I had ready to go and put them in the bank. Do you see? I forgot to make the deposit. The bank charged me $90.00 for three non-sufficient fund transgressions. (I consider NSF charges a highly offensive and aggressive form of punishment!) After that, it still took me two more days (post cleanse) to figure out, "Hey, Holly, you are ungrounded!" An entry in my *SRB* might look like this:

> *Detox care: think carefully before acting. Don't operate large machinery or make important decisions. Use cash instead of debit card.*

That's a Lightworking tool. If I learn the hard way, I don't want to do it twice so I make a note. If you work with a spiritual group, you can each start an SRB and share tools. In Psychic Development Circles, I teach this technique and we often share recommendations for books and healing techniques. You could make a list of anything that is helpful for you, movies, music or ... meditations.

Preparing for Meditation

For Lightworkers, meditation is a must. It's like showering or dusting your coffee table. You don't have to do it, but anyone that gets close is going to know.

I meditate in the morning because the energy is calmer. Try these simple but important suggestions: first, don't meditate lying down. Let me say that again: please don't meditate lying down. A straight spine with feet flat on the floor is more conducive to vertical energy. Imagine energy running up and down your spine. Consider grounding and connecting, staying in vertical energy. Second, try to create space so that you aren't disturbed. It took a long time for me to establish boundaries with my family so they wouldn't disturb my meditation. It took even longer to train myself not to answer the phone or jump up if I felt needed.

Meditating can lead to an interesting dilemma: people are attracted to Light. It is likely people will try to be near you when you meditate. A cat may want to sit on your lap, a child may need your attention, and your roommate/partner may assume you are available for conversation. I put a 'do not disturb' sign on the door when I meditate. My sign is highly effective unless a grown child, home from college, wants a smoothie. Yes, that actually happened. Light is attractive; in fact it's why you are meditating in the first place, right?

After careful consideration, I now ask Source to send Light and love when I am interrupted, but that wasn't always the case. Before I understood the attraction factor I felt aggravated by interruptions so I asked my guides to stop them, which didn't work... That gave me an opportunity to explore the situation from another perspective. What did these people want? My stepson likely wanted nurturing and care, and food, so much so that he didn't notice the 'do not disturb' sign. Sometimes people want connection, unconditional love. The Light provides so much, how would I know what is attracting someone. Finally, I realized it didn't matter. I could say a prayer for them to be blessed by what I am trying to connect with—our Creator. We are working to raise our frequencies and it's enticing. People are drawn to the Light. Don't be surprised when people are attracted to you and/or your Light. Just in case you have been interrupted, or if you are in an airport for two hours and want to meditate, this is a prayer to help you get centered:

Prayer for Centering

Father, Mother, God, Goddess, Creator, Source of All That Is; in this moment I call forth assistance to help me center.

I let go of my day, my worries and concerns.

I release all that I think is important to my guides and Angels, and I accept their help.

I allow the Light of God/Goddess to open within me and clear me of all that is less than pure Light. With this Light I release distraction and burden, I embrace love and healing. My doubts and insecurities are replaced with knowledge and strength.

I welcome peace. I am calm. I am relaxed.

I welcome alignment; I AM connected to Source and grounded to Earth.

I AM centered.

Thank you and Amen.

After I place my sign on the door, I get comfy. There are certain items I like to have nearby: pillows, blanket, water, crystals, pens and my journal. I am a minimalist; I like minimum three pillows.

Before I set *sacred space* for meditation or get vertical, I write in my journal. This includes downloading the previous day, my questions and intentions. I might write about thoughts, worries, current issues, whatever is on my mind. In *The Artist's Way*[8], author Julia Cameron suggests writing three longhand "morning pages". (You could add this book to a *Books to Check Out* page in your *SRB*.) I like the idea of releasing thoughts to something benign like a journal. Sometimes, I don't get to three pages or I type on my computer, but the technique is reputable. Writing sweeps our minds of small thoughts, our mental litter, crumbs and debris. Clear mind, clear meditation. After downloading my thoughts and mental clutter I write three or less intentions and/or questions. My guides explained to me that our questions look like grains of sand on a beach or, as it came through in a meditation class, a bowl of Cheerios! We think so much, so quickly. Don't expect your guides to sort through your grocery list, worries and desires. Be specific and direct. You may have to pull out one Cheerio and hold it up to your guides saying, "This is the one!" (One person asked if it could be Alpha-Bits; since they are much easier to read.)

After journaling, I set *sacred space* and get vertical using prayers from Chapters Two and Three. As I mentioned before, I never skip praying myself into *sacred space*, ever. Think about it, what part would you give up? Would you allow lesser beings to talk to you? Would you sacrifice *sacred space* and invite Divine Highest Light into a messy, negative thought filled place? What sacrifice is worth missing out on talking to God/Goddess? Why would we miss the opportunity to feel Divine Presence within ourselves? Writing this, it escapes me why or how I ever miss a morning meditation. But I have to admit, it happens. I am not a meditation fanatic, I am a believer.

I trust in the power of faith and prayer. If there is stress or I'm having a slow morning, I may take forty-five minutes simply setting space. Sometimes that is the extent of my meditation. If it takes too long to center, I will usually call it good. For that day, centering is the meditation. And then I close. Please don't forgot the power you have to open yourself to ethereal energy. What does each opening want? A closing! Don't forget to close your sacred space.

In addition to my journal, I have note paper nearby. If I keep remembering 'we need apples'; instead of resisting, I stop and write it down. This action says, "Thank you mind, I got the message, now be quiet."

Rock on, baby!

Rocks and crystals are ever near me because I love them. I love my Brazilian quartz Merkaba and the fist-sized natural citrine that I purchased in Mount Shasta, California. Grounding stones can also be helpful; try black tourmaline, stibnite, smoky quartz, petrified wood or pyrite. It is rare that I meditate without a crystal and many people ask me about choosing rocks. Metaphysical qualities are essential to me and I work with great books like *Love is in the Earth by Melody*[9], but picking a stone is much easier than that, I suggest you use your intuition. Pick a stone because you like it or ask your guides which would serve you best and follow your instinct.

When my friend Patty owned a bead and rock store she saw people do the funniest thing over and over. They would come in, get sucked into the vortex of healing energy coming off the mineral bead wall, walk toward it and pick something. Like a magnet they would be attracted to a certain color, shape or feel. After looking around, still holding their choice, these customers would wander over to Patty and ask, "Excuse me, but I am dealing with (blah, blah, blah). Do you know of any rocks that would be helpful?"

While grabbing her reference book, Patty would say, "Let me see." I am serious when I say this, her answer was usually, "You are holding it."

Who knows what you need? You do! So grab a rock and sit. Loose clothing is helpful, natural or low lighting and a comfortable chair may suit you as well. Play ethereal music, set space, get vertical and go. *Meditate!*

Meditation Styles

Are you practicing? Are you playing with the techniques and prayers? I hope so, because I am going into the next step, I presume you are ready. I use and teach a deep meditation technique called *Journey to Your Garden*. I learned this technique in a six-week course, which I took three times. It was powerful, and each time I wanted more, so I took it again. The first run through was intriguing, but I couldn't quite get the garden thing going. When the class came around again I was able to relax my mind/ego/mental body a bit more and the garden was visible. The third time I got it. I was able to ask questions and receive answers while in meditation.

Since we aren't able to have a six-week class, I will share what I can so that you can create your own sacred garden for meditation. Please note that I am offering advanced meditation instruction. It is up to you how you work with this information. I have found that diligence is its own reward. By meditating with the same technique daily or nearly daily, your vibration rises and that is what you want. At least that's what I think you want: Higher vibration, better communication with guides, a more guided-centered-balanced life. Is it? (Say, "Yes!") Meditation is the single most important tool of my work. It has helped me communicate with my guides, heal and clear. But going into your garden isn't the only way to meditate. Let's go over some options.

> *Free-style: Simply sit and get vertical. Empty your mind or concentrate on one thing like a word or your breath. You can do this anytime, anywhere. You can also listen; open yourself to your surroundings and simply listen.*
>
> *Walking: Intending to communicate with Source while you are walking can bring insight and internal conversation. Try it. If walking is not conducive, try another type of movement like swaying or nodding.*
>
> *Guided: Relaxing while someone describes a technique for meditation. A guided meditation is perfect for groups with focused intentions. (Hint: free meditations at www.LightworkersAlliance.com!)*

Journey: Journey meditations guide you into deeper realms of consciousness and awareness. Excellent for high frequency communication with Light Beings, personal healing and dimensional exploration.

The best way to find your favorite meditation is to experiment. There are so many to choose from; try local classes or CD's. Think of meditation as food for the Soul. Sometimes you need a nibble; other times you need a five-course meal. If you create the nibble, a short meditation you can do anywhere and anytime, then you have a tool to use even if you are busy or traveling. (Note: you might want to start a meditation section in your *SRB.*) A journey-style meditation can lead to past life recall or conversations with your guides which takes more time, like a five course meal. Decide how much time you have before you meditate. Let your guides know what you want by setting your intention, in writing. Trust me, it works.

Getting vertical and setting *sacred space* are the first steps. Next we will go into technique, so practice opening *sacred space* and using your vertical light to balance. At any time you can pray for information. Pray for access to what you know about meditation from other lifetimes and experiences. Above all, meditation is a practice. Dedication to meditation will raise your frequency, and when your frequency is higher, your pure consciousness is able to expand into your life. Imagine living free of lower energies like depression, hate, anger and disappointment. Practice and pray. You know how to do this because...

I swear I read Chapters Two & Three, and I am using the prayers!

After setting sacred space and expanding vertical light, check out that frequency! I expect you did some version of these prayers: Vertical Alignment Prayer, Prayer for Setting Space, Divine Accordance Prayer, Release Protocol, Choose to Remember, Prayer for Protection, Heart Protection Prayer, Highest Source of Light and Prayer for

Centering. Wow, that's a lot of work! But wait; let's talk about one more thing.

Watch your reactions. Your subconscious mind is a recording device. It was listening as you spoke the prayers, it paid attention while you were setting space and it now knows what you intend to do. Because your history is recorded, you might have emotions that you don't understand. While you were reading the prayers, did you have any resistance? Did you get defensive? Tired? Angry? This could be something from your past. If you get stuck, pretend that emotion is a big yellow highlighter. Pay attention. You may want to write down your reactions and ask for help in meditation. If there is a prayer, line or word that bothers you, don't get stuck trying to fix or heal, ask your guides and Angels to take care of it. Just remember, you are a human being, trying to clear out human trappings. Our reactions tell us where we are carrying something old.

Look for anything that needs attention. If you are creating *sacred space* and you sense a big hole in the wall of light (remember your *sacred space* was sealed off on the north, south, east, west, above and below) stop and address it. Your perceptions and intuition are noteworthy. Imagine setting space as if you are creating a foundation for a building where you go to talk to your guides. Why would you spend time and energy erecting a building on a foundation that won't hold? Pay attention to anything that doesn't seem perfect for your *sacred space*.

Let's get back to the raised frequency, and your *sacred space*, and all the healing you are opening for, and all the messages of Light you are receiving/perceiving—and whew, you are doing a lot of work! Remember when we talked about capitalizing the word, 'Light'? If I am speaking of light, little "l", it's simply light, like light from the sun. The capital "L" represents Source/Creator Light of the I Am Presence. In other words, its God Light, personal, empowered, God/Goddess/Source Energy. A Divine reference. That's what I choose to invoke. Just like in the *Vertical Alignment Technique*, from Source to you to Gaia/Earth, and back. A vibrating, pulsating *pillar of Light*. By the way, have you altered a prayer yet? Have you copied one in your own handwriting? Have you washed, dried, shrunk or stretched it? Yet?

I know you are busy, so let's do one more thing. You've probably heard the old Buddhist saying, "You should sit in meditation for twenty minutes every day, unless you are too busy. Then you should sit for an hour." Here are four methods of bringing Light to you; I call it *Light Raising*:

-Light comes into your solar plexus and extends up, down and out.
-Light from above enters your crown and spreads down through your body.
-Light comes from Gaia into your feet and reaches up through your body.
-Light bubbles up from the floor and moves up into your body.

After I set *sacred space*, I use a *Light Raising* to increase the frequency. This term and technique come through a former teacher, but it is universal. If you are interested in doing this with me, look on my website (www.LightworkersAlliance.com) under free meditations. It can take anywhere from five minutes to an hour. Imagine a bubbling pool of Light moving into you from below, filling your physical body; skin, flesh, muscles, blood, cells, bones, etc. It should also move into your organs, chakras and all systems. Infuse your endocrine, skeletal, muscular, cardiovascular, digestive, etc. Sometimes I love raising the Light so much that I spend extra time exploring each chakra, or a particular organ. When you are agitated, worried or stressed, use *Light Raising* to settle your energy. Schedule a short meditation in the morning or raise Light in the shower. Play with Light moving into pain, injury, etc. I love *Light Raising*, and along with the opening prayers, I never skip it. Before meditation, I do a *Light Raising*.

For a moment, I would like you to let your mind stretch around an idea. We aren't actually raising Light. We are Light. Nothing less. We are made of the same vitality Creator is made of. Remember those veils of incarnation? They put space between us and the truth. Using techniques like *Light Raising* pampers the mind, that part of us that believes we are separate. We allow ourselves to see an outside influence, like a bubbling pool of Light, moving into us and giving us something we don't have. Misnomer. It's already there. In a *Light Raising* you are simply activating your cells to wake up and dance the memory of what you know you are. Light.

For a visual references, I would love for you to find a picture, or create one, of what a *Light Raising* looks like; a perfect addition to your *SRB*.

I Am Light

It's okay to trick your mind into knowing what it knows. Think of soothing a child, your inner child, the child within. Use *Light Raising* with the consciousness that you are raising Light to activate the Light that you are. And once you are bubbling and dancing an ethereal dance of beauty, let that Light expand. Let the Light become a Pillar that extends from you to Source and from you to Gaia. I usually see my *pillar of Light* an arms width out around me. If you can't see it, use whatever sense is strongest for you. Even clairaudient (hearing) people can discern Light in its purest form. Feel into it, sense it. Get familiar with your way of *knowing* pure Christ Consciousness Light.

Sensing pure Light is a necessary tool in meditation, in fact I might go out on a limb (Nod to Shirley MacLaine[10]!) and say it is a *vital* tool. If you are visual, and a being appears in your meditation remember that if they have form, ask them to open it and show their Light. Animal, person, whatever, they must open themselves so that you can check their Light. If you sense anything less than absolute purity, they must go. Tell them to leave, tell them you only accept pure Christ Consciousness Light. If you are not visual, use your ability to sense. When you sense a presence, ask them, "Are you Pure Christ Consciousness Light? If you are, you may stay; if you are not, leave now." It is imperative that you develop a way to recognize pure Light. This is called *checking the lights*. For each person the awareness is different. Some people feel safe or pain-free; others smell apple pie or roses. When I sense the frequency of God/Creator, I have described it as the place of no questions. Thoughts and desires seem to melt into an all-knowing-one-frequency. In human terms I could call this unconditional love, but when it is the single sensation it becomes simply what *is*, and a name is useless because there is nothing else.

You will not offend a Light Being by insisting. They are graceful, open and endearing. Dismiss anything that is less. Allow only pure Christ Consciousness Light to work with you or through you. Your guides are calm, persistent and forgiving. They support and love you. Work with nothing less.

Always set your intention to work with Light. That is the *what* part of your opening prayers. There are many levels and layers of negative consciousness that can entrap or entice you. Beware. If you can, keep your mind free of ego-centered desires. Being fooled by entities on the other side is something I see often, unfortunately. Discipline and awareness are our greatest weapons against negative energies. What is a negative energy? Sometimes it is dark, lethargic, leaching, agitating, unhelpful, vampirical, depressing, heavy, lost or possessing. Negative energies can be entities, thoughts or lost Souls. Go cautiously, carefully forward. Take notes after you meditate and study them for interpretation. The beginning prayers are loaded with mystical, magical healing powers, and don't doubt the words that come to you during meditation.

Where are my guides? Soon, grasshopper, soon...

Prayers, prayers, prayers... After raising the Light (and frequency), it's time to meditate. I like to provide my mind real information when it comes to meditation. If my visuals are too ethereal, I tend to get distracted with thoughts like, "How is that supposed to happen?" If you have an active mind, employ your imagination to calm yourself. Give your mind permission to use magic, like flying carpets. Allow yourself to borrow from your memory. If you are suddenly walking by a lake and your mind says,

"How?" Give it an example, for instance, "We flew there with Luke Skywalker." I find that when I have information, it helps my mind relax.

After you set space/get vertical/raise light, you need a place to go. I use a lake in the Rocky Mountains, near where I live. Your place must be outside and Earthly; it should be quiet and have water. It can be a beach, park, childhood memory, a field high in the mountains next to a running creek; but again, make it Earth. Not the sky, not high in a tree, not on Mars; land, dirt, soil, etc. On Earth. Use your imagination to create this place; it does not need to be an actual physical location. And if it is, make alterations to suit meditation. For instance, my lake is near a road, so I changed it to be quiet and isolated, entirely for me. Also, I had to shrink the real lake. It was too big for me and I wanted to feel safe, which is appropriate because I call this the *safe place*. Like I said, my mind needs a plan.

Next we need a way to get to your *safe place*. Use transportation that suits you, but make it realistic. Try to avoid space ships, because we aren't leaving the planet. Make it Earthly, Earthling. Think bicycle, car, walk, ride. Your *safe place* should have ground, landscape and sky. After *Light Raising* I imagine that I go to my car, get in and drive to the nearby mountain lake. I imagine that I park, get out of my car and enter my *safe place*. Then I walk an earthen path. In classes, it is fascinating to listen to the variations students invent. You can borrow an idea; try a magic carpet, train, unicycle or skateboard. How will you get to your *safe place*?

Consider your *safe place* a sacred location where you are able to receive pure Light guests, messages, inspirations and healing. Let your mind create this place and give yourself permission to change it if you want. In the Rocky Mountains, outside of Lyons, Colorado, there is a big rock next to the South St. Vrain River. A friend showed me how to climb up on this rock and lay in the center, where water carved out a perfect hammock millions of years ago. You can stare at treetops and sky while listening to mountain run-off; it's incredible. That rock is in my *safe place*. Look at vacation pics, one client brought a photo of a park bench with wisteria hanging over it. Keep any references in your *SRB* to support the idea that this is real. Are you ready? Let's do it!

-set sacred space

-get vertical

-bubble up a *Light Raising*

-ask your guides/Angels/Ascended Masters to help create the perfect *safe place*

-come back using the same route and transportation

-release and close your *sacred space*

Just take a peak for now, jot down some notes, return and use *Closing Prayer*. If you received healing work, felt any psychic connections, located cords or anything that still feels connected, try *Closing the Space Prayer*. Like the opening prayers, I use both closing prayers organically every time I meditate, do a reading or open *sacred space* for any reason.

Closing the Space Prayer

I wish to thank all of the guides, Angels, Ascended Masters and Beings of Light that have joined me today for this meditation. As they release back to their realms of choice I ask that Source please bless these Beings with the highest frequencies of love, appreciation and gratitude on my behalf.*

I ask that Source please release and close the sacred space. I ask that all those invoked by name or thought be blessed and any cords or inappropriate energy connections be severed and healed. Please keep me grounded and connected to Source, in my pillar of Light.

Thank you and Amen.

**session, group, massage, healing work, etc.*

What happened?

Repeat after me, "I did a good job." And, "My meditation was perfect." In my classes, we share after everyone meditates. I love to listen to the experiences, but I don't like when people compare themselves to each other. Let your meditation be the most special, original, excellent experience ever. Please.

There were times that I felt the destination was more important than the journey. If you are running to the bathroom, it might be. But we are calmly exploring our connection to the Divine; so take your time, every single thing means something. Pay attention. When I learned to meditate I did not understand frequency changes. My experiences were visual and detailed, but I couldn't remember everything. After months of frustration, I began cheating. I started taking notes *during* meditation. I have done this for years now, and tell my meditation students to take notes during if you have/need/want to. It's simple; you can jot down a word to jog your memory. You can create a sentence or write the whole sequence. It doesn't matter if you actually see; write what you sense or feel: Elation, forgiveness, peace, release. Write the words. Watch for sensations, colors, noises. Feel into messages, changes or healing. Sense the landscape, water or weather. Notice trees; are they pine/oak/apple? Are leaves thirsty, waving in the wind, rustling, opening? Can you smell something? Are there any *animals*? Later, when you have closed your meditation, you can read your notes and mull over what each message means to you. The Internet is a fabulous resource for research, but continue to open to any meaning your guides might generate relating to your personal experience.

You might be curious about guides and Angels. If so, let that move to the bottom of the list, for now. If we put the cart before the horse, we move a lot slower. The horse will lead; it knows how without you knowing how it knows how... grasshopper[11].

The Messages

Make sure you are familiar enough with the path to your *safe place*, and the transportation you choose (donkey cart?), so much so that you notice any changes (like a new sky color). Remember to mentally note or write down anything that catches your attention; you will love reading it later. You may want to start a file in your *SRB*. Small little details can unfold into gigantic subconscious messages that heal something hidden, like a past life. If writing during meditation distracts you, it's okay to write afterward.

There was a time that I repeatedly saw a moose in my *safe place*. He/she would eat grass and mostly ignore me. Finally, I looked up the meaning in *Animal-Speak*. Did you know that moose represent the Divine Feminine? I was surprised. Guess what I was working on? Honoring the Divine Feminine Light within myself. My guides were speaking to me with a visualization from which I could research and learn. A visual and interpretive language I could hear with my spiritual ear.

Concerning any beings that might pop in before you *officially* invite them, remember: check the lights, check the lights, check the lights! When you are familiar with how you sense, feel or see in your *safe place*, it is imperative that you check everything. Make sure you are experiencing true and pure Light. Check the lights. *Don't forget* or get overly impressed with anyone or anything. They must open their form. I have expelled, commanded out, banished and exiled beings/entities. My guides told me, "It is better to be safe, the Light will return." And it's true. When fear orients my senses I banish to be sure, if the Light returns I check it again. Your guides won't be overly assertive, bossy or pushy. I find that my guides rarely give advice unless I ask. Watch for too much enthusiasm or guidance, it may be from a less than Christ Consciousness place.

While you invoke the presence of your guides during the opening prayers, there should be an additional invitation. *Ask for what you want.* For instance: go to your *safe place*, experience it, be with it and get to know it, THEN (a few weeks later) say,

"I welcome my Guardian Angel to come forth through the Divine Light of the I Am Presence." I know it's tempting to invite four Ascended Masters and Archangel Michael. But it's not wise. You are a powerful Being of Light; don't underestimate the delicious aroma and radiant Light you are emitting. This can attract lesser beings. If you work with *your* specific beings first, you can get to know them, and most of all *trust* them. They will then become part of your protection. I have been meditating for years and when my Ethereal Teacher comes forth I *still* check his light.

Did you say, *Ethereal Teacher*?

Why yes, I did. But let's talk about that in a minute. Visit your *safe place* in meditation every day at the most. Don't force yourself to move ahead too quickly. This technique is designed to help you release blocks and raise your vibration. If you don't give yourself the opportunity to do this by going slowly and paying attention, the frequency will not be appropriate. Pace yourself, grasshopper. It will pay off.

Visualize the walk to your *safe place*, it's like walking up the sidewalk to your home. If getting inside the house is a challenge (it's getting dark, the mailman talks to you, toys and garden supplies all over the place), you will likely feel happy when you finally get inside the house after stepping over all the obstacles; then your eyes can adjust to the light (metaphor alert). After comfort settles in you will probably start looking around. This is a pretend house, you don't have to rush in and start cooking, cleaning or returning phone calls.

The *safe place* isn't going anywhere; it's a metaphor for your subconscious mind. If there's an obstacle in the way, step over it and take a mental note for later examination. Go slow and easy. Give yourself a moment to listen, feel, and take a look around. Stay by the door and get used to the metaphorical house. Sit down, relax, feed the cat later. (Just kidding, note to self: no hungry pets in meditation garden.)

If you ever feel you are imagining too much and not seeing enough, reframe those thoughts. Quiet your mind and tell yourself that imagination is your key to information; all you need is interpretation. I once worried about my over-active, artist imagination. My guides told me that imagining actually awakens and strengthens the third eye, our sixth chakra, it's a pre-requisite to increased clairvoyance (clear seeing). They asked me, "Where do you think your imagination comes from?" Everything comes from Source! So I let go of my judgment and let my imagination fly. There are times when I question myself, but that is normal. If I let the question sit, my guides usually provide another example so that I can discern what could be learned, and what could be released. Our guides will use any and all methods to help us, including our imaginations. Have you heard fake it until you make it? Imagine seeing until you do.

Now, about those guides, Angels, Ascended Masters and ancestors and all the healers, teachers, sages and gurus on the other side... take a deep breath. When you do your opening prayer, you invoke everyone that you need. We have invited Beings of Light, the I Am Presence/Source/God, Angels, guides and Archangels; protection, guardians and Light with a big L; and truth and purity—all in their highest forms. This is a lot of Light; you have a virtual *army* of Light Beings between you and Source. I find that asking Source to send the best one for the job helps, "Please send forth the most *appropriate* Being of Light." You could ask, "Appropriate for what?" That would be a useful question. Remember the journaling you did before you set *sacred space* with prayer? What questions did you ask? What healing did you invoke? Besides all of the beings that you need for safe communication in your meditation, there might be another for something specific. For general purposes, I want these two beings with me for meditation: my Guardian Angel and my Ethereal Teacher.

You should invoke and meet them separately, without exception *check their lights*. To give you an example of less than light frequencies, this is a meditation entry from my personal journal:

He is resplendent, glowing violet with an ornate staff. I sit next to him and he stares straight ahead. "Beloved, kneel." I do and he touches his staff lightly on each shoulder and my head. Am I knighted? I wonder, and then I ask to see his lights.

The lights bloom. White and violet and awesomeness. I stay with the vision, I watch it and when the light begins to move out there is something in the center. It looks like a form that is not light; I am suspicious. I banish it from my meditation. A vortex forms and the entire energy is sucked out.

I sit on my heels, as I look for any residue of that energy. Then I hear, "It is not all that bad, beloved." I see my Ethereal Teacher as he sits upon the bench, in human form. But, again, I must see his lights. He closes his eyes, sits erect and his body begins to change and shift forms rapidly. I know what I am seeing, all the many forms I have known him. Not always friend, not always known, form and formless. The violet light begins to form and I watch cautiously now. The energy is different, less drama, more softness. As I look deeply to make sure no strange energy is there I sense something completely different from last time. I sense warmth, like hug or holding, coming into me. I sense a mother's womb, a sense of security.

I stay with this and I realize that the other was sensational, or sensationalism. This is slower and calmer, no agenda, simply being. I let myself walk into it and I am held so deeply, so purely. I want to cry, from joy.

Asking to see lights is necessary. If you do not have clairvoyance in your *safe place* (and many people don't) you must find a way to sense or feel pure Christ Conscious Light. There will be another way to know the highest form of Light, one you discover (or remember) on your own. How you know is not as important as knowing. Set your intentions high when it comes to working with ethereal beings. Work with only those that support you and your agenda from a Soul perspective. Leave behind, banish or ignore anything that comes to you with ideas, too much instruction or suspicious behavior.

Are you ready to meet your Guardian Angel? I have been told that Guardian Angels are never Archangels. If you invoke your Guardian Angel and sense an Archangel, it may be because they have similar names or vibrations. Vibration is like a signature; if you hear a song once and then hear a similar song you might not be able to tell them apart. If you heard both songs many times you would likely be able to distinguish between the two. As you get familiar with ethereal frequencies, you will notice subtle differences. But for now, rely on checking their lights and your feeling.

Make a special intention to meet your Guardian Angel. Invite him/her by writing that intention. It might look like this:

> *Today I want to meet my Guardian Angel. I am excited and ask for all of my guides to help me to be open to receive this great gift. Guardian Angel, I invite you into my safe place. I welcome my Guardian Angel to come forth now. I accept only pure Christ Consciousness Light.*
>
> *Thank you and Amen.*

Do *Vertical Alignment Technique* and set *sacred space* with prayers you have chosen (or re-crafted into your personal opening). Do a *Light Raising*. Take a nice, slow journey to your *safe place*. Feel, sense or see the surroundings then make a statement to invite your Guardian Angel. Imagine a beautiful Light comes to you, you check it (check the light, check the light). Imagine that you bask in the energy and love emanating. You know that this can happen over and over, so you don't worry about asking questions or receiving information. When complete, you return, close and release.

You may have to adapt to the new frequency. If you do not sense or see your

Guardian Angel, wait until the next meditation and try again. Sometimes we need to clear before we are able to raise frequencies to a high enough place for visions or communication, think of it as an elevator in a high rise. Your Guardian Angel may be on floor twelve and you are only getting to floor ten. Use the prayers that are presented throughout this book, then come back and try again. Be patient. Meditation is a *practice.* Show up and do the work, the rewards will come in time.

After you meet you Guardian Angel, and you are ready to open yourself to something extraordinary, using the same process ask to meet your Ethereal Teacher! Use the same technique, set your intention and write the invitation. When your teacher arrives, check his or her light (check the light, check the light). Your teacher will feel completely different from your Guardian Angel, my teacher feels a little more like an authority figure. My Guardian Angel feels supportive and loving, someone I could not offend or disappoint. But the Teacher is, well, a teacher. There's an air of expectation, work and support. Move forward slowly with your new communication so that you form trust and faith in yourself, you will learn to work outside of your mind. Dedication, discipline, responsibility and protocol. You've got this one; I have faith in you.

While Guardian Angels are not Archangels, Ethereal Teachers can be Ascended Masters. If you are curious about Archangels and Ascended Masters I recommend, *Archangels and Ascended Masters* by Doreen Virtue[12]. This book is a comprehensive reference guide for beings that come into your meditation. The Internet is also helpful, remember to trust YOU first and everyone else second!

When you experience your Ethereal Teacher, you may wish to ask a question. If you move to large questions too fast your ego-mind might take over. And sometimes they don't answer. When someone asked about the Big Bang Theory in a reading, the guides did not give any information. I learned that the question was not asked from heart-felt desire; it was a mental body question. It was a challenge formed from doubt, it was a question to test me and gain information for the ego. The guides ignored it. Always ask from the heart; be open to receiving the love and light that Creator can bless you with in that moment. Below is a list of questions that have worked well for me.

-What is your name?
-Is there anything I can work on right now to heal myself?
-How can I be of service to the Light?
-Is there anything I can do right now for ________?
-Is there anyone I can forgive right now?
-Will you help me with ______?
-Have we been together before?

I like to prepare my questions early and be focused, but there are times when my meditation takes a complete different turn. In that case, I pray, "I allow all healing through Divine Light."

Closing the space...

Create a way into your *safe place* and return via the same route, every single time. Treat the *safe place* like your home. You would not let strangers in without reason. You would protect your place of comfort and pay attention to anything suspicious. When you complete your meditation, consider that you have journeyed therefore you need to return. Offer gratitude and travel back exactly the way you came, all the way back to find yourself occupying your body. End your session by closing the *sacred space* and releasing your wonderful guides with closing prayers. No matter how grounded you assume you are, it is likely you aren't. Why do you think they call this woo-woo? Take a little time, or eat something to help you adjust as you anchor back into reality. Did I mention that this is your chosen reality? You *chose* to incarnate and be here. La-la land is enticing and feels good, but you can't be your smart, manifesting self with one foot in the ethers. *Get grounded after each meditation.* When you get used to accessing your higher mind, it will start manifesting in your daily life. My guides have told me more than once, "How you meditate today will be how you are in the future." I have meditated long enough to know that this is true. My peace and ease and comfort are present now, but years ago I had to meditate to get fifteen minutes of what I live in now.

After meditating, wiggle your toes. Send some love and appreciation to your wonderful third-dimensional vehicle/body. Write what you saw, felt and heard. Were there symbols, colors, words, impressions or anything of significance? What we understand in a higher frequency does not generally stay in our minds when we come back. Write it down immediately. When you read your journal later, you might be surprised at your insight. Remember, if you were meant to be in meditation all the time, you would be. Get grounded, be responsible. Put away your tools, like good boys and girls.

Release completely from your meditation. If there are energies/thoughts/feelings that you would like to have in your life, spend some time in contemplation. Consider how to integrate the blessings you received.

PS: Did you notice the redundant message about getting grounded? In the classes I have taught the most common problem is not visualizing or hearing, it's coming back. It is necessary to get grounded, get grounded, get grounded. Your shampoo bottle says rinse and repeat, doesn't it? You don't do it, do you? Do this. You will be happy that you did. Thank you and Amen.

Chapter Five

Happy New Year!

We discussed meditation, are you open to further Lightworking tools? If so, expand your toolboxes friends, because it's time to clear and heal!

Where I live, every December people start asking about New Year's Resolutions. One year, I gave up the idea of some supernatural current of energy swooping down and making my wish come true at the exact second one year ended and another began. Because it's ridiculous. (This from someone that talks to dead people?!) If New Year's Resolutions worked, we would all be extraordinarily fit super models with paid off credit cards, vacation homes and master's degrees. I would be a size four, cellulite free, tri-athlete with a landscaped yard.

On TV once, I heard the actress Mo'Nique say that she doesn't want all those physical changes popular in Hollywood. She wants St. Peter to recognize her at the gates of heaven, cellulite, flabby arms, gray hair and all. That's inspirational to me and I hope my confidence gets as strong as Mo'Nique's someday, but I am willing to admit that I have unfulfilled requests waiting for that one special night when I can make a wish, and it comes true. Besides that, I am wondering, "What's up with resolutions?" Do I avoid setting goals because I resist advertising and Hollywood-style judgment or did I experience disappointment and get lazy? What is blocking me from setting intentions? What is preventing what I *resolve* to do?

Fast forward to a local seminar where I wanted to be incognito (you know, not-the-psychic-girl) except the event was hosted by one of my clients. She gave me a wonderful review on stage, which I loved, but I was no longer covert. We separated into groups so that each person could share an issue while the others listened; then listeners would offer ideas and support. As an outed psychic/intuitive I seemed to be the fall back when no one wanted to speak. They kept looking at me, or to me, for opinions. This made me uncomfortable because I fly solo, unless my guides get invoked. I am serious about responsibility and protocol; and I don't offer advice unless I am asked, but every once in a while there is an exception to that rule.

In this case, a young writer and life coach talked about finding peace and success by not having expectations, she suggested it for everyone, release your expectations. My inner voice emerges, and I recognize my guides showing up unannounced. (No Angelic horns blowing?)

But let me digress for a minute. It took me quite a while to understand my limitation; my need for structure and control versus being in service to The Divine. In the beginning of random psychic happenings, I spilled the beans hoping to help someone. That didn't work, I recognized after thousands of tries, so I changed my ways. Instead of spewing drops of incredibly-special information, I decided this: forget it. If people don't like what I have to say, I won't talk at all. There must be some Taurus in my astrological chart.

In the eighties and nineties there was this guy in Boulder, Colorado that could tell you the zip code of any town. He would hang out at the outdoor mall and people would give him dollars and coins for entertainment. One day I challenged him with my small Missouri town and he nailed it. I thought, "Wow, how does he do that?" And my guides replied, "He has access to a part of his brain that you do not." What? And wow!

A few weeks later, I see this guy in an office where I was meeting someone. We were talking and I said, "You know that you are normal, right?" He looked at me strangely; he was quite odd, probably not a lot of social support from his peers. So I said, "You have access to a part of your brain that most people don't, it helps you remember things, especially numbers." He did not talk to me anymore. I was embarrassed.

What happened? You have part of this lesson, I trespassed. I asked a question, which was answered, but I was not asked to tell him how his brain worked, that was my idea of being social. After that I had this great inspiration, *a corral.* I asked my guides to create an energy corral around me so that I was not privy to information based on my curiosity. This worked great, until I ran into someone that needed/wanted/prayed for help more that I wanted control. Remember the tap that becomes a push that can turn into a shove? As I sat in that seminar, at the table of women who were looking for help and information, the energy tap turned into a push.

Her speech about releasing expectations wasn't sitting right. I thought about it and I realized that we create through our expectations. So I asked this bright-eyed writer for permission to give my opinion—which was hardly adequate because the poor woman was about to be knocked off her security pedestal. (Those are the pedestals we create specifically to be knocked off of, by the way.) She welcomed my perspective, tentatively I said, "I am wondering, is there any possibility that you are avoiding expectations to prevent disappoint because you had a bad experience in the past?"

I knew I had pushed too much when her eyes welled up and she looked down. It was such a harmless question, but I could feel the energy behind her emotional reaction, something was up for healing. Silently, I asked my guides to shift this reaction and help her. Out loud I am still talking. Words come out that smooth the reaction and hopefully help her through the emotional pain. It was a little awkward for the writer, but everyone else at the table jumped at the chance to participate. We all asked for release of anything blocking expectations or any reaction to disappointment. (You can ask for this, too.)

There's a saying that I use when this happens: *I hope the foot in my mouth was God's foot.* Outside of worry over offending the writer and a strong desire to run, I came to a realization. It's an epidemic. We are steered by our fear. I have disappointment interfering with my goals and resolutions. *Especially* New Year's Resolutions.

What do you do when you know fear and/or disappointment are in the way? I decided to take it to my guides. I journaled about resentment, failure, fear and disappointment; then went into meditation. I asked my Ethereal Teacher about New Year's Resolutions, why I might resist them. I asked about disappointment, was there anything causing me to not apply myself? What about fear, where does it stop me? And failure; is there some historical happening, in this life or another, that makes me afraid? Do you want to know what I was told? One word: *addictions.*

Addiction? I was confused. To me, my habits were mild, harmless. How could addiction affect something like goal setting or expectations? What could I be addicted to? Gently, my Ethereal Teacher showed me that addictions, from an energetic perspective, can be addressed as a whole. When a person gets caught in a cause and reaction loop, they might create a way to cope. *Issue, reaction, cope.* Repeat.

This is common in drug and alcohol addictions. An *issue*, like self-doubt can surface as a *reaction*: insecurity or social anxiety. To *cope* one might use alcohol or narcotics. *Issue, reaction, coping.* A circle of action that is hard to break. If you have dealt with counseling, therapy or a twelve-step program, you know that therapists are really hunters. They arm themselves with information, they watch for *reactions* so that they can find the *issue.* Attacking what one does to *cope* is not helpful. If there is a leak in the roof, you can cope by using a bucket. Or you can fix the issue: the roof.

With the writer I mentioned, you can see the cycle. We may not know the exact circumstance, but an issue resulting in self-doubt is quite evident. The reaction was to create a protective thought, although her mental body was too involved and protection became a bit defensive. Rather than seek help for the issue, she tried to trump it by inventing an idea: *avoid expectations, prevent disappointment*. This might be a novel idea for someone willing to sit and watch life go by. Maybe a writer that wants to shelf their work, or a hermit never planning to be seen.

However, we are Lightworkers. Being seen is inevitable. Be prepared to feel inside out at times. The work that chooses us aligns each of us with a higher power. The road to clarity and spiritual communication is only hard because we resist delving into our issues. We fear the pain or exposure. The odd thing is, the issue isn't usually what hurts us, its years of coping behavior. It's the *reaction* that we are ashamed of.

When people bring memories into sessions, I ask for healing for the memory and anything connected to it. Sometimes there are deeper issues that can be healed and cleared via the surfacing memory, or any coping/addiction resulting. I have worked with clients that don't understand their addictions, but they use *Sustenance Prayer for Addiction* and heal.

Can you see the connection between New Year's Resolution and addiction? Addictions, and/or negative energies attached to them, can impede Light. Consider someone addicted to shame or guilt. If they receive too much positive attention, they might fall into a downward spiral of embarrassment or regret, resulting in depression (reaction). Naturally, one would avoid creating depression, if they could. That means stay out of the limelight, don't excel, don't succeed, don't be noticed or commended or blessed (coping). So the subconscious mind tries to protect, it reads situations and when it recognizes danger it sends a message, "Avoid attention it leads to depression." The mind puts up a roadblock for protection, "You are not worthy of positive attention, you are (fill in the blank)." Fill in the blank with whatever childhood/past life idea you have that stops you from radiating your light. Until you find the issue, you are stuck in the reaction and try to cope.

I can imagine someone's head hanging in sadness; it's such a circle of frustration. If you throw past lives and genetic inheritances into the mix you have a bevy of issues from which to choose. My Ethereal Teacher pointed out that you don't have to know any details of the original issue. Use *Sustenance Prayer for Addiction,* it works on patterns and coping behavior.

When I examined my resistance to making a New Year's Resolution, I was shown that every year my desires were the same, and so were the blocks. It was true. I made the same requests every year, and felt the same failure when my resolution proved naught. I thought of a new idea: wouldn't it be wonderful to release issues blocking my desire? I encourage you to use this prayer even if you are not aware of addictions or restrictive behavior.

Sustenance Prayer for Addiction

Father, Mother, God, Goddess, Creator, Source of All That Is; please assist me, I am willing to absorb Light so that I may heal. I am willing to release any frequency less than one-hundred percent unconditional love causing me to use any source for less than optimal advantage.

If I partake in anything out of habit I ask, command and allow that all negative frequencies from that source be immediately transformed to Light, and all positive frequencies from that source be utilized by my High-Self for my highest and best good.

To all engineering forces that guide my desires, cravings or focus: I release you into the Light. I allow my will to be the Will of God/Goddess. I allow clarity from my guidance concerning addiction. I allow wholeness, goodness, health and balance to be my goals and manifest SELF.

Thank you and Amen.

(Note: The words 'forces that guide' refer to entities or negative energies that might be influencing your thoughts or actions.)

Assorted Energetic Distractions

Now you know how to stay vertical, set space, meditate, invoke guidance, check lights and release addictions; let's throw a few energetic curve balls into the mix. We live in a multi-dimensional world. I love the explanation of dimensions offered in *The Light Shall Set You Free*[13], an excellent read if you are doing any type of Lightwork. Remember the explanation from Chapter Two? First dimension: rocks and Earth, second dimension: animals and plants, third: human realm, fourth: astral plane, fifth: heaven, sixth and higher dimensions: guides and Angels. If you explore any dimension stay in your *pillar of Light*, remember that everything can come to you, every experience, every vision, every piece of information.

Dimensional travel, astral travel, bi-locating and other forms of separating from your physical body are *not* something I recommend. I have learned from my own experience and through my Ethereal Teachers that we don't need to explore through separation. If you learn to meditate, and use your *pillar of Light* for protection, you can experience everything. It takes practice; learn to understand your particular gifts and you will have the keys to the kingdom. Albert Einstein said, "The separation between past, present, and future is only an illusion, although a convincing one[14]." Albert Einstein gave us the Theory of Relativity, and with it the concept of a time/space continuum. If there is no time or space outside of the third dimension, where would we travel? I encourage you to study this. Einstein anchored energy for us all to open to higher minds, use your own higher thinking to discover how you can experience another time without actually traveling there. To explain what happens when we astral travel, read this metaphorical story:

Imagine a great forest, it's beautiful, green and lush. It is a magical example of Earth, pulsing with Gaia's heartbeat. It draws you in. You're pretty smart, you don't get lost easy. So as you journey into this inviting place you skirt along the edge and keep sight of something familiar. But what if you see a precious little bunny hopping along? Ohh, it's so cute! You follow it. It lets you get close, but then it hops away. Then you see blooming flowers and tall trees with low limbs you can climb on. The bunny, still teasing you, draws you further into the forest. It lets you get very close and you almost pet it. Warm sunshine streams through trees hitting the forest floor in dashes and lines, scents of flowers tickle your nose. These sensations distract you; euphoric, you walk further into the forest.

You sense a place you can heal. The energy is wonderful; your communion with Spirit is strong; you ground, connect and meditate. When you release and become aware of your surroundings something is odd, you realize that you are lost. Every direction looks the same. You follow a trail for a while, then another, and then another. Frustrated and tired, finally, you find your way out.

Emerging from the forest you are so happy to be free that you don't realize what came with you, or more importantly, what you left behind. Your scarf is missing, and an earring. There are bugs on you, small little hitchhikers that you don't even notice, and there is one black poisonous spider on your back.

What does getting lost in the forest have to do with dimensional travel? You can see that when one's curiosity is peeked (Can I pet a wild rabbit?), one might forget to be careful. (Also known as being distracted.) The scarf and earring represent your personal energy. One might accidentally leave something behind when visiting the ethereal realms. Shamans are trained for many years to traverse the underworlds; take this into consideration. Whether you are meditating or visiting with your dead uncle, use precautions. How would you prevent leaving something behind? Don't go in loaded. The metaphorical scarf is a flowing piece of fabric. Visualize thought forms, they trail behind us like ethereal scarves. If we go visiting, do we need to bring them? And, if we leave them behind, can we psychically still be connected to them? This can get confusing, but pay attention. If a negative entity acquires your scarf/scarf-like energy what exactly is the impact to you?

If you know exactly what you are made of and what you might leave behind, fine. You can make sure you come out as you went in, without additions or deletions. But do any of us truly know that much about ourselves? Our multi-dimensional, ever-expanding selves made in the image of God? We don't, at least not yet.

Let's address the issue of what you pick up, the additions. The way we collect energy in our ethereal fields is largely what keeps me in business. Many years ago I swore I would never deal with entities, ghosts or clearing work, which is primarily what I do now. (I hear laughter from beyond. Gentle, loving laughter; but laughter none-the-less.) Remember the hitchhiking bugs? They can be shaken off, that's a simple metaphor for lesser energies. But that poisonous spider can bite if he gets scared. He represents a conscious and calculating entity, something with an intention. (My apologies to arachnid fans, it's simply an easy example.)

If you meditate, stray into unsafe territory and pick up a big, scary, toxic energy, I hope you run straight for help. You can personally deal with something of potential danger by asking for assistance from your guides. Ask them to gently move that little friend off your back and send him back to where he came from. Use your *SRB.* (If you haven't already started a page on 'things to do if you feel unclear', please do so.) If you meditate and feel strange after, you may have crossed into the forest, or visited the perimeter, and picked up a little bug. When doing Lightwork it is of the utmost importance that we navigate and explore at a comfortable pace, and please, if you are going into the forest, take your GPS. Using *Prayer for Lightworkers* is like putting an imaginary GPS in your guides' hands. We might call it a 'galactic positioning system'.

Prayer for Lightworkers

Father, Mother, God, Goddess, Creator, Source of All That Is; it is my intention to be of service to the Light. I am in surrender; God's will be done. Thy will is my will, we are one. Please, see that I am complete on all levels, vibrations and frequencies, and in all bodies. If I am fragmented from any part of my Self, I command and demand those fragments to return now in complete form with no alteration or additions.

Please remove anything dark or negative from any of my bodies or aspects of myself, known or unknown to me, and return these to their creator. In asking that this is done, I know it is so.

I ask for assistance in my Lightwork and in all aspects of my life and growth. Please guide me to do what is in accordance with my Divine Plan. Please assist me in staying in my heart center and using Creator as a guide. It is my intention to work and listen to pure Christ Consciousness Light and only Christ Consciousness Light.

Thank you and Amen.

Working Together

If you want to raise the frequency of any meditation or communication with your guides, why not ask a friend to help you *hold space*? Holding space means that someone holds the same intention that you hold. We can hold space for one another to embrace a specific frequency or intention. If someone I care about is having surgery, I will offer to hold space for them during the procedure. I envision them in Light and ask for their Angels and guides to protect them while they are under anesthesia. Holding space can help in many situations, but the Soul is in charge. Don't feel disappointed if your prayers aren't answered, we must hold the highest in mind, which may or may not be what we want.

Truly, I am a believer. But it still gets me excited when I think of how common energy attracts people. In classes, when I have advertised a theme, people show up to learn about that specific idea. I have watched the guides come in and work. Sometimes I can see that the theme is what we are all working on, but other times I wonder if it's a ruse to gather Lightworkers and help us clear something completely different. Once I advertised a group on *remembering who you are*. The class was underway; I was talking about the theme and noticed that each person was releasing an orange energy. Interesting, I thought, that everyone has the same issue (identified by me as orange). When I looked closer, I felt it had a maternal feeling, woven through with stifled creativity, and then it was gone. Wow! I witnessed a second chakra healing for our entire group; a healing that was due to a current of common need, but it had nothing to do with our subject. Or did it? After that, I looked for what might be happening in groups while we focused on the advertised subject. I joke about it now, saying that we could discuss our grocery lists and Creator will do what our Souls intend. Sometimes I tell everyone, "While you are holding space for our subject, thank your guides for helping you release any impeding energies that block your desires and ability to manifest." Or, I remain quiet and smile.

What draws us into groups for healing? We are all psychic! Next time you ask yourself, "What on Earth am I doing here?" Look around. If you have judgment of anyone, ask God/Goddess/Creator to extract every little critical thought from your mind. That's the trick to healing. Find the love; find the common thread of Light, ignore annoying behavior. Start asking for blessings from The Divine for everyone and see if you can raise the frequency of the group or situation. If you are gathered to heal, open space so it can happen. If possible, ask permission to set *sacred space* so that everyone can hold the intention together.

These days, people are sending out prayers and meditations over the Internet to gather forces for Lightwork. We can focus on one idea together and bring healing to any situation. (Did you get the one where everyone prayed for a particular lake? That water must be fantastic!) But how do you focus the energy with so many people and so many ideas? *Creation Divine* prayer, which is next, helps wash away the mental interference. It helps you isolate ego body ideas for clearing. This opens space for Divine Inspiration. Use it to center before workshops, seminars and group happenings so Light can do the work. Gathering together, we anchor love into our beautiful planet.

Creation Divine

Blessed be the inspirations that feed our minds and hearts. Through them we create motivation and desire. We call forth to Source Light Inspiration and offer ourselves in service.

God/Goddess, awaken our Lights to their true purpose. Align our senses to Divine Knowledge and Truth. Let our service become Universal Law. Those who serve as one create as one.

Creation Divine, Creation Pure, Will of All, The Absolute, Source; guide us to the path of enrichment and consciousness as our hearts, minds, bodies, Spirits and Souls remember oneness, responsibility and truth.

We recognize that thought begets and forgives. We are one, unified and creating together through intention and action. As one, "I love, I forgive, I Am."

Thank you and Amen.

Are we healing you or me?

Working with energy can be daunting. It takes strong focus to hold space so that Source can pour in Light and release negative energy. Your focus is necessary whether you are meditating on your personal questions or working with someone else. I have mentioned, and will likely continue to mention, responsibility and protocol. When our guides are deciding which entrance to use (front door, side door, cracked window, chimney) we sometimes get hung up on technique or verbiage. Occasionally, when we are working so hard, we forget to wait patiently for them to decide when, where and how they will work with us. We begin to direct, thinking we are efficient.

There is so much to understand when you work with ethereal beings. I guess you could say the same of human beings. Interpretation can cause problems. I want to take this opportunity to share something with you; something that has helped me immensely with interpretation. When my client Faye asked for help with her unruly teenager I received two ideas from our guides, and I have used both of these often. First, when someone tells you something, ask them, *"What do you mean?"*

I have found *"What do you mean?"* to be a profound question. Ask it sometime and see what happens. Almost every time I ask, I am enlightened. I have asked my husband, admittedly when I don't like his last remarks. However, when he explains what he means, I find myself wide-eyed with embarrassment. I assume too much; I listen and (unethically) use my psychic energy to hurry conversation by assuming his intentions and answering what he has not asked. All this based on an opening statement.

Out in the world I have asked and learned what someone actually *meant*. Humans are not always the best communicators. When asked, they tend to get more specific. That greatly helps getting the results one wants, whether that one is you or someone else.

Second, when someone is complaining about an issue, especially when you want to offer a solution, try, *"Oh my, what are you going to do about that?"* This lets the person know that you believe they have tools, and you see them as capable of solving their own issues. Unless someone asks for your help, especially a teenager, don't offer it. Ask questions. If they really want your help and you choose to offer it, then make sure you have a very specific request. Many problems are rudimentary. We don't always need to offer answers, sometimes the best resource is to direct the person to their own inner knowing. From those two simple ideas I learned that I don't have to solve all the issues, and I don't have to guess what people mean. That frees up quite a bit of time and creates more authentic conversations.

Those two spiritual questions/suggestions from Faye's session would make another great page for your *SRB*. Start a "help" or "great ideas for communication" page. If you have trouble remembering, use sticky notes or index cards to help; eventually you will find your subconscious automatically asking, "What do they mean?"

If you find yourself stuck in a situation where you have assumed something, step back and ask for healing. Assess the interpretation you focused on and try to release it. We can get attached to our assumptions. It's a mental body reaction, we love to be right. A little joke I play with myself is that I know I need to work on my need to be right, but my business is based on accuracy. Therefore, I do love to be right.

When the mental body/ego takes over, we are in trouble. Love your mental body, it is a useful and necessary part of you. A spiritual guide once told me that it is my physical body that tells me I am hungry, but my mental body drives the car and decides where to shop. God/Goddess bless our mental bodies! Love your mental body, listen to your mental body, but don't let it take over. It's easy for our egos get out of control if they aren't managed. Maybe you have experienced a situation that left you hurt, only to later find out that you blew it out of proportion. (Also known as: over-reacting, a primary skill of the mental body.) We have all assumed or misinterpreted someone's thoughts. *Interpretation Prayer* can help you open your heart to the possibility that you have access to God's understanding and love. (Dear God, What the heck did they mean?)

Just in case this point isn't clear, here is another perspective. Words from people can hurt us. We can strive to understand cruelty and aggression. We can work on why something happened, and clear the issue. But we are delicate flowers in a big, wide world of experience. Imagine yourself in Divine Light, see that you are the perfect image of the I Am Presence and you are opening like a blooming rose. You are beautiful, soft and as sensitive as delicate petals. But every time someone feels jealous of you, a petal falls. Someone is rude to you, another petal falls. Each time someone challenges your thinking, you release a petal. Negative thoughts cause a petal to drop. Soon you are a drooping, extinguishing, former rose.

That's dangerous! We must learn to override the opinions of others and look to the heart frequencies within. We are strong and full of Light that transmutes. With compassion and understanding we are less affected by cruel, flippant comments or the exaggerations of our own minds. Use *Interpretation Prayer* to find grace and nurture your beautiful, blooming self. Keep your petals, let Source interpret and deliver your messages.

Interpretation Prayer

Father, Mother, God, Goddess, Creator, Source of All That Is; I call forth your assistance in understanding my interaction with ______. Please help me understand the meaning of all words and actions, from all participants in this situation including myself. Please help me see* *why I created this and what I intend to learn. I allow all anger, jealousy, shame and resentment to evaporate with this understanding. I Am love. I Am Light.*

Thank you and Amen.

**Use this space for someone's name, a feeling or circumstance.*

The Story of the Prayer for Balance

One day I was looking for something on my computer and I ran across a file that I didn't recognize. I opened it and read what I now call *Prayer for Balance*. It made me cry. Where did this writing come from? I couldn't remember anything about it, but I knew I needed it and should read it every day. *Prayer for Balance* touched me deeply, it was so beautiful and rich; it felt like forgiveness, compassion and understanding from The Divine. I wanted to live the words, to remember where everything within me came from, to surrender and know at the same time.

After a few days of reading the prayer, I had a flashback. Months earlier, while typing I was reflecting on *Serenity Prayer*[15] when writing came to me, which I saved and forgot. I wrote it! I wrote *Prayer for Balance*. Are you familiar with *Serenity Prayer*?

God, grant me the serenity to accept the things I cannot change;
The courage to change the things I can;
And wisdom to know the difference.

Reinhold Niebuhr[16] is quoted as saying, "The prayer may have been spooking around for years, even centuries, but I don't think so. I honestly do believe that I wrote it myself." I think Niebuhr may have channeled *Serenity Prayer*. Further research indicates that there are other possible sources, but none as solid as Niebuhr. We may never officially know what inspired Niebuhr or *Prayer for Balance* for that matter. What I know, and feel, is that the reason for both prayers is to let go and let God. Surrender to your higher power knowing that you are not separate, you are One.

New confidence came for me the day I remembered writing the *Prayer for Balance*. I don't know how I typed something, saved it in a file on my computer and then completely forgot about it. When the memory came back it dawned on me. *It dawned on me*. The sun came up, and I got it. The *Prayer for Balance* came from within me. Walking a spiritual road has taught me that if you have a Divine experience, don't get attached to how it happened. If it tastes good—eat it with gratitude. If it feels good, accept it with gratitude. Every time I read *Prayer for Balance* I feel God/Goddess/Creator/Source and I feel good. It's a delicious source of Light and I am so grateful to be the conduit of such a blessing.

Channeling, bringing information from another source, is challenging to prove, especially to one's self. When I read *Prayer for Balance*, I felt Oneness. I felt overwhelming Light and love unify within me. *Me*. At the time, I thought myself as least likely to channel; least likely to be clear or worthy or listened to. My faith and trust in the Divine changed that very moment of remembering. It wasn't that I remembered I wrote it (or typed it), that came later; it was that I remembered something inside. Maybe I found a spark of Light, or an essence of the Divine. Whatever it was, I began to associate myself with God… and God with me. As one. I felt the Divine in me. *Me*.

Of course, when you read it, I don't expect you to see my Divinity. Hopefully you can read it without sensing me at all. Think of yourself, *your* Divinity, your oneness, your ability to fall into the arms of Angels and be accepted without question. Can a prayer do that? Each time I read it my mind settles, my heart opens and that unfathomable proposal, WE ARE ONE, seems solid. Not because I can channel, but because I can believe. Because I can rest. I can live. I can know. It's an odd confidence. There's nothing solid about knowing God. You can't hold it with your arms, but you can feel as if you've eternally held it. You can't photograph yourself on vacation with God, but you can adventure with God in your heart and remember.

In sessions I often hear: *Thinking everything is a message is more important than missing one message.* Aha! Maybe I am not so foolish after all. And, if I am, I forgive myself! I seek balance. I ask God to help me remember that I am human. I sing, I talk, I vow and I forget. I witness, I see, I assume and I forgive. If I tune into my pure Light guidance I have the ultimate resource for everything that I need. Information can drop out of the clear blue sky into my consciousness. When I set appropriate space, align myself with Creator and listen, we become One. That is balance. That is beauty.

Prayer for Balance

God, grant me the vision to see that everything placed in front of me is from Spirit so that I may embrace every happening and every moment in my life as a gift.

Grant me memory to use when I think I am doing something; help me to remember it is the oneness of all that truly does the work.

God, please help me remember that I am the oneness, all power that moves through me is a sign of my investment in the purpose of my life and the intention of my purpose is to be the perfect expression of the Will of God, which is truly the will of all, and therefore my will.

God, please continue in your valiant efforts, which are my efforts, to bring surrender into my heart, mind and body so that I may experience the Spirit of all in this physical manifestation.

God, I pray that I can uphold my end of the bargain by completely forgetting all of my ideas and remember that each perfect moment is another example of an expression of the highest teaching and the highest truth.

Let me see opportunity to forgive and to know that forgiveness comes from my heart easily and ceaselessly for all I encounter and, with all my power, for myself.

Let my love and forgiveness for myself become the beacon that others see, and let that beacon lead them to their own awareness of self-love.

Thank you and Amen.

The Alignment Continues

Releasing negative thinking seems to be a theme for our culture. It's finally popular to be in love with you! In the 1980's Cybill Shepard starred in hair color commercials where she said, "Because I'm worth it!" I remember feeling embarrassed; to me, it seemed so vain to love yourself. A popular insult for young women at the time was, "She's conceited." Well, times have changed. Now it's popular to be a b-word, it's good to love yourself the most and narcissism is a fad. With social pressure, I suppose we act more confident, but are we? If one buys expensive hair products and flashes a confident smile, does that mean all the negativity is gone? No, it doesn't. We've grown smarter about hiding. And that is exactly why we have to excavate our subconscious minds.

It doesn't matter whether your negative voice comes from a childhood experience or a past life, you can use prayer to heal it. The first step is to take responsibility. Stop using blame and projection; both create further issues *and* both are perpetuated in our society. People want to know how mean your mother was, how absent your father was. Watch for this; if you are exposing an issue, make sure it is for healing, not sport.

Let's start with the mirror. Many times I have heard my guides tell clients to look in the mirror and compliment themselves. Louise Hay recommends this as well, calling it *mirror work*[17]. Some of the most confident people squirm at this idea. From my own experience, I found the idea challenging. I practiced with quick glances and short comments. I encourage you to give yourself this assignment. Here are the rules:

1. Eye contact. You must look directly into your own eyes as you speak.
2. All compliments must be spoken out loud. No mental telepathy, whispering or notes. (Although you can add those later, we can all use a sticky note that says: Hi, Beautiful!)
3. Giggling, squirming, crying and eye rolling *are* allowed. Give yourself permission to be uncomfortable, then release it and start over.

Incidentally, if you are having a hard time looking yourself in the eyes, try to find out if eye contact is an issue overall. Can you hold someone's eyes while talking, or do you look away? If so, practice with your own image to improve. I challenge you to try this exercise. Look into your eyes and love yourself. Be vocal and appreciative and loving. Compliment your eye color, your hair style, your voice. Tell yourself you are successful and engaging, reliable and honest. Go for it! And maybe, if you are feeling adventurous, create a collage for your *SRB* dedicated to compliments. I use a piece of card stock and old magazines. It's fun.

Is self-love our greatest challenge? Are we afraid to admire, enjoy and compliment ourselves? If we are, how can we trust ourselves? Learning to trust self is learning to trust God/Goddess/Source and the voice of Spirit that comes through each one of us. What do spiritual messages mean if you, yourself do not trust the person receiving them, *which is you*!? Use the *Prayer for Positive Thinking* to realign your thoughts to the positive.

I am positively sure that I love and appreciate myself. I am positively sure that I love and appreciate mySelf. I AM POSITIVELY SURE THAT I LOVE AND APPRECIATE MYSELF!! (your turn...)

Prayer for Positive Thinking

Father, Mother, God, Goddess, Creator, Source of All That Is; it is my intention to think positive, expressive, helpful thoughts. Be it known now that I Am increasing my positive energy in every moment.

I Am an expression of positive thinking. I Am a reflection of positive thinking. I Am a magnet for positive thinking. I welcome and enjoy positive thinking. I love positive thinking.

My thoughts reflect my positive self-image and esteem. My smile spreads positive emotions and confidence. I Am positive. Be it so, through my own self-empowerment I grant myself grace, and bless myself into the new me... POSITIVE!

Thank you and Amen.

Expanding Your Wisdom

Before I knew how energy is archived, I felt like there was some residual pool in the sky that held information. I would ask people if they felt it, this residual pool, in the sky... Back then, before I could hear my guides clearly, prior to the prayers and encounters with Angels, all I had were these strange ideas and a lot of confusion. It can be difficult, trying to understand something that exists in another dimension.

We have quite a few Earth terms that don't make sense from an ethereal perspective. Without time or space, we don't need linear concepts like *vertical energy*. There is no up or down, and truly, if you want to know... God/Goddess/Creator/Source does not live in the sky; your Divine and True Source is within you. And if there is no time or space, then where (and how) is everything archived? How is Karma kept track of? There are no libraries, vaults or file cabinets of information that hold the archives of our past lives, right? Well, that depends. Remember in Chapter Three when I mentioned the Akashic Records? That is the archive of everything.

Many people have asked about the Akashic Records; during one session my guides explained to a client that there is an energetic archive that holds all happenings and events. The client asked if every lie, even a small white lie, would be remembered. We were told where truth is concerned, each reckoning holds a specific weight; truth is the lightest and non-truths the heaviest. If one were to tell a lie that hurt many people, it would have an impact, or memory, that is conclusive and therefore held as a viable energy. That energy has a weight to it and maintains its currency.

We would term that as archived—which would create Karma, requiring balance. Contemplate small happenings, incidentals, as if they are written on tissue paper; and large happenings, major events, as if they are inscribed in stone. Tissue paper dissipates; stone lasts. When we look back, we see the stone archives first. These create our Karma, what we work on in each lifetime.

The Akashic Records are our ethereal library. If you meditate and see a past life, you are retrieving that information from the Akashic Records. That means that there is a resource for all information, every happening and, believe it or not, every perspective. When you work with a client or even talk to someone, there can be barriers. Language can be an issue, and so can understanding. My aunt told me that where she grew up in Tennessee people would say "I don't care to" and it meant "I don't mind". If I asked my Aunt to pick up apples at the store and she replied, "I don't care to," that would indicate I get apples. If I said, "I don't care to," that means no apples.

When you are working with people, or when you are listening to your guides, verbiage may have a different meaning than what you are accustomed. That is why I like to ask for my clarification to be assisted via Source. I have my mind; my experiences, past and knowledge, but I also have access to the Akashic Records, which is essentially all experiences and all knowledge.

Access to the Akashic Records is not exclusive or limited to experienced Lightworkers. It is likely that you are already using the records in your daily life. Expand your awareness with the following prayer. *Prayer for New Knowledge* will help you align to a higher and more expansive part of yourself; a place where you can access knowledge without limiting your ability to learn.

Prayer for New Knowledge

Father, Mother, God, Goddess, Creator, Source of All That Is; I request assistance to understand the evolution of knowledge. Please assist me in releasing any blocks to learning and comprehending. Please assist me in accepting all wisdom and learning pertaining to new knowledge. I pray for understanding while my mind releases and my connection to Source gains strength. I accept all this as an example of further truth that we are all One.

I allow my mind, body and Spirit to integrate knowledge, wisdom and understanding from all sources of one-hundred percent Christ Consciousness Light, truth and unconditional love. I acknowledge myself as guided, guarded and protected on my journey.

Thank you and Amen.

Oh no, not another Divine learning experience!

Again, with the responsibility! This time it is regarding healing. Are we actually manifesting everything? Yes. Do thoughts truly create? Yes.

When you do readings, or if you have a reading, what is read is the energy. For me, these energies are another language. Like snowflakes, ethereal beings appear the same, yet no two are alike. I have been told that our spiritual guides do not exchange words in the ethers; they communicate with thought. Without physical bodies, there are no voice boxes; therefore, if I am hearing words it must be due to an interpretation on my behalf. I asked my guides if this was true and they gave me two answers. Yes and no. That is the most common answer that I hear from spiritual guides, and to be honest, it can be a little annoying.

I am making fun of the desire I have to get answers. That yearning is present, but I do my best to use surrender so that I can remain clear. When I do readings, I have learned to be aware of subtle changes so that if something less than Christ Consciousness comes in, I can notice and check the lights. I pay attention to the message, or the snowflake. The origin is in my periphery; I am aware of it. But I can't bring accurate messages through if I am distracted by trying to figure out where the snowflakes originate. That job is for the Beings of Light that you work with in meditation and those that help you create *sacred space*.

My guides generally work with suggestion, rather than answers. For instance, I was going on a trip and I wanted to write. My laptop is on the heavy side and I toyed with buying a new one. In meditation I asked, "Should I take a computer." The answer was, "You won't use it." Not, "No". The decision was mine; they gave me information. I could decide, do I want to buckle down and write or surrender to what is coming and leave the heavy laptop at home? They don't try to create dependency so that I rely on them for every decision. On the contrary they are there, without judgment, to teach. They gave me an answer and a way to get to know myself better. I choose not to bring the laptop on my trip and it worked out that when I wanted to write, there was a computer at my disposal.

At this point you may still be wondering, does one actually hear their guides? Or is it all interpretation? I hear my Beings of Light. In the beginning I heard words, as if a human were speaking. I would share the information with my clients as carefully and clearly as I could. Eventually, the words became so fast I could not relay the entire message. When I learned to surrender into the energy, the information became a knowing that I could speak. The energetic exchange happens at my High-Self level. There, I can rely on my ethereal beings to manage Christ Consciousness Light. After years of practice, I am aware of slight shifts of energy. If warranted, I will stop the session to ask for clearing—or anything that is necessary to maintain Christ Consciousness Light.

It didn't start this way. It took me years to allow information to flow without a pause between them talking and me listening. This connection was developed primarily through my meditation practice, and secondarily through readings. I call it *channeling*. Some people don't like that word, but I see myself as a *conduit*, a pipe or resource or channel; imagine an antenna held up high, receiving and then sharing. It's not the term channeling that I question; it's the intent and whether one works with pure Christ Consciousness Light. Before I work with an ethereal being, I identify the frequency, signature or vibration in meditation where I am in control of surrounding energies, not in readings. If a frequency is recognizable to me (and I still check Lights) because I have meditated and used a familiar environment to learn about it, I will work with it. I do not allow random guides or any other entity in my sessions. This is not done unconsciously; it is not random. I work with ethereal beings in a state of surrender, *via responsibility and protocol*, after I have *set space* and in *vertical light*. This never wavers, it takes time and effort to be diligent. Sacrificing the protocol reduces my purity and clarity.

Some ethereal beings have voices. If an Ascended Master has had an incarnation, and many have, they might use that particular voice or image. What works best for me is to continue checking the lights and let the voice be what it is. Rather than worry about a genuine voice/voice box I focus on the message and its clarity. I watch the energy. I check the frequency. And lights. (Maybe a bumper sticker should come with this book: Check the Light!)

When someone comes for spiritual work and asks about their physical body I ask my guides to look. (We are not doctors, we do not replace doctors. I am speaking of energy.) Sometimes I see dark energy; this can be a message to look for something. Remember, we don't have to label what we see. It can be blue, cloudy, dense or smelly. Before asking the guides anything, I ask if the client would like clearing. For instance, "There is something heavy feeling and dark, would you like me to ask for clearing?" This is very important! Sometimes they don't want it. I once asked a client if she was ready to give up her autoimmune issues. She was on disability and saw her current journey changing when she discovered the root cause of her illness. She said, "I don't know if I am ready." It was an honest answer. Souls have their journeys; we are here to assist each other not interfere.

For those that *want* healing offered by spiritual beings (not by me, I am the conduit—not the healer), I ask the guides to clear the energy that I am shown. This means that I don't direct. It is essential that we honor each other's paths. Interference does not bode well energetically. If you cross boundaries, you will pay. It's like the person who went walking in the woods. You don't want to be a magnet for dark energy by walking in and saying *go away*. It doesn't work with mosquitoes or entities. You may be the only other light in the forest (or room). There is an easier way and it is in these pages. By taking responsibility we honor that someone may not want to heal right now, by using protocol we check to see where that decision originates. If it's from an entity, a possession or some other dark force, we can help alleviate discomfort by creating high frequency, protected *sacred space*. At least then the person can have some relief, and if appropriate, the guides can work. If it is a decision from the Soul, we can honor each other and our sometimes karma-laden journeys.

Psychics and intuitives can be shown energetic issues that may be the psychosomatic cause of a future illness or disease. These are hard to prove, but an experienced energy reader will recognize an illness frequency. Illnesses have signatures, an identifiable vibration. Incidentally, so does everything. Addictive drugs have signatures, as do harmful experiences like rape or abuse. We learn these signatures through experience, either our own or through someone else.

If you discover a signature and the client is not having symptoms, there is a great possibility that the energy can be released before it becomes a physical issue; much healing happens like this. Have you ever received healing work and walked away feeling a great relief? You may have released something tiny before it manifested into a virus/illness/disease.

If an issue is beyond energetic, if there is a physical symptom, we might need additional help. We are not doctors (unless, of course, you are a doctor). I want what is best for myself and my client. During one such session someone complained of fatigue and poor focus. I asked the guides for information and they suggested a dental issue. My client went to the dentist twice yearly but decided to take the advice. It turned out that she had a bacterial infection in her mouth and it was compromising her immune system, making her tired.

Occasionally, I will work with another person to create a duo of healing and informational flow. One such time, Andrea made an appointment and I believe a miracle happened. Andrea explained that her nose was broken after a recent fall; however, she said that wasn't important because her hip was hurting, causing a problem with exercise. We set *sacred space* and her guides joined us bringing powerful healing energy. I didn't pay attention exactly, I simply held space while watching the light show. Then information came through about Andrea's nose and what the damage could do to future breathing; in fact, the guides were more concerned about her nose than her hip. After the session Andrea left for home feeling great.

I did not hear from Andrea for about six months. Which isn't unusual, healed wings often fly away. When she called to reschedule she casually said, "Oh, yeah, I forgot to tell you, after our last session my hip healed and so did my nose!"

Although Andrea's intention was to heal her hip, she mentioned her broken nose and the guides took the opportunity to direct energy to both places. Clients have reported changes in x-rays, shrinking tumors, disappearances and reconnections, events that cannot be explained. Regardless, I am careful about healing. The client must hold the intention; I try to look only where I am directed. No peeking. My favorite healings are when something is purged from the subconscious mind; when habits change, fears release and life gets happy. I have learned not to hope for healing, but to listen and ask Source for direction. Andrea wanted to heal and she did. But there are occasions when one needs to hold onto something for an unknown reason. The *Willingness to Heal Prayer* is used to open us. It's an issue can-opener. If you find the blanks awkward, rewrite the prayer with specifics for your intention.

Willingness to Heal Prayer

(fill in blank with what you wish to heal from)

Source Light, through my Divine Manifestation I have managed to produce __________. I am no longer in denial. I embrace __________ as the sacred messenger it is.

As __________ teaches me I release __________ from any further obligation to be with me. I command my body and mind to recognize its ability to be free of __________.

I am willing myself to heal. I open my heart and Soul to the Divine Origination of my perfection. Like a fine machine I open myself to operating perfectly. I allow myself care and cooperation in this endeavor.

I am healthy, healed and awake. I am astounded, amazed and surprised at my ability to heal quickly. I am alive, loved, embraced and guided. I am One.

Thank you and Amen.

When illness threatens life, Lightworkers have other tools to offer help. One particular case was brought to my doorstep through family circumstances. Jessica (not her real name), an eleven-year-old, was diagnosed with lymphoma and needed a bone marrow transplant. Jessica's prognosis was grim, her therapies life threatening. During meditation and prayer, I saw her inner Light, which led me to trust that she would survive the treatment; that, and a message from my guides. While Jessica and her mother were visiting, I asked Source how I could be in service, they suggested shopping. Not my usual assignment.

But I took the idea and ran with hit. After asking Jessica's mom, I hunted down coupons for a popular kid's store. We had a blast. I watched Jessica, how her Light affected everyone. Cancer in children is heart wrenching. You see their small frames and pale skin, bald heads; yet, under all that Jessica was like a little sun. People weren't afraid of her, they talked to her and she told them anything they wanted to know. I craved, yearned to bring forth healing and see Jessica recover. Yet, when I meditated the message was clear: Jessica was with God and her destiny was between them.

Since the cancer diagnosis Jessica's mom spent every night with her. She did not leave her once during repeated hospital stays; not one mental health day or reprieve for a tired care-taker. I arranged for an overnight stay at a famous hotel in the area, knowing Jessica may decide not to be there without her mama. But she was delighted to have a special girl's night. As the chaperone to three young ladies, I was the entertainment committee. We made jewelry and Jessica modeled the new clothes she purchased on our shopping trip. What I thought was a treat for Jessica was more likely a much needed break for her mom.

During the time I spent with Jessica her mom noticed significant healing of an open wound. These wounds are common with Jessica's treatment; they can take months to heal. Jessica was more energetic than usual. Through it all, not once did I ask to be a channel of healing or move from the tasks I was given by Source. It was hard, unbelievably hard. When I look back, it was a series of moments. Memories for our family. Jessica is in her twenties now, still living and creating happy moments.

I was blessed by the grace that came with Jessica's visit and how I could be of service. She beat lymphoma and a few other issues, and still shines her Light today.

This prayer was written for Jessica. Please change the name to suit your needs.

Prayer for Someone Ill

Father, Mother, God, Goddess, Creator, Source of All That Is; we ask for assistance for Jessica. Please bless her with harmony of heart, to endure her path. Please bless her with peace of mind, to understand. Please help her eyes shine with God's Light so that all who love Jessica see her inner peace and beauty.

We pray for Jessica's pain-free recovery. We visualize her good health and joyous future. We acknowledge her as God's child, a child that is loved and cared for by an army of Angels, a wealth of Light.

Through the Light of God let our prayers be answered, let Jessica heal.

Thank you and Amen.

Chapter Six

Understanding Clearing Work

Remember when I mentioned that meditating is like showering, or dusting your coffee table? People will know if you don't do it. Let's say that you didn't meditate for a while. Life is going along fast and then it gets a little faster. You begin to move through days like a teenage driver speeding through town while singing with the radio, occasionally crossing double yellow lines. In youthful splendor, wind is blowing through your hair as you drive with a carefree heart, all the stoplights are—never mind, what stoplights? You're spontaneous, lighthearted, a little sweaty. Imagine that happy-go-lucky teenager that doesn't have to make rent or a house payment, driving down the road as if nothing matters.

But it's a fleeting moment. The teenager in us will eventually have to accept that others say we are irresponsible, late, unconscious or oblivious. What? Why would anyone ruin a perfectly harmless daydream? Because, dear Lightworker, it isn't harmless. Why the dramatic comparison? Metaphorically, it's not that far from the truth. Double yellow lines represent parameters and boundaries. Traffic lights remind us of proper timing. What are most teenagers learning about? Discipline and responsibility. Although this isn't about actual teenagers; it's about the immaturity in all of us. Meditation/spiritual practice teaches us discipline to stay centered and create our learning experiences consciously, with peace, ease and comfort.

Know this: *Source protects the novice.* If you are beginning on your spiritual path, you may feel like you are safely bouncing against rubber walls. This happens for the exact amount of time necessary, then the walls turn to *wood* or *drywall* or *concrete.* That's when I feel like someone is saying, "Quit fooling around." Also know this: when you are no longer a novice, it can feel abrupt. Somehow, I doubt that you are a novice; it is likely that you are experienced. I would guess that you have fallen down and scraped your ethereal knees while dabbling in psychic matters. The spiritual path is available to everyone and we each have a unique route. Yours may be a path of pebbles, grass or even flagstone. You may feel dirt between your toes or an escalator to the sky. Visualize your path to Source and create an image. It can be a deeply rooted tree, a high-rise building or a flying carpet. When you choose an image you give yourself something you can check every day. If the escalator isn't running, your guides may be trying to tell you something.

It might also be helpful to create a collage as a physical representation of your chosen image and add it to your *SRB.* I have collected pictures and words from magazine and junk mail for pages in my *SRB.* I feel that the physical representation reinforces my mental picture. The prayers in this chapter could be in there, too. Metaphysical issues reflect in our physical world. If you use your own mind power through vision and creativity, you are messaging yourself from physical world to non-physical. Imagery is directly connected to clairvoyance. Using your imagination opens up venues for spiritual communication.

By having a visual concept, you can train your brain to watch for distortion. This works as a reference so that you can notice interference. Most of us are suffering some type of interference. It might be from a past life, childhood experience or even inherited. Regardless of origin, we must clear out negative baggage so that we are open to our guides and Light Beings. Spiritual guidance is not hidden or restricted based on some criteria. It's on the other side of a barrier. We can release barriers to our spiritual guidance by clearing negativity.

Clearing negativity isn't as hard as it sounds. It begins with identification. When I first learned about negative energy, it scared me and I swore I would never deal with it. I was like a kid throwing a fit: no clearings, no entities, no ghosts and *absolutely no dead people*. My visceral response was a clue. Guess what I do now? It's ironic how what frightens us or what seems impossible is what we have potential doing. Here are a few examples of that:

> *I once saw a client's eyes bug out in shock. It was a relatively normal session, not an exorcism or anything. The bugging happened when I relayed a message about her working with teenagers. No, she informed me; she was in graduate school to become a therapist but absolutely not for teenagers, after all she had raised three boys. Eventually, she graduated and her work led to helping teens.*
>
> *In another reading, I spoke to a young man about going back to school to become a chef. No way—that wasn't going to happen; although he wanted to, he certainly couldn't afford it. I explained that there was energy there, I could see school happening. And I could see a resource for tuition, possibly from his former stepfather. Yes, his mother's ex-husband! It didn't sound likely, possible or plausible. Time went by. His mother remarried her ex-husband, who paid for school. My client graduated and now works as a chef.*
>
> *Another person hated talking in front of people. She became nervous, jumbled her words and felt inadequate. She never imagined what*

clearing negative energy would allow. We worked on issues prohibiting her self-confidence. She is now a yoga teacher who does readings and healings.

Hint: pay attention to where and when you say "never".

I could offer you inspirational quotes about fear, what there is to fear, how we fear and the potential of fear, but it won't make a difference. Not wanting to do something isn't about being afraid. Let me explain. The therapist I mentioned was already spiritual. Her resistance to her destiny had nothing to do with her connection to Source, her guides or Angels. The resistance, our resistance, is there because it's where the path narrows. Our world gets tight and we become hyper-aware of our surroundings. We feel constricted.

Imagine yourself as a pipe. If there is a clog, and you want something to go through, it won't. It can't, there is an obstruction. The clog isn't fear, it's back-up. Something is stuck. There are two great opportunities when it comes to clearing obstructions. *One:* shove it down roto-rooter style. Push hard and barrel through. This is likely the most painful choice, but effective. *Two:* identify what the clog is and find out what makes it smaller. You can be aggressive, fight and conquer or you can identity and proceed with your intelligence. Guess which one makes for an easier life? And aren't we all about peace, ease and comfort?

Our dreams and desires are highly charged energetic opportunities. They come with lessons. When my work progressed, I had to face the real reason I didn't want to talk to dead people.

Through meditation, and guidance from others, I discovered that my resistance to dead people had many levels. I was worried about being fooled, about being wrong. I felt that dead people haunted. I was afraid of being connected to the astral field. And what about possession? Remember that many ethereal beings were once alive. Many

Ascended Masters have lived on Earth. Jesus walked here. Essentially, Ascended Masters *are* dead people. So if I was to do my work at all, I would have to move this particular judgment aside or risk not being clear.

Eventually, I was doing a reading and someone asked about a deceased relative. In that moment, I could see Divine Light come forth and was able to receive a message. I learned that with *sacred space*, vertical light and surrender, talking to dead people was no different than working with Angels.

Are you ready to deal with some clogs? At this point, I strongly suggest a sit-down with your guides. It took me a long time to establish peace, ease and comfort as my theme because I was already branded with "School of Hard Knocks". I had to rewrite the script. (I am trying hard not to say it.) The next time you meditate, remind your guides that you wish to live in peace, with great ease and comfort. (Because you are...) Stand in your truth, know what you want. Understand that doing Lightwork means clearing out what stops you from being the Divinity that you are. In your vertical *pillar of Light* make a statement about your creation. (I know you remember!) It's all about... *responsibility and protocol.* (There, I said it!) If I created that clogged pipe, I can clear it out. Thank you and amen.

It's time to delve deeper into prayer and healing, release and integration. It might feel a tad confrontational. You may not clear as fast as you would like to; you may need to do homework. Write or talk things out. Address stuckness, desire, regret, anger, resistance or whatever you experience via meditation with your guides or with someone that you trust. Take your questions into your *safe place* and ask your guides/Creator for support. Demand it! Stomp your feet and claim it. Don't give up, you are worth healing, I promise.

Teamwork

Your guides won't judge or be angry with you, ever. Spiritual guides and Angels do not give up, and they are never impatient. If your Angel is tapping her foot, if your guides are raising their eyebrows; send them on their merry way. (Banished!) Pray and request pure Christ Consciousness Light guides, your true guides, and wait until your heart fills with love and your ethereal eyes open to see the Divine Truth they represent. Have patience with your particular *clair*. You may never see your guides, but that doesn't mean they aren't there. Each of us can learn our guides' energetic signature. Try this: get four friends together. Have someone sit in a chair wearing a blindfold. Take turns standing behind that person and see if she/he can guess who is there by feeling. Play games with yourself so that you can learn to feel energy. Trust me, you are already identifying by how you feel. This is taking that intuition to the next level.

I play a game with my mail. We are on the end of a delivery route, which sometimes becomes the beginning of another route. Therefore, my mail can come very early or very late. Or somewhere in between. When I wonder if it has arrived, I envision my mailbox. Is it full? Empty? I feel the inside with my mind. I am right most of the time, but ironically, I still check the box to see.

Wrong or right, psychic or oblivious, it doesn't matter. Each life choice is an opportunity for us to choose, and our guides are the fan club in the stands. They are not fair-weather fans; they will not leave before the game ends. On the contrary, they are omnipresent, dedicated and unconditionally loving. They will consistently assist us in clear, unhindered, creative lives; no matter what type of trouble we create for ourselves.

We, the humans, who have capped our vision and hidden our gifts, make mistakes. Our spiritual messages can be blatant, the lessons obvious; but we don't always get it, not while we are there, suffering, complaining and trying to change.

When I began opening spiritually I was in great resistance (which I may have mentioned). I was looking hard toward God. I had hate in my eyes because my friend Nancy was murdered. I blamed, accused, reprimanded, threatened and challenged Source. I was not kind or in service (at least not consciously). Depression came; I could not imagine a harder place to exist. I wanted out, I wanted off this planet and out of this painful, uncomfortable life. There were all these voices in my head and no help; at least that is what I thought. In hindsight, the help was there but it had to swim up-current in a river of piranhas. I was stuck, surrounded by muck that needed to be cleared. I had created my own personal hell.

Apparently, my High-Self had an agenda. Every single experience, including the resistance and anger, was teaching me about my spiritual path. Everything I went through was part of my education. That hard road, that school of hard knocks, made me compassionate and alert to the struggles *we* go through. Who are we? Lightworkers. We are the spiritualists, the helpers, the fixers. When we are out of sorts, encumbered with negativity or restricted, we are less than our light. We must be our Light. We must shine and do our work and be who we are. It's exhausting to be anything else. True freedom for a Lightworker is to do the work regardless of the reward. (Note: I said reward, not exchange.) Lightworkers live in a pay-it-forward world. We have to; the Universe is the only one that can afford to reward us with what we want. And what is that? At one time, I assumed it was enlightenment, but not anymore. My guides have taught me that we all come from an enlightened place and are not separate from our enlightened Souls. What do I want? It might be *living* the enlightenment; it's definitely living a heart-centered, conscious life utilizing my spiritual help, feeling the Oneness that I Am.

When I began writing this book, I debated on whether to include my personal journey. Initially I wrote it all, edited some, deleted most of it, added it back, worried too much was coming from my ego, and then stopped writing. When I asked my friends for their opinions, they told me that depersonalizing my writing made it generic and separate. Each friend encouraged me to add more of myself; they liked the stories. It took me a long time, but I realized my experience is who I am. Keep in mind... it's not random. Everything I went through, I created for a reason. I am taking responsibility so that I can use the experiences as a foundation for growth.

My journey began with thousands of voices. I felt watched, spied upon. I knew the symptoms of schizophrenia and did not mention my feelings to anyone for fear of being locked up or ridiculed. Then I discovered that some of those voices could be eliminated. As this happened my mind cleared and I became less of a puck in a psychic hockey game. My horizontal energy began to ground into the Earth, consequently I felt more supported. When timing, contracts, energy and Light aligned, I heard one clear voice. That's when my journey gained focused and my work emerged. But it took ten years—*ten years!*

In my twenties and early thirties, I had some spiritual experiences and healings; I bought Medicine Cards[18], collected feathers and rocks, and got a few readings, but nothing dispelled the chaos in my head except to abstain from tuning into the inner voice(s). Then I met a man. A friend talked me into going to a group where this man spoke. His name was Rick Lewis[19] and he channeled Kuthumi, an Ascended Master.

We went to someone's house. It was weird. I mean sublimely weird because the house was average and the twelve seekers hoping for a spiritual message seemed normal. There were no signs of a cult; no one burned sage or wore hoods or even ohm-ed. We sat in a circle, on furniture and pillows. The lights were low; it was evening. People waited. All eyes were on Rick, who was imposingly tall, six-foot-four or so, and serious. I felt anxious. Rick prepared to channel and as the frequency rose, I was able to feel and see more and more. It was overwhelming—so I wrote everything. Luckily I had a pad of paper.

Rick closed his eyes and spoke in a funny voice that I thought was ridiculous. I would never, ever do something so silly. I felt embarrassed for him. My stomach tumbled with nervous energy and I wanted to talk. As a Sagittarius, I usually want to talk, it's a nervous habit. Then something strange transpired, *he made sense.* He helped people. I sat incredulous, with my mouth open, watching emotional reactions accompanied by tears of relief. So I joined Rick's cultish group and went to his meetings every two weeks. Just to check it out, you know, see if they served Kool-Aid.

Over time, Rick began helping me clear negativity, insecurity and what I now call a serious case of horizontal energy. He would point above my head and say, "What's that?"

Scared out of my wits, I didn't care; I would say, "Just get rid of it!" I released negative thought forms and entities and who knows what else. Then a weird thing occurred, I began to hear an odd voice in my head, it sounded like Rick's voice channeling Kuthumi. It was like an echo of the group meetings. Confused, I booked a private session with Rick and told him about the voice. The conversation went something like this: (remember I am very naïve at this point)

"When I hear Kuthumi's voice—"

"What?"

"Well, I wanted to make sure he was telling me the right thing—"

"What? You hear him?"

"Well, yes, doesn't everyone in the group? Isn't that what happens?"

"Seriously, you hear him?"

Rick became excited; apparently his guides told him that someone with similar gifts was coming to help him, and he was so glad I was finally there! Great, except for one thing: I was the least likely to channel. Don't think about where I am now, imagine a person who doubted, scoffed and had little experience. There were people in Rick's group that were long time spiritual students, I was a novice. There were people that wanted to hear their guides so badly; I didn't know what I wanted. In fact, I was pretty sure it wasn't to hear voices in my head; yup, pretty sure of that. But there I was, clearly hearing Spirit.

From where I am now I can look back and see two things. One, the guides had been speaking to me for a long time, since I was young. And two, drum roll please, I fought them all the way. In fact, I cursed at the voices and told them to leave me alone, I had to raise children—not be crazy. Two days after the youngest child, my daughter, turned eighteen... I met Rick. *Two days* after my official child rearing duties ended. That was July 2001.

When the other group members learned that Kuthumi spoke to me, I gained a reluctant fan club. I am serious when I say I was least likely to channel. There were those attracted to the energy I channeled, but I am not sure they liked the vehicle: me. Regardless of their questions and requests, my insecurities blocked confidence. It was a rocky start for a confused participant. I felt excited to finally be doing something that felt right but my path was unclear.

Because my mental body purged when I was in any type of elevated frequency, my mind went wild. I would spend hours writing about small experiences that seemed overwhelming. It might be something Rick said, or an argument with a family member. I would write and write and write and then guess what happened? I would write a prayer. It was like a tiny sliver of light amongst the chaos.

Then one day in early 2002, after knowing Rick for seven months, I experienced a bank of clouds, in my bed.

This is a personal and sacred story. Briefly (I could talk about this for hours), I met my High-Self Council. It was early morning; my husband was in the shower. While waiting for my turn, I sat in bed. Sitting up, awake, and not meditating, I relaxed and closed my eyes. Suddenly I was surrounded with clouds. I opened my eyes, no clouds; closed my eyes, clouds. It was a strange dream because I was not asleep. I could see light, it was above me, in fact a hand was reaching down for me so I stretched my arm up (I actually did this) and within seconds I was in a circle of Light Beings. The one that led me there was next to me, he seemed to be some sort of guide or leader so I asked his name. I heard, "St. Germain". There were others, twelve of them, and I was told they were my High-Self Council, St. Germain was the spokesperson. I saw each being as a figure of Light. Then I came back and found myself sitting in my bed.

At the time, I knew hardly anything about St. Germain and I wanted confirmation on my experience so I began asking people about this mysterious ethereal being. Here is where Source teaches me resign my fears and learn to trust.

Before the vision, I had about two years of odd happenings. Each one would become a piece to the puzzle of my High-Self introduction, or should I say reunion. For instance, about a year earlier I became obsessed with the Native American known as Crazy Horse. I wanted to know more about this mysterious historical man so I searched for books, information and a purported photo. I never found the photo, but read that Crazy Horse had curly hair, like me, and was known to his friends as "Curly". During my search a pain developed in my back, above where my ribs end on the right side. I had no luck with chiropractic visits and felt frustrated. Then I read something: Crazy Horse died from a wound in the same area. Very interesting. Even more interesting, after I read how he died—the pain disappeared. I was bewildered and thought about a psychosomatic connection. Did I already know how he died and intuit the pain? Maybe from a movie or story I'd forgotten? To this day I don't know. I put the book away and soon forgot the incident.

Just after my vision, during conversation with a friend, I gathered my strength and asked, "Have you heard of St. Germain?" She ran to get a book with information. (Unfortunately, I don't know what book.) As she read the description, she looked at me and said, "You know he was Crazy Horse in a past life, right?" I did not. I didn't know anything about him! However, the mention of Crazy Horse brought back memories of my passion and research. It was a message that I was on the right track.

Another memory surfaced from years earlier. In 1993, my husband's back was hurting and interfering with his work. One night, I woke up while it was still dark. Awake and pondering Bobby's pain, I heard a voice say, "Use the violet light." What violet light? I was told to place my hands on Bobby's lower back, so I did. When I closed my eyes I could see a violet light going into his body, coming from my hands! I fell asleep, and didn't remember what happened until the next day when Bobby came home from work and announced he did not have back pain that day. Oh! I remembered and told him what happened. He said do it again, I tried but nothing happened so I eventually gave up.

When I asked another person about who this St. Germain character was, they asked if I knew about the Violet Flame. Violet Flame? I remembered the violet light, Bobby's pain-free day, and I started to feel like maybe I was actually aligning with an Ascended Master. Every time I asked someone about St. Germain a similar coincidence occurred; puzzle pieces fell into place one-by-one until my doubt was defeated.

That was the beginning of my conscious communication with guides, apparently Kathumi paved the way. Afterward I was able to recreate the contact and receive information, if I stayed clear. Anytime my ego got in the way, or if I got overwhelmed, or if I was not clear, the connection would diminish.

Overwhelm & Clearing

Have you ever seen a vacant lot overgrown with weeds, and thought, "Wow, that would be great place for a garden or home?" Where would you start? How would you make a garden or home there? Would you dig first, draft house plans, buy seeds, get a permit, buy the lot, talk to the neighbors? The enormity of a task like that reminds me of clearing. There are so many ways to start, sometimes you have to step back and evaluate before you take action.

You could begin clearing by assessing your symptoms. What are your primary complaints? *Make a list.* Are they mental, emotional, physical or spiritual? (As a side note an easy way to remember the four main bodies is M-E-P-S, which is not their order, but I can remember MEPS easily. The order is physical, mental, emotional, spiritual.) Here are some common symptoms I see among Lightworkers:

> *Mental: agitation, harsh judgment, hate, disillusion, confusion, projection, guilt, desperation, lack of focus/completion, frustration,*

fear of persecution, inability to let go, control, fear, lack, anxiety, victimhood, loss

Emotional: crying, sadness, up and downs, depression, anger, rage, inadequacy, disconnect, pity, empathy, inability to focus, feeling closed down, loneliness, unclear thoughts, fear, confusion, blame, projection, worry

Physical: fatigue, aches, headaches, spine/neck issues, insomnia, hyperactivity, solar plexus agitation, drowsy, tired, odd sensations, hearing voices, tinnitus, heaviness, dehydration, adrenal imbalance, endocrine issues

Spiritual: strange information in meditation, new guides that offer too much direction, feeling disconnected from Source, faithlessness, doubt, worry about connection to Source, inability to meditate, ungrounded/horizontal, entities

NOTE: You might notice that some of these symptoms could be from a legitimate medical issue. You must learn to recognize whether your issue is something that needs medical attention. Go to your doctor if necessary, you can say a prayer in the waiting room. Please consider if something is physical you may need to deal with it in a physical way. There should be no guilt or shame in getting a checkup or seeking help from a doctor.

Making a list of symptoms for spiritual healing may seem contrary to positive thinking, but it isn't. If your mind balks at the idea do this: First, tell your mind that the list is for your ego, Light doesn't need direction, but we do. Second, transform your complaints into affirmations. Your list will give you direction, and more importantly, it will give your guides and Angels direction.

"Don't they already know? Haven't I complained and whined and cried and demanded help?"

Yes, you have; I have, we all have. However, did you know that our conscious mind is less than ten percent of our total mind? *That means that ninety percent or more of your mind in subconscious.* Your dominating force in subliminal! I have heard this bit of spiritually enlightening information from psychiatrists, read it in books and located it on the net. Think about it, your focused thought, no matter how powerful is at its absolute best ten percent. *Ten percent.* The good news is we aren't shooting for one-hundred percent; we are literally attempting dominance. When do the scales tip? At fifty-one percent; it's called *critical mass.* In a conference room of one-hundred people, fifty-one people can vote yes on something and get it.

No matter how many affirmations you say, and they are good—don't get me wrong, they may not heal a block/hurdle/mass/obstruction or a brewing volcano/mental tsunami/chakra-impacting-past-life that could be the engineering cause of an issue.

Does that sound dramatic? Yes! But aren't we the actors in the play of our lives? If you feel dramatic or act dramatic, look inside. The subconscious mind is a network of little archives. I use two metaphors for my subconscious mind. The first is a *file cabinet.* It nicely holds the Akashic Records, our ethereal library. If I need help I might ask my guides to show me one file that I can heal right now. Try it in meditation. Ask to see a file on the issue you would like to address; ask your guides, Angels and Light Beings if there is anything in your subconscious mind creating this particular issue, tell them you are ready to release and clear.

The second image for my subconscious mind is a *cave.* I learned this when it came through in a reading for a client. Her guides said to imagine the subconscious mind as a cave with small caverns all along the walls, each representing pockets of memories. Imagine each cavern protected by a door, or gate, and a guard. They said to ask for what was appropriate to heal in this moment, and she would be taken to that experience. Some memories will remain safely tucked in; they don't all need to clear. For instance, if you touched a hot stove when you were three, you probably want to keep that reminder for later use, yes? No need to burn your finger every few years because you insisted on some type of massive subconscious clearing. When working with the subconscious mind, I yield to my guides, asking them to show me what needs to be released, understood, healed, etc. through the Divine Light of the I Am Presence. This prevents me from using my ego to decide what needs healing and clearing. Imagine if I erased all difficult healing? I would not have met Rick Lewis. Conversely, I would not have decided to stop the bumpy road and live gracefully.

> *During a session with a man in his 50's, let's call him John, we called in our guides (and Lighted company) to clear overwhelm and thoughts of burden. An interesting experience came through. I saw a past life where John lived on a peaceful planet with his wife and daughter. The life was simple and happy until their village was bombed. A school was hit and many children died, including John's daughter in that life. John and his wife were overwhelmed with grief. While the wife worked with her community to rebuild the school, John vowed revenge. He left in a vehicle, to fight the evil bombers and restore peace to his beloved planet and home.*
>
> *Far away from his home, John and many others fought the enemy while friends and family rebuilt what they could and tried to recover from the loss of lives and property. When the fighting calmed down many returned to what was left of their families, but John did not. He was obsessed with hunting down the bombers, the killers. Many years went by with John coming home occasionally to see his wife. Grief and abandonment wore on her, she died lonely and sick. John found out about her death during a visit, after years of traveling. He did not*

have his revenge; his heart was broken again.

Now, many lifetimes later, John experienced confusing feelings around responsibility. He felt burdened with family obligations and wanted to leave, but wouldn't let himself. Work, bills, communication and responsibility overwhelmed him. Can you see the parallel? John suffered guilt because he left his wife and home in the former lifetime. He struggled with duplicating the circumstances, chasing those he blamed for his pain.

Why would he leave, again? We sometimes re-create the past to give ourselves another chance to heal. Maybe we make better decisions, sometimes we actually do it all again, hurt the same people; go through the same pain attempting heal.

John didn't heal the first time and I didn't see this playing out well. I called on the ethereal guides, Angels and Source and with John's permission asked for them to heal the past, present and future concerning burden, loss, confusion, grief, abandonment and regret. We asked that the healing be blessed to all involved through their *pillar of Light* via Source to avoid any horizontal energy connections and honor the choices of all involved.

The root of John's grief and confusion was hiding in his subconscious mind. Some part of him lived with a daily reminder that he could or would abandon his family, that he could or would grieve his family. The circumstances were hidden so John applied the feelings to his current life. Once the past life was exposed, John was able to heal.

What do the guides say when clients ask about their subconscious minds? "Look around." If you want to know what's going on inside, take a good look at your life. Remember, that ninety percent (subconscious) is manifesting. If you are poor and want money, you may have a subliminal resonance with poverty consciousness or a historic vow of poverty. These are common among Lightworkers. Another common issue among us is fear of persecution. It's likely this isn't your first rodeo. In your next meditation ask your guides to clear and heal every persecution you have participated in whether it be past, present or future. Remember to ask for clearing and healing for both sides; that means the persecutor and persecuted, all family members, witnesses, informants, judges, hangmen, fire starters, liars, torturers, etc.

The subconscious mind is steering the vehicle; your vehicle, my vehicle and every vehicle. If you want to change, you must address the archives of your subconscious mind. It's simple: meditate and ask your ethereal guides to help.

Entities

In this chapter, there are specific prayers for a handful of issues, but you are a unique individual. There are so many aspects of you and every single one of those aspects is significant enough to be cared for. We could talk about clearing your ethereal bodies, the psychosomatic causes of illness or, in case you are bored, entities. My particular favorite it would seem.

My work with entity release began when I learned what was making me feel overwhelmed, encumbered and depressed. This was before I understood what I heard and where it came from. Since then I have grown to believe that we all have an ear to the other side. If it's not evident to you right now, ask yourself these questions:

-do you ever hear your name called when you are alone?

-do the hairs on your neck ever stand up?

-do you ever feel spooked or watched or uneasy for no apparent reason?

-do you have random thoughts that are not in character for you?

-do you ever see odd things out of the corner of your eye?

If you answered yes, oh yeah, sure or uh-huh to any of these questions, you might know an entity. But what is an entity anyway?

An entity is something that does not have a physical body, or material existence, although it may or may not have consciousness. I use the word entity to describe beings outside of the third dimension that are not pure Light. This includes those that have crossed over and did not go into the Light; anything with ill or possessive intent, negative agenda or discordant energy. Entities can be ghosts or lost spirits. In my spiritual world, I use the word to describe something I do not want to be attached to me. But in proper English, an entity can describe practically anything.

To clear entities, I ask my ethereal guides to clear and remove anything less than *Christ Consciousness Light*. You have likely noticed these words in many of the prayers in this book.

Long ago, my guides gave someone this explanation and I still use it:

> *If you died suddenly, you may be confused and not believe what happened; you could be dreaming, after all. Imagine that Source sends forth a deceased relative in their Light form to help you cross over, like your grandfather or grandmother. But you have the choice to stay or go. Not realizing you are in your Spirit-body in the astral field you might decide to stay close to those that are still alive. In fact, you could stay so close to someone in their physical form that you become attached to them.*

This would be a benign entity, a lost one. There are numerous lost ones, old and young, aware and unaware. *We can channel these entities.* They can be accurate and reliable, but their agenda can become twisted and that is what gets us into trouble. If you are in service to the purest, truest Divine Light—your Creator and Source of All Things and what you channel is not, there can be a conflict. Call in your guides, ask them to protect you from lost ones and all entities that are not pure Light. This is why *sacred space* is essential. It is difficult to tell the difference between a lower dimensional entity and an Ascended Master.

Not all entities are benign. Some have ill intent like possession. There are those that seek to control us. Others simply seek energy or power. This information is not brought forth to cause worry or fear. Your empowerment and protection are through your vertical *pillar of Light*. Your best efforts to stay entity free are preventative. Remember to keep your frequency high via meditation and prayer. I hope by now you have written your opening prayers for setting *sacred space* and placed a copy in your *SRB*. I read my prayers aloud for a long time, and I changed them often. Own those prayers! And if by chance you get entangled in negative energy, write down what helped you get free. Keep notes on what supports your clarity. Because unfortunately, when we need help we can't always think clearly. Have a quick reference, and use it!

Focus on Light

The most consistent thing I have found in healing and clearing work is that when our frequencies of Light increase, healing happens. In fact, when I set *sacred space* for sessions some negativity clears as soon as the frequency elevates. It's like inviting cleaning people to your house and their mere presence alleviates dust. I haven't personally experienced dust disappearing, but I will keep you posted.

Symptoms, causes, all of our lists and labels are important, but not as necessary as the actual healing. Our ten-percent-or-less conscious mind can get hyper focused. When you experience elevated frequency, as in meditation, things release and clear without labels or identity. Do your best to allow them to leave; let them go. If we need to understand something, it will stick around and become more of an issue.

My mind doesn't always allow baggage to leave, it says, "Hey! Information is good; it leads to wisdom and understanding. I want to be wise and smart and proficient and resourceful. I want to heal and feel good about my work in the world. Wait, what is that? Bring it back."

To my mind I reply, "Hello mind. I love you. And you are worthy of my focused attention (minds like that). I allow you to work in the world, to be in service and acknowledged, but know, the Light does the work, okay? And sometimes you need to let things go."

> *My guides give this analogy: Imagine that you receive a big clearing. Your issues, entities, etc. are releasing in bursts of energy that look like helium balloons floating up in the sky. You watch them as you gratefully release old stuff. But wait, you might think. That's my stuff. At the last second, you jump up and grab a string. It's your balloon and you want it. The mind wants information, the ego wants purpose, the heart wants healing. Sometimes, we have a hard time letting go. That ugly, horrible, annoying, distracting thing is mine. I'm simply not ready.*
>
> *Now there's you, clutching balloons and feeling like a thief. And there's Source/Creator/God, waiting patiently with no judgment. Creator soothes the ego, comforts the heart and reminds the mind that you have access to everything. There is nothing in those lessons that will disappear. If you haven't learned something, it will return. If you are losing something, you will find it again.*
>
> *You slowly release, again; this time you breathe through it. You allow high frequencies to transmute. You relax, giving Light the opportunity to cleanse, clear and heal. Ahhhh-men.*

Our third-dimensional bodies are in great need of bridges between our physical selves and our ethereal selves. If you work to balance the four main bodies (MEPS), you will find yourself releasing things that are less than Christ Consciousness Frequency into the Light. *Including entities!* You can be clearer as a channel.

If you work as a healer, you know that we do not do the work. Creator Light is the power behind healing. We may try to understand how healing happens, but we won't.

When it comes to spiritual formats, faith and trust are better philosophies. There are too many venues for us to manage how things happen. You may use a tool that your guides give you once, for a specific client and never again. Why learn the details when you can be free and clear for new tools. Lightwork happens most accurately when we focus on Light. As the Lightworker, your job is to make sure *sacred space* is apparent so that Light Beings can do the work.

Teachers

One day when I was complaining to Cindy, my favorite third-dimensional teacher, she asked me, "Who are your teachers?" I scrambled to find the right answer, mentally making a list of people who have helped or taught me something. Oh there are so many, now which one should I tell her is my teacher? First, I must assess what is being taught, right? If it's meditation, well that's Cindy. But if it's about clearing, that might Rick. Oh my spinning-mental-body-goodness, who are my teachers? Wait, what about the reading I had with so-and-so, she is a good teacher.

Cindy let me fret about this for a few minutes. Then she said, "Holly, your teachers are ethereal."

When she forges this question, the question I have heard so many times since the first time years ago, I still develop confusion. Over years on my spiritual path, I have investigated many modalities. During one of these *opportunities* I decided to get a reading by someone that seemed to have her career together; she had a cable show and was a published author. Sounds like someone I can learn from, right? I did learn from her, but the entire experience backfired. Let's call her Carol.

I arrived to an old home. The newer model car outside had vanity plates with Carol's business name. I knocked, and she let me into her house which was being worked on, but no contractors were present.

The welcome wagon was absent; what I mean is I felt out of place, as if I were there on the wrong day. She told me to go upstairs, but not to which room so I waited in the hall wondering which door was the right one. When she came upstairs she made a face and I felt dumb for stand there, waiting. We sat and while she dealt with the end of her breakfast (it was in her teeth, she said it was nothing...) we chatted. Mostly about her. I was not impressed.

Since she was someone to me, and I was nobody to me, I went back two more times. My hope was to glean that special information that was there, somewhere, on a recording or in her words or through a healing. There must be something because I was drawn to her.

Later, there was a metaphysical show in town; Carol had a booth. I went to buy her book and say hello; she treated me strangely. It was as if she didn't know me. When she turned her back to me I stood there, she conversed with another woman that she seemed to know. I felt not special, not important, not relevant. So I walked away.

When I complained to Cindy about the experience she asked me why I choose to see Carol. My reply was, "To learn." It should have been a red flag that I felt slightly defensive after Cindy's question; it wasn't until later that I realized I was not *guided* to see Carol. I simply wanted to; I was looking for something, maybe a mentor. Carol represented experience to me, something I lacked. I thought I would learn about me with her help, and I did, but not in the way I thought a spiritual advisor would teach.

Carol taught me quite a bit, inadvertently; through my vulnerability. I learned how to treat clients because I wanted to feel special and welcomed. I learned that little details, like running late or not being prepared can affect a client. Simple offerings, like specific directions about where to sit are important to someone getting a reading. Through my disappointment, I began taking better care of my clients. My work is about them, for them. Their comfort and safety matter to me.

I also learned that I should check in with my guides about my own education. For instance, "Would it be helpful for me to have a reading with Carol?" Later, it became obvious that I was a little star-struck and not following my best advisor: me. If I had to pick the most noteworthy thing that I forgot, I would have to say it was learning with peace, ease and comfort. I chose to look outside of myself and saw another person as greater than me.

Rick Lewis once said, "Don't put me on a pedestal, because you will be the one to knock me off and I'll get hurt." I have used that phrase with students and clients trying to save myself the pain of falling off the proverbial pedestal. But what did I do with Carol? I put her on the pedestal, then knocked her off.

With Cindy's help I was able to learn (for the umpteenth time) that the teacher with the truest alignment to my Divinity is my High-Self. The answer to Cindy's question, "Who are your teachers?" is, "My teachers are ethereal." This answer not only aligns the consciousness within the *pillar of Light* it puts mind and mental body at ease; they don't have to search high and low for a being of human form to supply answers. Another bonus is that your High-Self does not demand one being to supply information; everything is done through frequency. If you check the Light of each guide or feeling or sensation you will find that you are working with an aspect of the Divine, not a human ego or hierarchy of belief.

Ultimately, I am grateful to Carol and what I learned. Since then, I have released my control over when and how I learn. I try to surrender to peaceful interactions that come organically. True, I have learned from many in the third dimension, haven't you? But consider this, don't they come because (on some level) you call them? Moreover, don't you put pieces together from every teacher you have ever had to form the puzzle of your knowledge? We need our guides to fit all those tiny pieces together. I admit my human intelligence does not know how to hold my vast expanse of experience. There are my conscious learnings, my past lives and my DNA connection to every life ever lived on this planet. That kind of information deserves a team. Luckily, we are all in possession of such a team; it's the High-Self Council. A team of ethereal beings specifically put in place to help me. Or, in your case, you.

Soul Healing

When my guides showed me a Soul, I thought it looked like a disco ball. You know, the silver thing hanging from the ceiling at a seventies dance club? It was round with many facets. I began referring to the tiny facets as Soul aspects. I was shown that when we incarnate we use maybe ten percent of our Soul aspects. Ten percent can make us who we are! That is incredible. I was also shown that through integrations we can become approximately thirty to forty percent of our Soul. This information amazed me. What is the rest of my Soul doing? That was about the time Connie called. She was in Iowa and having a hard time. Connie was afraid and felt an eminent dark energy around her. She had inexplicable insomnia and a sense of loss.

> *We began a session by getting vertical and setting space. I was guided to lead Connie into a meditation, where I was immediately aware of a different place. I saw terrain that did not look like Earth and light that did not come from our Sun. Another planet. My focus was on a woman. She was hiding in a long ditch with dirt piled up on one side, like a military fox hole. She was tired, badly hurt and desperate, radiating great distress. I could see other beings lying around her, men and women. They all wore the same uniform.*
>
> *Everyone, except this woman, was dead or gravely wounded. Through her, I felt the ground shake; I felt terror. I could see large beasts running on two legs; information flooded into my mind; I sensed a planetary attack, death to all and barbaric treatment to dead*

and living alike. Bodies dismembered, aggression, savage destruction. Suddenly, the woman got up and ran. I watched her run from what was coming, keenly aware that what I watched run was not her physical form. Her physical body was lying in the ditch. As she ran I saw what she was running toward, it was Connie. I watched as the woman's form began to fade, she seemed to be slowly disappearing. Still headed toward Connie, the woman's fuzzy form walked into a great light where Connie waited. They were united.

Knowing that I was there to see this unification, I disconnected from what happened to the physical presence still lying in the ditch, even though she was dead. Curiosity gnawed at me, but after disconnecting from the vision I felt a surge of relief.

My guides spoke to me then. They explained the woman was a parallel life for Connie, each incarnated from the same Soul. Drawn to each other so strongly, the Soul attempted to reunite through a horizontal integration. The woman in the ditch ran for something safe.

Connie, very psychic and perceptive, was unable to turn away from the clarion call and couldn't separate her human emotions from what was happening ethereally. I prayed for help and was guided how to best assist Connie. I was told that a horizontal integration could impact Connie with fear or other feelings the woman had at death. These integrations must be clear and clean of and mind or mental status that might be present at one's death.

We continued following directions from our guides. I asked that the integration happen via Source Light, vertically. We requested all work be done for the highest and best good for Connie, the woman and all involved. With prayer, and invocation of every guide, Ascended Master and Archangel we could recall, I saw Light fade from the woman's body in the ditch and move up to Source; where Connie waited and the reunion happened via pure Christ Consciousness Light.

I believe this experience was brought forth to teach Connie and me about Soul Integration. Connie was experiencing the parallel life empathically, and she needed help to bring the integration to a higher level for the clearing and healing needed. They merged and now experience as one, resulting in a higher percentage of Connie's Soul present for her current life experience.

In my experience with Soul integrations I have found that when someone requires more presence of Light in their life a clarion call goes out to the Universe. Connie made that call by needing more of herself for this life; it was answered by a parallel life. The uniformed woman did not choose to be born into a new body; she joined Cindy's life which was already in progress. The woman's clarion call was answered by Connie, she needed help releasing from her life of war. This unification resulted in a higher Soul percentage present for Connie. But keep in mind, I have found no evidence showing that a conscious-mind decision makes any difference to the Soul. Soul choices happen at a much higher level. So if I decide to call in more Soul, it's a mental request with not a lot of energy behind it.

You have read about reasons we need clearing and healing. You can address issues through your own prayer by asking for help with your daily life and manifestation. The rest of this chapter focuses on what I call *general clearing*. It's a good idea to use the following five prayers to rebalance your multi-dimensional self in times of difficulty.

Remember, we often manifest situations to heal. If your neighbor is bothering you, pray to heal your issues. If your mother is annoying, pray to heal *your* issues. If your job craters... pray to heal your own personal issues. *Vertical Soul Integration* addresses clearing past and future Soul Integrations and any residual fear. I like to imagine that the hand of God comes from above, and then moves under lower frequencies, lifting them to the heavens. Visualize horizontal energy becoming vertical, clarifying all negativity.

Sometimes, even after clearing, we have fear that doesn't make sense. If you have an unreasonable fear use *Prayer for Help With Fear*. Consider that it may be the result of something you don't remember or understand; either conscious, subconscious or otherwise. *Vertical Soul Integration* and *Prayer for Help With Fear* work well together.

Vertical Soul Integration

Father, Mother, God, Goddess, Creator, Source of All That Is; I call upon Divine Will, Source Light and the Alignment of Christ Consciousness Frequency. Please assist me, I ask for a Soul clearing and healing. Please remove any negative attributes or attachments from any Soul integration I have experienced. Please clean, clear and heal my Soul, now. Help me to ground all appropriate energies, and release what no longer serves my Light. Please help me to relate to my Soul in its entire expanse and recognize what I have chosen to work with at this time.

I allow Soul integrations through Divine Light, Divine Will and via Christ Consciousness Frequency. I ask and allow my guides and Angels, my High-Self Council and Ascended Masters to assist me in all awakenings concerning my Soul or any aspect of my Self, known or unknown to me.

I ask that this work be done through all time, space and dimension. I command this work to be done peacefully, easily and comfortably.

Thank you and Amen.

Prayer for Help With Fear

Father, Mother, God, Goddess, Creator, Source of All That Is; please assist me in discovering why I fear ______. I am willing to understand the beginning of this fear. I am willing to release the root cause of this fear. I wholeheartedly ask my guides to bring forth any and all help concerning my fear of______.*

I allow this work peacefully, easily and comfortably according to my highest and best good.

Thank you and Amen.

**This prayer is easily adapted to any emotion. If you are experiencing anxiety, agitation, etc. simply change the word fear to what you are feeling. You may also replace 'fear of' with 'experience'.*

A message from Spirit: Our faith in the wisdom and memory of humankind is yours to use as you wish. Ask to borrow it if you feel inadequate or doubtful. We work with you, for you, beside you. Blessings dear ones, you do not journey alone.

Soul Responsibility

While doing a reading for Irena we talked about the responsibility she felt toward her family. There were four main characters: Irena, her mother, step-father and husband. The energetic resonance between them was intense and deeply rooted, more so than one lifetime would generate. I checked with my guides, and was told yes, they had experienced many lifetimes together.

Think of that for a moment, because this likely affects you. Immediate family members, to my knowledge, are always Soul family members. So instead of one lifetime of history, you have many lifetimes of history with each person you are related to.

Several years before our work, Irena's husband passed away. Two years later, her mother died and most recently her stepfather, Greg, passed. Since Greg's death, Irena often felt lethargic or sick, sometimes unable to get out of bed. We were told that she was the last incarnated member of her immediate Soul family. Feeling abandoned and lonely for her human family, Irena began unconsciously using her Soul connection to find Greg.

With your knowledge about sacred space and vertical connection, can you imagine what happened? Irena unconsciously sought Greg as she knew him in life, without raising frequency. An astral field connection occurred. Through this connection, Irena felt a plea from Greg. He was upset. In our session, Greg explained his worry about unfulfilled karma. Irena did something generous; she took on 263 Soul contracts that Greg left incomplete.

Soul contracts are pre-life agreements made Soul-to-Soul, upholding a much higher consciousness than our humanness allows. Irena's subconscious tendency was to help first and ask questions later. In the reading, we discussed the repercussions of this behavior. If we take on extra contracts, it should not be out of family obligation, even if it is Soul family. These burdens can be heavy, sometimes toxic. The burden of additional contracts was overwhelming to Irena, so much so that her grief was pushed aside as she nearly became catatonic. After our session, her energy returned quickly, as well as her ability to grieve.

Women, due to years of genetic programming, often volunteer to help. When you couple this genetic condition with intuition the result can be a much burdened being; one who might *intuit* the need to help, which is what Irena did. She reached out for a family connection and found work; somehow she interpreted the work as hers. It felt like having her stepfather back. But we must remember, we are governed by a higher power and that higher power is capable of redistributing contracts, if that is what is needed. Regardless of gender, we don't have to "take one for the team".

Irena released her burden of soul contracts, but watch for other types of burden. Our society pressures people to spend more money than they earn, which creates the encumbrance of debt. In our day and age of national debt and over-purchasing, we can easily feel overwhelmed. When clients talk of arduous, heavy feelings I watch for dense energy that might find relief with *Release of Burden* prayer.

Release of Burden

Father, Mother, God, Goddess, Creator, Source of All That Is; via Divine Accordance Prayer I call forth to God force frequencies of Light for release of all burdens. Through this release I request karmic healing for all my lineages of Light; past, present and future.*

Please assist all bodies in understanding only real, current and true responsibilities. As I gain perspective of my possibilities I release all burdens from the past, present and future.

I embrace all gifts from past occurrences and release all burdens. I allow all burdens, responsibilities and anger to be filtered from my mind. Help me open to resolution.

Furthermore, I release all mental body patterns holding me in a place of stagnation or accumulation of negative energy. I release old patterns and clear resentment, burden and overwhelm. I welcome love, Light and understanding to integrate with all my God given gifts. My chosen reality is here. I am free, I am abundant, I am well.

Thank you and Amen.

Karma

One of the reasons we might take on responsibility is a misplaced sense of karma. Karma, defined, is the idea that we are governed by cause and effect. Your Soul, preincarnate, may have decided to experience an event or emotion due to a past life experience. This sounds reasonable, but have you considered *self-imposed karma*? Self-imposed karma is a condition created when one decides to take on something from a lesser place, versus a Soul assignment from Divine Resources. If a close relative or friend died, you might take on a karmic burden due to some connection or sense of obligation that is subconscious. This may have been why Irena was so eager to help her stepfather. Subconsciously, she seized an opportunity to balance and connect. But it was not by Soul agreement through the Divine and therefore self-imposed karma.

If you sense conflict, doubt or even delusion with another person, try *Understanding Karma Prayer*. It indicates that relationships are karmically based. Remember to assume responsibility to help your mind understand that ultimately, you are the creator. But even as the Divine Creator, we need help from our ethereal guides so that we are not working from subconscious fears. Self-imposed karma is quite common. Not only do we tend to help our family and soul members, there are energies that profess that *not* doing so will anger the gods. This prayer can also help release old religious misunderstandings pertaining to any dogma that has encouraged subconscious karma.

Understanding Karma Prayer

Father, Mother, God, Goddess, Creator, Source of All That Is; please assist me in realizing all reasons for my interaction with ______. It is my full intention to participate in any outworking that is my design; peacefully, easily and comfortably. Through my empowerment to create I call forth Source to assist me in creating with responsibility and kindness to my Self and others.*

I ask that I be blessed with understanding that will help me feel grateful and appreciative towards those teaching me through all karmic experiences. I allow agitation and fear to be transmuted by Light while I embrace unconditional love for all those assisting my life on this planet.

Thank you and Amen.

**Use name of person, situation, feeling, place, etc.*

Besides taking on karma, or self-imposing, there is another way for us to burden ourselves unnecessarily. When burden or an energetic encumbrance is passed down through the DNA, we call it genetic. You may have received feelings from great, great grandparents. You may have adopted karma, even self-imposed karma from your ancestors.

One might carry on a passion that is held by their mother or hurt where their father had pain. We can hold prejudices, wars, enemies, beliefs, misunderstandings, illnesses and more in our genetic memory. These energies are considered part of our *lineage*. We were born with them. During my own clearing of genetic connections to burden, Spirit gave me the following prayer: *Genetic Filtration*. If you choose to participate in a clearing of this caliber, please take it seriously. When you begin this clearing process, use the prayer often. Request Divine blessings for those that teach you, meaning your ancestors—the exact connections you are dissolving. My verbiage is: *All involved through all time, space and dimension*. I have worked with this prayer many times and have found it to be quite transitional. Again, please consider this clearing and healing carefully. You may need time to rest and release during the days that follow this work.

PS: The previous paragraph is significant. The repercussions of this prayer are intense. I have learned this through my personal experience and via clients. Please take the warning seriously.

Genetic Filtration Technique

Set sacred space and get vertical. Center yourself. Feel your energy. Sense the Light within you and your connection to the Divine.

Call forth protection from the highest sources of Light, use Divine Accordance Prayer. Ask for clearing of less than Christ Consciousness frequencies, use Release Protocol.

Ask your guides, Angels, ancestors and all appropriate Pure Light Beings for assistance in healing any lineage patterns of transfer. Say this:

"Through the Light of God, I ask for assistance in filtering all lineage transfers. Please create a filter so that all transfers happen through Source. My High-Self is the guardian of all receptors concerning lineage transfer, energy and genetic pattern. Let this be so through the Highest Source of Light and Truth in the most appropriate form. With grace and ease I allow this change. With comfort and appropriate timing I allow resolution. It is so. Thank you and Amen."

When I worked with Irena I saw something incredible. While communicating and focusing on being a clear conduit for my guides and Irena's guides, Greg came into our session. As I explained to Irena the information about the contracts and Soul family connections, Greg went into the Light. After he crossed over his Soul spoke to me with contentment and peace. Yet there was part of him still here, I could sense his presence here on Earth. I was told that his Spirit was still in the fourth dimension. From there he would be able to finish what he felt was undone on Earth. He would release when he felt it was appropriate. Then he would merge into his Soul for the next journey.

After a long day of work, Lightwork that is...

When you are finishing any Lightwork, the opening, or portal, that allowed the inter-dimensional connection/communication should be closed, unless you want to use it for something else. And by that I mean, close it. If you are finished with your work, close everything. This is important to understand. We so desire to be in touch with the other side that we will sometimes utilize lesser forms of communication and circumvent our own ability to be in touch with Source via High-Self. Don't let those yearnings confuse you. Make sure to request all entrances, exits, openings, doors, etc. that were created for your communication be closed, healed and sealed, as appropriate through Divine Light. You may want to use *Closing Prayer* from Chapter Three. I say this is important but it's so much more, it is essential.

On occasion, I find that I need further clearing to close these openings. This may happen after doing readings or even if I visit a busy place, like an airport or hospital. *Bath of Light* was given to me for a workshop I was teaching, it was recommended to all students for their healing and clearing process. I use *Bath of Light* often, varying the oils and herbs as I am guided. To eliminate confusion, I have divided the process into *technique* and *prayer*. Please don't underestimate your ability to open ethereal doorways. It happens when frequency raises. Once, I was leaving a restaurant and I had the distinct feeling that I left something. When I checked in, my guides told me that my friends and I opened a doorway to higher realms. Since then, whether I find out something is open or not, if a spiritual conversation happened... I ask for all openings to be closed.

Bath of Light Technique

Place in a nylon or muslin sack or like container:
Epsom Salt (1 tsp – 1cup)
Baking Soda (1 tsp – 1 cup)

Lemon (shave/grate skin or slice, squeeze juice into bath)
Orange (optional, but treat as the lemon or eat while in the bath)
Rose Oil (2 drops in salt for distribution)

For tub:
Black Tourmaline (place under root chakra during bath)
4 Crystals (place in four corners around tub)
White Candle (lit safely during bath)
Essential Oil of your choice (use for connecting and centering)

During bath:
Set sacred space; use Vertical Alignment Technique and/or chant, "I am, I am, I am, I am, I am, I am..." for a few minutes.
Read 'Bath of Light Prayer' three times.

Concerning substitutions: The original recipe is most effective, but not doing the bath would be least effective. It is recommended to substitute anything you don't have on hand with something you do have. You may have lemon essential oil or lemon juice instead of a lemon. Use anything that you intuit to substitute any ingredient. Additionally you might want to include: fresh mint leaves, sea salt, sea weed or classical music (without words).

Bath of Light Prayer

Beloved Presence, I have offered my assistance in service to the Divine, now I request clearing and balancing.

-Please align all new energies to integrate in a comfortable manner. (Pause for this to happen.)

-Please help me release what I have unlocked, completely, including anything hidden or subconscious.

-Please align all my bodies to my vertical pillar of Light.

I recognize now... I am an evolution. I am safe in change. I am a welcome aspect of Light in my community and among my friends and family.

My old attachments are freely released for transmutation.

In my new freedom I am _______. (Healthy, happy, clear, wise, in surrender, healed, grounded, joyful, safe, etc.)

I am comfortable with my changes. My self-expression is also an evolution.

I welcome my new reflection in the world.

I am a Divine Carrier of Light. I am a Divine Healer and I Am Divinely healed.

Thank you and Amen.

Clearing the Vicinity

There is one more essential step in Lightwork, one I consider mandatory. This step involves clearing your personal space, and in some circumstances someone else's space. Maybe it's your house, office or car. It could be a client's house or a friend's office. You will need to use your awareness; any 'clair' ability you have can be used to sense subtle messages about how an area feels. Pay attention to any unusual sensations, electrical pulses, pain, confusion, anger or suspicious happenings. This might include: headaches, nausea, paper cuts, bruises, down computers, forgetfulness, lost or moved items, dripping faucets, light bulb issues, quickly drained batteries or cell phone problems. As a Lightworker it is your responsibility to make sure that your space is clear of anything you, or a client, may have released. To make this issue more complex you may have released, or helped someone release, during a simple conversation. Lightwork is not always intentional. For instance, if you talk to your mail carrier for five minutes your Light may have assisted a negative thought form in releasing. How would you know?

Again, it is your responsibility to pay close attention to the world around you. If anything seems suspicious call forth to your guides. Say *Release and Clearing Space Prayer* immediately. Work with this prayer with care. These are important questions to ask your guidance when it comes to any type of clearing, but particularly when clearing someone else's space. Make sure you get a "yes" to each question before continuing:

-Can I? Do I have the ability?

-May I? Do I have permission from the High-Self of each being involved?

-Should I? Is it safe for me? Will I become encumbered with what I want to release or clear?

-Will my guides/Light Beings do the work? Have I sufficiently set my ego aside?

Release and Clearing Space Prayer

Father, Mother, God, Goddess, Creator, Source of All That Is; I acknowledge the Light I carry within. I allow this Light to grow; larger, greater, wider, and brighter until it encompasses my entire body. Within this Light I command the clearing of all frequencies less than one-hundred percent Christ Consciousness Light. Please release and clear anything causing fear or stress within my body or surroundings to the Light.

HOME or OFFICE: I ask that this Light continue to grow clearing this space, room and building. I call forth to the High-Self of the owner of this building and ask permission for this clearing. I call forth to the Soul of this building for permission and assistance. Please clear all inanimate objects connected to this home/office, building or property.

CAR: I ask that this Light continue to grow clearing this vehicle and neutralizing all negativity on inanimate objects within. Please adjust all electrical currents and do whatever is necessary to keep this car protected safe and in perfect working order.

ALL: I allow all of this work to follow Divine Accordance; the highest good for all with surrender to Divine Will. I command that all released go to the Light or their highest outworkings using Release Protocol. I AM guided, guarded, protected and loved.

Thank you and Amen.

Chapter Seven

Drama and Trauma

When you are upon your path of Lightwork, whether working with clients or on yourself, these begin to show up: drama and trauma. You might find yourself in a conversation where someone is gossiping. In the past, you may have added a little comment to be polite; but once you have attained a certain level of consciousness you will have a higher frequency presenting new thoughts. It's something we all go through, so don't despair if you find yourself regretting gossip. If that happens, pray your way back to vertical energy and ask Creator to bless all involved. The best response to gossip is compassion, for yourself and others.

Please do not make the mistake of accusing and blaming others for complaining, gossiping or having lower frequency reactions. We are vibrating beings, and we create our surroundings. If an angry person is complaining, look within yourself to clear anything that is causing the situation. The more you take responsibility, the easier it is to recognize the true cause of uncomfortable situations.

When Patricia came for a session, we talked about a buyer that was preparing to make an offer on her business. Patricia had planned an excursion later that day with her potential buyer. During our session, she admitted that she did not want to go. We talked of how to make it easier, because Patricia did intend on going and following through with her commitment. However, Patricia's subconscious mind did not get the message. After Patricia left our session, she ran an errand where she sprained and dislocated her big toe on the right foot.

If you are a fan of author Louise Hay, you might be evaluating that Patricia injured her *right* foot, which is the masculine side. Feet can represent where we might be stepping, the injury could suggest that Patricia stop stepping, or moving forward. Patricia did stop, she had too because the injury required attention. Then she took responsibility for not listening to her inner self. This is an example of drama that leads to trauma. Later, Patricia had plenty of time for rest and contemplation; she had a boot-cast on her foot and could not walk far.

There are a few spiritual messages that have become staples in my work, classes and readings. During healing, releasing and clearing one particular phrase keeps surfacing. That phrase is *responsibility and protocol.* Have you heard it? Maybe once or twice? Repeatedly, I have seen human problems appear because we avoid taking responsibility. When we follow a spiritual protocol and take responsibility, we can be free of limitations, pains and most importantly *victimhood.* When we feel as if something *happened* to us, we relay the story as a victim. By expanding our conscious understanding that we are the creators, we can embrace the empowering creative ability we each have. Not one of us is a victim; we absolutely must expand our inner vision so that we can see from a higher perspective. In some cases, this information can be overwhelming; some of us have experienced great pain on Earth. For this reason, I do not bring up responsibility and protocol lightly. I also do not use abrasive, aggressive or invasive techniques to force people into this idea.

If you witness someone creating drama, consider what will happen if you point out his or her situation. Even if they ask! Always check in with your guides, seek the peaceful resolution. When I feel uneasy about someone's pain, I ask my guides what to do next. They are resourceful, wise and prudent. I have often heard the guides say, "If the front door is closed, we will go to the back door. If the back door does not open, we will try a window. We will not give up on you." When help is requested, they will find a way.

Many times clients have released drama or trauma during sessions simply by grounding and experiencing elevated frequencies. Prayer and meditation are your most significant tools. Have you ever felt so intricately woven into an experience that pliers are necessary to pry away the ropey, ethereal cords? Lightwork can heal trauma and the energy cords that come with it; I have seen this happen many times. And remember, when I mention Lightwork I refer to what is strongest in you. Or, who you choose for help. Sometimes, we resist the idea that we may be as messed up as our neighbors. And healers often feel that they must appear healed of what their clients need. We all have puzzle pieces for each other. Trust that you are a vehicle of Light, because you are.

You can be a remarkable healer no matter where you are in your spiritual growth. Your ability to communicate with Spirit is not measured. Neither is where you are on your path to enlightenment; there is no contest. If you are willing to put aside mind, ego and mental body (*Divine Accordance Prayer*) and allow yourself to be a clear spiritual conduit, messages will come through. Our problems sometimes steer us to help or to receive help, occasionally at the same time. If we approach these situations with our hearts, instead of our fears, we can heal together.

Make your choice, call in your guides and bravely move forth. Facing our issues is a daunting task, but I have faith in you. We must have faith in each other to heal together. Try this mantra, or alter it to suit your situation:

> *I choose to be a clear and concise channel for Christ Consciousness Light; I ask that all healing come forth for my client and me. Thank you and Amen.*

The next prayer came through as a message from my guides about our favorite subject, responsibility and protocol. The words became the prayer.

Responsibility and Protocol Affirmation

> *We are the Divine Creators of our realities. Everything we see is a mirror, a reflection of what is inside of us. We attract all situations, happenings, conversations, events and circumstances. We understand the Law of Attraction. We know we are not separate from God/Goddess, but part of the One. We are healing and healed. We walk a path of Light. We are pure, open and awake. Amen.*

Problems

If we are such wonderful, light-filled messengers, why do we have problems? Let's talk about common Lightworking problems. Occasionally, when doing Lightwork we help someone release something that (inadvertently) sticks to us. My friends and I refer to this as "picking up something." Think of yourself as flypaper for entities. Does that sound too intense? Good. As a Lightworker, you are a bright light attracting all types of energy; *awareness requires responsibility*.

Maybe we forget to disconnect properly from our clients after a session, leaving a little bridge for stray energy to move back and forth. Do you remember the story about seeing the cute rabbit in the woods? There are so many unknown levels of energetic exchange. "Picking up something" can happen during a conversation that elevates in frequency, I have experienced that many times. It is easy to pick up energy if we accidentally use our intentions instead of the client's (or friend's) intentions. By assuming what they need, we override our guidance. Instead of allowing Light Beings the opportunity to offer advice, we go off on our own, writing ethereal prescriptions and chasing off entities.

Do you have the ability to chase off entities? Yes, it is likely that you do. The problems emerge when the entities dislodge. Where do they go? There are three likely places: First, they may leave and later return to the host. I have watched entities hover right outside of my *sacred space*, waiting to reunite. Second, they may go into the Light, the proper Light; not just an attractive light, like you. Third, they look for the nearest *safe place*, which is likely the Lightworker dislodging them. After experiencing a few cases of, "Where did this come from?" My spiritual guides taught me that *I* am not to release entities. I can call for Light Beings, Ascended Masters, Angels, etc. to come help, surrendering the decision to a higher level than my conscious mind. It is a tricky balancing act, learning to meditate, receive information, understand high frequency messages with the conscious mind and then, via responsibility and protocol, decide how to proceed.

If you find yourself feeling icky, wondering about a psychic attack or recognizing an unwanted frequency around you, I recommend heading straight for prayer. Use your intuition to pick a prayer or try *Release Protocol.*

I have a method so that my personal drama does not escalate. Always, I watch for initial signs. Remember the tap that turns into a push that becomes the shove? Here are some taps: red lights, long bank lines, paper cuts, cranky grocery store checkers, can't find my shoes, dropping things, stubbing toes, paper cuts, mismanaged time. As the Divine Creator that I Am, I realize that I am completely responsible for all my experiences. I pay close attention to small details so that my guides do not have to hit me over the head with anything. This took me approximately thirty-five to forty years (and I do not know how many lifetimes) to understand. I am a quick study.

I did not learn about drama, trauma and problems by watching soap operas. I could have, my mom is a big fan of *Days of Our Lives*[20]. As a child I remember thinking, "Why don't they tell the truth?" All my lessons were there, on the television. But no, I forged into adulthood creating my own messes. I manifested hormone trouble, endometriosis and a hysterectomy. After surgery I launched into menopause, or mental-pause as I like to call it, which eats memory for lunch. I cannot even remember how forgetful I am! (Did I actually just affirm that?) Maybe I just notice it more, when I was younger occurrences seemed so simple to remember. Not now. These days if I don't have a note or calendar, things don't happen. Woe is me. Imagine a slim figure fallen on the sofa, back of hand to forehead, forlorn, weary, exasperated. That is not me, but I like the picture. Anyway, she is desperately preoccupied with what she cannot remember and therefore does not have the slightest clue how to heal herself.

Woe.

Whoa!

You can see how easy it is to fall *victim* to our own dramas. When you feel something, it seems real, becoming a story. Now imagine an *empathic psychic*, he or she listens and feels at the same time. Think about that. Imagine listening to someone tell their story while you are empathing how they feel. The exception being that the telling and feeling don't match. If you sprinkle that mess with a little "I want to help" you have a recipe for drama. Whether it is your client/friend, or you, boundaries can be crossed. Why not just reach inside your psychic toolbox to find a little help for someone? That seems harmless, right? However, it is not harmless, in fact it's trespassing.

If someone directs you to a dramatic issue in voice, if they actually say *this* is happening, that is where you must look; even if you know it's a false belief. Let your guides show you how to use compassion and care to keep your client/friend comfortable while healing happens. Otherwise the client/friend may feel affronted. Before you know it you have a little drama dancing into trauma. We protect ourselves with our stories. Just because you can see through someone's version of their life, it does not give you license to point it out to them. Doing this can lead to negative energy dislodging and attaching to you. Now their drama is your drama.

If you are not already watching for subtle signs out in the world, please do. Another way to watch for your personal drama alerts is by knowing how you react. Are your reactions outward: fit-throwing, cussing, aggressiveness or anger? Maybe you prefer the polarity: smiling, condescending, evasive or insincerely nice. Both types (and any other reaction) are distracting you from the real issue. It is easy to address the behavior versus the cause. Know your signs and watch for them.

We are Lightworkers. That does not mean we have to be emotionless and phlegmatic. Our emotions are a spiritual gauge; if something bothers you, maybe it wants healing. My guides tell us, "If you want to know what is happening in your subconscious mind, look around." We are constantly manifesting, every single moment. If you are experiencing drama and/or trauma, go meditate and look within. Assess yourself; is it you or someone else? Do you need clearing or healing? (Note: It is okay to ask for both! And by now I hope you are thinking of a page in your *SRB* that reflects ideas for healing and clearing when there is drama and/or trauma.)

Our surroundings speak to us constantly. Friends, family, books, songs and co-workers are reflecting energy to us all day long. Pay attention to your reactions. What do you do when you are sad, off or out-of-sorts? I go to the store of depression in the bargain basement of my worst memories where everything is cheap and if you leave, you can take everything with you. Uck. It is a desperate place of hunger, wanting and un-fulfillment. Have you read *Eat, Pray, Love*[21]? Elizabeth Gilbert hung out there a lot, before she ate her way to spirituality and love.

Healer, Heal Thy Self

This chapter is full of references for your *Spiritual Response Book*. Remember; make this book *before* you feel bad. One section of my *SRB* is for *Healing Techniques* where I write about modalities I hear about and keep business cards I collect. You can list any favorite things you do for yourself. Do you like to see energy healers, massage therapists, hypnotherapists, acupuncturists and people who work on the body? Are you a spa person? Do you heal from a long hike? Although it might sound menial right now, you will be relieved to have a Table of Contents with words like "depressed, tired, anxious, etc." for later if you need help. If you feel achy, you can look under 'A' and find a list of wonderful healers that can help. You can list anyone or anything you want. I have a page called *Inspiration*. A good friend uses the word *passionated*, what about a page for what encourages your passion? Do you love to walk in the park, skip rocks, visit friends with animals or donate time to a local charity? Don't forget about smelling roses. Even in the dead of winter, you can go to a florist and smell roses, its brilliant therapy for feelings of depression.

Your *SRB* can include poems, prayers, songs, movies, websites, artwork, photos or anything inspirational. Have you ever felt emotional and unable to release? Try including a page for *Emotional Movement*. It might include movies, like *Terms of Endearment*[22] or *Gone With the Wind*[23]. Make sure your *SRB* includes things that are free, in case your problems coincide with financial challenges. For instance: soothing bath, listening to inspirational music or web talks; drawing, painting, reading old thank you notes or calling a dear friend from your past.

Your *Grounding Page* will probably be long, since Lightworkers tend to launch into the ethers when they are upset or uncomfortable. My hope is that you take care of yourself, that you catch energy issues early and find a way to release them, pre-drama/trauma. And lastly, get vertical! It is imperative to feel connected and supported. You can access the Light via prayer and energy work, but to hold on to it, you... must... be... grounded!

Taking Chapter Two to Another Level

Much Lightwork happens in ethereal realms. When one finds it challenging to move back and forth between the physical and ethereal he or she can become ungrounded, sometimes called "airy-fairy." Avoid feeling spacey by identifying the issue and looking for a solution. We are strong, capable and reliable. Groundedness may seem far away from God, but it does not disconnect us from Source. We use linear thinking so that we can visualize, but the truth is we are never separate from the I Am Presence. We are connected, we are *One*. When grounding is challenging try *Grounding Prayer* for a quick fix or meditate with *Light Anchor Visualization*.

Grounding Prayer

Father/Mother/God/Goddess, Creator, Source of All That Is; please assist me in grounding and connecting deeply with Earth and Gaia. I ask for assistance in grounding as appropriate for my highest and best good. I command all negative and/or interfering energies to be surrounded with Light and taken on to their highest outworkings. I offer myself in service to Divine Light, Source of all that Is, and allow myself to be the highest expression of Light possible.

Thank you and Amen.

You have read about getting vertical, listened to advice and created thoughts about your connection to Source and the core of Earth. Now, take a few moments to expand your concentrated efforts with *Light Anchor Visualization*. Even practiced meditators will ask me to do this as a guided visualization. You can make a recording and listen to these words once a day. Try it. Try enhancing your connection.

Light Anchor Visualization

In a quiet, comfortable place, prepare for meditation. Ask your guides to help you visualize and experience the following exercise.

Place your hands over your high heart, which is between your throat and physical heart. Take a deep breath and focus on your high heart. Imagine that there is a glowing light within. Feel the Light of*

Source expand within your chest. Feel beautiful, bright, clear golden Light.

Imagine that the pure golden Light becomes an anchor within your high heart. Feel it as it becomes heavy. Feel the weight of your anchor pulled by gravity. As you let the anchor descend, you see an ever-lengthening golden Light cord extending from your high heart.

The anchor seems to gain heaviness as Earth pulls it with gravity. You can feel your anchor move as it is guided by Source to the core of Earth. Feel it move through rock, sediment, water. It disturbs nothing, it is disturbed by nothing. Feel your anchor of Light move directly to the center of Earth, to the great Light waiting for you there.

If you lose your way, do not worry. Source is guiding and Earth is receiving. Release your ideas of completion and allow your natural connection to awaken. Feel your pillar of Light protecting you, your guides showing you the way. Sense the great Light at the core of Earth. Ground, connect.

Remember: Between Earth and Source, we exist in a pillar of Light. Feel this connection daily. Let the knowledge become natural for you.

It is from this place we manifest. If your truest desire is to be who you are, know yourself as a vast light, perfect in creation, full of wisdom and love.

Thank you and Amen.

**You can also start with your solar plexus/third chakra.*

If you meditate, talk to friends and still can't shake the blues, read *Ten Things To Do When You Are Feeling Bogged Down.* The title refers to how Lightworkers feel when they have done too much energy clearing and are under it. The energy, I mean. Don't forget, let your guides guide you, it's what they are here to do.

Ten Things To Do When You Are Feeling Bogged Down

1. Get vertical... (yes, again!) Visualize this: you pick up a pot of coffee to pour yourself a cup and the liquid goes all over the counter, there's no cup! This is what your energy looks like when you aren't vertical. Remember the energetic pancake from Chapter Two? There is no container for your protection; no boundaries for your gifts and talents to honor. Vertical alignment serves us. Within our *pillar of Light*, we have protection from our own mindless explorations and the haphazard energies of others.

Ask Source to help you ground and connect to the highest Light possible. Visualize yourself in a giant *pillar of Light* filled with unconditional love. Reread Chapter Two!

2. Cut cords... If you are feeling extra energy around you, and suspect that it is not yours, you might need some extra help to cut energy cords. If you aren't already, get vertical. Set space and prepare for communication with your guides. Use great confidence as you call to your favorite Light being, I often request Archangel Michael. For instance, "I call forth to Archangel Michael, or the most appropriate Christ Consciousness Light being to assist me." When feel a presence, check the lights.

Remember the five w's from Chapter Three? A standard for any invitation: who, what, when, where and why. I usually throw in 'how' for good measure. Your prayer might continue like this, "Please help me, I am feeling bogged down and I request healing and assistance. Please cut all negative or inappropriate energy cords around, above and below me, now. I ask for any energy cords and/or connections to be sent to their creator and for all learning to be peaceful, easy and comfortable." *Discord Prayer* (Chapter Eight) is also a great way to do this, with added bonuses like helping one take responsibility for making a mess in the first place.

One note, cutting cords is a term that describes getting free of unwanted energy. In meditation, you might see swords, fire, scissors, machetes, etc. These are metaphoric images. Cords release with Light. Your guides will call in high frequency beings to help you, when you ask.

3. Call in the big guns... Are you fighting a major war with a squirt gun? My big guns include acupuncture, massage, readings, meditation, friends with good listening skills, chiropractor adjustments, energy work, healers, people who love me and art. As well as Archangels, Ascended Masters and spiritual Lighted ethereal beings. I heard from a friend that Sonia Choquette[24] says every Lightworker should have a list of twelve support-type people. How many can you name? (Good idea: Start making a list right now for you *SRB*, work on it until you have twelve reliable people, and never let this list wane.)

Check out this suggestion that came through for Linda, it was during a session right before her birthday. Linda is involved with a group of women she calls "the coven" that gather monthly and for special occasions. Lately, Linda noticed her group did not feel as loving as they once had. She felt one member in particular was challenging. This woman, let's call her Jan, made a few remarks that were less than positive. Afterward, Linda took them personally and felt inadequate.

During my work with Linda, I found no energetic evidence of dislike or disrespect directed toward her from anyone in the coven, not even Jan. On the contrary, I saw respect and honor, but maybe a little jealousy. Enter jealousy; a green-eyed creature emerges from the depth of insecurity, able to eat words and spit them out in a different order with just enough wasabi to create chaos.

Because Linda's birthday was around the corner, the guides suggested that she make a request of her friends before the next coven meeting. We were told, "Ask your friends to tell you what they like about you." She blanched and became emotional just imagining it. Yikes, I thought, that is a tough homework assignment. So tough that I didn't expect her to follow the advice.

Despite her fears of rejection, Linda completed the task. She asked each coven member to write down something that was liked about her as a birthday gift and bring it to her birthday celebration. How brave! Can you imagine sitting in a group listening to compliments about your heart and Soul and personality? (Say "yes!") Linda did it! Linda discovered what they each found wonderful, loving and beautiful about her.

When Jan spoke she mentioned admiration and envy; Linda discovered that it was jealousy she reacted to earlier, not dislike.

I hope you will try it. I did suggest this for another birthday girl. She asked her sister to make the request to friends and family; it worked out wonderfully. Sometimes, endearing thoughts from others are the big guns against sadness. Look for joy in words; know what makes your heart sing.

4. Water yourself... Is there anything worse than a dry Lightworker? (Now, that's funny!) Water is a conduit for us. We need to drink it, absorb it, touch it. Water clears, releases and rejuvenates. If I do readings at a metaphysical show, I take a bath that night. (See Chapter Six for *Bath of Light Prayer and Technique* which include ingredients for a wonderful clearing soak.) Our cells need to stay hydrated for Lightwork. It's mandatory!

Do you feel a little bogged down, like you have something to release? Try washing your hands in cool water. For an energy clearing bath include two cups baking soda and two cups Epsom salt (or the amount perfect for you) and soak to demagnetize negativity. (You might want to rinse after.) Try reading a prayer while soaking, or do a *Light Raising* (Chapter Four), please stay awake if you are meditating.

Guides often mention water during readings and sessions. "Get your feet in a creek, sit by water, listen to an ocean CD, swim, hydrate." It's all about the water. We need it, we want it, again—it's mandatory. Drink, drink, drink. Use clear, filtered water if possible. Follow the rules: humans need water. We may even feel hungry without enough water. Some hydrating ideas are coconut water, watermelon or other juicy fruits, and drinks with electrolytes. Also, try less caffeine and sugar. Water the Divine Being that you are.

5. Check your energy... Two common methods for checking one's own energy are dowsing with a pendulum or muscle testing. Muscle testing is a way of checking the flow of energy through the strength of your muscles, looking for resistance or weakness, also called kinesiology. A good reference for muscle testing is *Power vs. Force:*

The Hidden Determinants of Human Behavior[25]. One can muscle test with fingers by closing a forefinger and thumb loop with one hand and using the other forefinger to pull through the loop. If the loop holds, your answer is yes, if the loop is weak your answer is no.

I prefer using a pendulum. You can purchase a pendulum or create your own. A pendulum is simply a weight on a string that is able to swing freely; a metal washer works great. Metal and glass items are best, as they do not collect energy like minerals. Dowsing has a long history, including the use of rods for finding water. Miners have used dowsing for decades; many cities have a Dowsing Society for such talent.

Using a pendulum is simple, if you can get out of the way. Imagine your guides using your arm as a conduit for energy and, in the words of Hanna Kroeger[26], "Let go and let God." Start by learning what means "yes" and what means "no". I use a forward/backward swing as "yes" and a left/right swing as "no". Many use clockwise and counter clockwise circles, but I find the former much faster. Learn your pendulum language. Don't worry if this doesn't happen immediately. Have faith and keep trying.

Another helpful tool is a half circle pendulum chart, which looks like a protractor, or half of a circle. You can easily draw this. Turn a piece of paper sideways, long side down. Draw a straight line across the bottom edge, then from one end of the line to the other draw an arc making a large half circle. The half circle will represent a 0-100% chart. Please mark zero on the extreme left of your line; and one-hundred percent on the extreme right. Put your pencil in the center of the flat line, this is *center point*; draw a line from *center point* straight up to the top of the arc. This centerline is half way between zero and one-hundred therefore it is fifty percent; write 50% at the top of the centerline. From *center point* to the arc mark off lines for 10, 20, 30, 40, (50 is done), 60, 70, 80, and 90% (100 is done, as well). Label each line along the arc so that you have a half circle that resembles a wheel with spokes. You can hold your pendulum at *center point*, ask a question and then watch where on the arc the pendulum points.

Before you use the chart, do a few simple things to ensure the quality of your answers. Begin by setting space, getting vertical and asking Source to do everything. Use *Prayer for Centering, Divine Accordance Prayer, Release Protocol, Interpretation Prayer, Prayer for Balance* or any prayer you are drawn to. I use these words before swinging a pendulum:

Pendulum Prayer

Father, Mother, God, Goddess, Creator, Source of All That Is; please assist me in receiving information. I offer myself in service to the Divine Will of God and ask for clear and concise answers to my questions via this pendulum. Please clear any interfering energies. Please send forth the appropriate guides, Angels, Ascended Masters and teachers. I allow only pure Christ Consciousness Light Beings, none other.

Can I receive answers to my questions? (Wait for positive swing from pendulum.)

May I ask these questions? (Wait for positive swing from pendulum.)

Should I continue with these questions? (Wait for positive swing from pendulum.)

Thank you for your guidance and answers. Amen.

If ever there is a "no" to can I, may I, or should I; the work cannot continue. Trust your guides! There may be a good reason you can-not, may-not or should-not continue. These reasons have your best interest in mind. Think of it this way: Can I?—do I have the ability? May I?—do I have permission from all who participate to receive this answer? Should I?—am I safe and protected in this action? I never skip these questions.

If you have never used a pendulum, start with your elbow on a table for stability. Begin without your chart, learning your personal yes and no responses. Ask simple questions. For instance, "Is my name _______?" When you feel your answers are coming through clearly, ask questions in which you seek guidance.

If you are ready to further your communication, grab your chart. When I discovered the half circle chart, I fell in love. Yes and no answers never seemed to give me enough information. For instance, I once asked about the energy of going to a party. I wanted to go, but felt something was off. It was inexplicable and, quite honestly, aggravating. So I grabbed my half circle chart, set *sacred space* and said the *Pendulum Prayer*. I asked, "Please show me the positive energy of going to this party." With my pendulum at *center point*, it began to move toward 80%. Eighty percent! That is terrific positive energy. Then I asked, "Please show me the negative energy of going to this party." From *center point*, the pendulum swung to 90%.

I released my guides, with gratitude, and closed my *sacred space*. If the positive energy were eighty percent, I would have a wonderful time. However, if the negative is ninety percent, something unfortunate is possible. Remember, each question is asked on zero to one-hundred scales. If you are seventy percent positive, it does not mean you are thirty percent negative because they are two separate questions. Nothing deflates a grand time like a flat tire on the way home.

When you receive high percentages of negative energy, you may ask your guides to do a clearing. It is possible your own fears are creating your future. I have asked for clearing and healing and watched my pendulum swing to lower percentages. Personally, I address any negative energy over fifteen percent.

Please, keep in mind that pendulums and muscle testing are highly susceptible to you; your mind, ego and mental body can interfere. Ask questions to cross-reference your answers. In addition, calling a friend and doing a blind test is helpful. I will sometimes dowse my vitamins, then have a friend do the same. However, I hide the labels! Always conclude by releasing your guides and expressing your gratitude.

Dowsing, muscle testing and other types of physical tests are not completely reliable and are for use with great care and caution. Use common sense and street smarts with tools like these. Using a pendulum is perfect for checking one's self for negative energy to clear, but there are other ways to check. I have heard that early Native Americans used gambling. A winner was sure to have good medicine. We do not have to go to that length, but if you feel unlucky, you might have a problem with negative energy.

6. Pray... Prayer is a subtle and personal art. When people ask me to help them learn to pray we work on inner dialogue; that inside, on-going conversation. Those words are your unconscious prayers. Praying is an art that requires kindness, respect and sincerity, whether you are communicating with Source or thinking to yourself. Watch your thoughts; re-script them into prayer. If you catch yourself saying, "I hate when I do that!" Stop for a moment and create a new, more prayerful phrase, for instance, "God, Goddess, Creator, please assist me in releasing any reason why I did that!" *Think on purpose, pray on purpose.*

I love to use the prayers in this book. They are gifts from Source and I remember that each time I read them. Do not be afraid to re-word prayers. Make them personal, full of your wants, needs or desires. Note them on paper, create something for your *SRB*. Write an index card. Draw something on your mirror. Make prayer normal, intuitive and easy.

7. Play... Have you stopped playing? Most of us have had play trained out and work engrained. Let's start a player's society for the betterment of humanity. I double-dog-dare-you to do something fun today! For the next month write a big "F" on your calendar every time you have *fun*. This is the new "F", not the old one from report cards. Take L out of flunky and make it funky. Get weird, loud, creative, excited, curious, jumpy.

Sometimes we need to do something amusing to remind us that we can have fun. Go ride go-karts, swing or see a comedy. I find that children are professional fun-havers. If you don't have a kid handy, offer a parent-friend some free time, take their kids to the park and watch them laugh. It's free! If you aren't into responsibility and car seats, go to a playground and try to figure out what all that fun screaming is about. Watch a child cry in frustration then laugh in glee. Go bowling. Take five dollars to a dollar store and spend it on toys. (You can donate them when the fun wears off.)

This is a true story: Someone I know got in trouble at a card store for laughing too loud with a friend. I won't say who, because I don't want to look ridiculous. Okay, it was me. And it was a very funny card! I was with the same friend at a local brewery; we were drinking iced tea and eating lunch. I was telling a funny story and we were laughing up a storm. The server came over and told us to be quiet or we would have to leave. The sound of laughter almost got us kicked out of a bar. Now, that's funny!

Ask your heart where, when and how you can play. Who are your playing friends? Mine, obviously, is the card store friend. We still go read greeting cards for kicks and laugh way too loud.

8. Cross the county line... This idea comes from when my kids were young, and I didn't have extra money for relaxing spa days. When I was able to carve out special time for myself, I would often take a drive. I noticed that my problems seemed to ease when I got out of town; I began to crave crossing the county line. I would drive to my regular grocery store in another town. There I could take deep breaths, stop for a walk, visit a lake or occasionally, have lunch in a cemetery.

Sometimes we absolutely need to get out of our home energy. Before the internet, I would use phone books to make a list of parks and take my kids out of town for picnics, or to a new library. We all participated in leaving home energy behind and enjoying something new.

Ultimately, I like a good road trip or a vacation. Whether you are able to take a week or an hour, try getting a little farther away from home, say across the county line, and enjoy some energy unencumbered by routine. Short vision quests are available if we can get motivated enough to take the journey.

9. Exercise... I might be the last to say, "Hey, let's climb a fourteener!" (That's a mountain term meaning 14,000 feet or higher; in Colorado, anything less is 'just a hike'.) Yet I know that when I am frustrated or depressed a walk helps. Our bodies respond to movement. Our muscles and ligaments enjoy stretching and releasing. Make sure to pay special attention to your physical needs. Gently, carefully, move yourself in the way you feel comfortable. Take care if you have any health issues.

Yoga, in its gentle form, is exceptional for Lightworkers. Keep your limitations and goals in mind. It's about movement, not injury.

Tai Chi, as well as other gentle martial arts, is renowned for health and meditation benefits. Try your local recreation center for a swimming class or search the Internet for a walking group. Nature is out there; don't let her hide from you. Plus you can find special gifts on walks like feathers, rocks and... money. I found a dollar once in the field near my house.

10. Buy a clue...or not... There are free clues, but they are not as valuable as ones you have to buy. Right? (This is a trick question.) Why is it people value possessions so much more when they pay? I have jeans from a thrift store that retail for over $100, I paid $7. There is another pair in my closet that I bought for $80, from a mall. The mall jeans don't fit well (some skinny, young thing said it was cool to have that belly fat showing, aka muffin top) and I can't get them out of my closet! I paid for them and maybe someday they will fit better and they were... blah, blah, blah. My thrift store jeans fit *great*; but they feel worthless, like $7 jeans. They are cheap, so I painted in them. Does this make sense?

Advertising is a way of life for most of us. Companies place name brands on or around beautiful people, and then show them to us on television, in magazines, online and via billboards. Our brains equate one to the other. Beautiful-young-pretty female gets a diamond ring. If we want a diamond, subconsciously we think, "I must look younger, prettier. What should I do?" Tall, dark-haired man in a suit gets a sports car. We believe, "No gray hair, lose some weight and I get the car." Does this sound ridiculous? Look around. We are all trying to look/be/act different. I once mentioned to my friend Chetan[27] that I desperately want to be my true self. He said, "Advertising is against it."

Ads tell us that we must change. Have you ever read an ad that said, "If you want something, *go pray about it*? Or a billboard that reads: *Tell your guides and wait*. Not likely, but those are the true messages. Try those suggestions and if what you want does not come, see if there is a block in your emotional body. Check for subconscious beliefs of unworthiness. We live in a material world; therefore, we must develop a balancing system to wade our way through the BS. (My guides claim BS means *belief system*!)

If you have debt from over-purchasing, please take a moment to breathe through any guilt, then ask yourself, "Am I better because I bought this?" The answer, as you know, is: *No*. You are not a better person because you drive an expensive car or wear a new shirt. I am not different in any way if I own expensive denim jeans. Consider your definition of value; if you have to pay to feel that something is worthwhile, send me a dollar! Ask yourself if your value system is entangled with advertising and/or spending.

Make sure that material items do not reflect your self-esteem. We are innately valuable to the Divine because we are the Divine. When you feel worthless, without worth, read the following: (All caps for emphasis, speak this aloud...)

I AM A CHILD OF THE SUPREME LIGHT.

I AM BEAUTIFUL.

MY EYES ARE TAKING IN THE WORLD AND SENDING IT TO THE HEART OF GOD/GODDESS.

MY BREATH PULLS IN SOURCE LIGHT AND EXPELS ALL THAT I DESIRE TO

RELEASE.

EVERYTHING LESS THAN PERFECT IS A SMALL MESSAGE THAT I AM LEARNING TO CREATE AND I ACCEPT THE RESPONSIBILITY THAT I AM CREATING AND THEREFORE, CREATOR.

MY LIFE IS AN EXAMPLE THAT LIGHT CAN LEARN.

MY CHOICES ARE AN EVER GROWING MENU OF WONDERFUL NEW IDEAS READY TO EXPRESS MY WONDERFUL TALENT.

I AM A FABULOUS LIGHTWORKER.

I AM PERFECT THE WAY I AM.

I AM LOVED. I AM LOVED. I AM LOVED.

No more caps... they are so intense. Can you feel the words above? They are worth the dollar, right? Invest in your well-being, your centeredness with action. Meditate, converse with your guides, trust that answers will come. Ask for the free clues, the real ones.

Remember, each moment is the time for a new effort. You can change everything, but it starts with changing your mind. Express your creative desires by changing one thought. Thank God/Goddess when the results show up. Gratitude is a sweet breeze on a hot day!

A friend told me this, *"Source, show me a Divine creation. Now show me one step toward it."* That phrase came from a reading I did for her. I did not remember what the guides said, but it came back to me anyway. I am grateful for that reminder, because sometimes my goals are so far away the direction is imperceptible.

THANK YOU, SOURCE LIGHT THAT I AM! (Say that aloud, it heals!)

Lastly, if you are feeling bogged down, please surround yourself with loving and caring people. If you cannot find Divinity within yourself, find someone you trust and ask for help. Remember the birthday party assignment, "What do you like about me?" You are a worthy being, and love is your inheritance. Do not hide from the exciting, special, beautiful being that you are.

Healing Surprise Emotion

Have you ever noticed how our moods can shift with a song? Or a movie? Are we truly that impressionable? I know more than one person that can Jekyll/Hyde[28] on a dime. Why are we so affected by what is around us? One reason is empathy. Lightworkers tend to feel almost as much as they see. We live in a physical body that is bombarded by an influx of... well, everything. Occasionally, we might hear or see something that triggers an old emotion, and suddenly our mood shifts.

Perhaps our ability to sense so much at once requires a filtering system for the enormous container called the *emotional body*. Consider it. If you are standing in a group of people with your psychic antennae up, how many feelings do you perceive? What are you picking up? The enormity of that is confounding. If each person has four main bodies giving emotions, thoughts and feelings to anyone that will listen, and you are developing your psychic abilities, it is likely that you are picking up enough ethereal energy to Hyde-out when you where so calmly being Jekyll.

To keep some semblance of order you will need to organize your abilities to perceive. You can relax, there isn't a list here because your guides already know what you need. It is their job. They *are* the filtering system. While we act as emotional vacuum cleaners, often vulnerable in our ignorance and the desire to enhance intuition, our guides are working to prioritize our experiences. Have faith that this works in a systematic manner, I promise you that it does. But you must do some of the work. Namely, you will feel that guidance most effectively through *surrender*. My experience is that when I interfere, I displace Divine Order.

Through friends, I met Alex when he was twenty-one. This was years ago, before I knew about my spiritual gifts. However, people could sense something and would often confide in me. Alex told me his friend died. She was in the car with him and two other people. He was driving; the accident was his fault. Alex suffered emotional trauma from grief and the legal issues that came after the accident. Although he was found to be innocent of his friend's death, Alex's heart was heavily burdened with guilt. He once told me that he saw himself as a big bucket of water. Each drop of water in the bucket came from an experience with emotions. In time, the bucket got full. So full that when a new emotional experience dropped into the bucket, it caused water to displace and release a random drop.

If someone called Alex a jerk, he may cry because the "jerk raindrop" forced a two month old "broken heart raindrop" out of the bucket. Alex believed that he did not have control over what came out, he was completely overwhelmed and victim to his full bucket.

I could be walking down the street when suddenly someone bumps into me. My initial feeling is aggravation then suddenly (imagine displaced water forced out of the bucket) I feel angry, very angry. I want to yell at the rude maniac that pushed me! Aggravation made a nice opening in my emotional body for anger to surface. We are creative when it comes to supporting our feelings, so if I am not careful, I can bend the situation to support whatever I want to conclude. For instance, "That guy is an idiot! He should watch where he is going!" However if I pay attention, I will see that I have emotion to deal with—and I can start by looking at why I projected anger on someone who inadvertently bumped me. Being overwhelmed by emotion often leads to misplaced anger, with the potential for blame and projection.

Creating a section in your *SRB* for emotional support might be helpful. When you heal emotion, you are engaging in a type of communication that is specific to you. Don't let this imperative knowledge slip away, jot a note in your *SRB* under "Emotional Body Support". We are unique in how we respond to healing, your *SRB* is the key to opening the chest of treasure that you are. Every time you figure out how to heal, take note, for yourself or possibly to share with someone else. (*Or* maybe you will write a book about it someday!) It can be hard to identify projection and over-reacting, we feel justified in feeling what we feel. Use Alex's idea; ask yourself if you are experiencing the reaction to a current action or an old one.

If you find a drop of water escaping from your bucket, explore it as an opportunity. Your guides may be directing you to release or heal a block to your Divine happiness, or some other unfulfilled request. Also, meditate on the concept of healing the past; you might be able to diffuse old hurts before they sneak up on you. When I am working, and healing comes through for a client, I often ask for the same healing. I don't search for why I might need it, I simply ask:

> *If this is appropriate for the highest and best good and Divine Accordance Prayer, may I please have this healing. Thank you and Amen.*

When you find yourself in need of help because of a new emotion that you don't understand, try this: Set space. Get vertical. Take five or ten minutes to get to your *safe place.* Ask for a guide of Christ Consciousness Light (check their Light) to come forth to help you release an old, pent-up emotion. Use the bucket or your own metaphor. Ask for the memory to change, heal or repair. Ask for any healing that is possible to help you release anger. Thank and release your guides, come back. (Don't forget to ground and close!)

Resting

Lightwork may appear easy. It may seem like you can sit in a chair and talk, or move your hands in the air to heal, and then walk away ready to exercise. That is not likely to happen. During healing sessions, even a quick phone call with someone under stress, we use energy. If you are channeling, receiving energy and offering it at the same time, your physical body uses resources. We have physical requirements. Part of our refueling process includes sleep. As we clear, heal others—and ourselves—we use energy that replenishes when we rest. When I hear someone complain about insomnia, I am sympathetic. My early journey as a Lightworker left me with many sleepless nights. Lack of sleep can sabotage memory, mood, perspective, relationships, health and more. Being *under*-rested is like having a block of wood under your gas pedal, you can't quite get up to speed.

Please keep in mind that if you have recurring insomnia it may be a medical issue, for medical issues consult a licensed physician.

Because of my own issues with insomnia, I began to ask for sleep blessings at the end of evening spiritual groups. I found even the worst insomniacs sleep after a group channeling! I would ask Source to bless each person with a safe drive home and a good night's sleep. It sounds like this:

> *(Closing prayer.) ... "Please bless each person here with a safe drive home and a wonderful night's sleep. I ask that they wake feeling rested, rejuvenated and rejoicing. Thank you and Amen."*

After I attend a spiritual workshop, I often experience super-charged energy—the kind that causes insomnia. I call it a "workshop high". Sounds fantastic, doesn't it?

Except for the inevitable, the post-workshop low. When clients float in after a grand experience I often ask for guides to help create a nice smooth road instead of a record-setting roller coaster. This includes a serious night's sleep.

The following prayers have worked for many over the years. They are helpful if you have tapped into an interfering energy, have too much energy or need a cleared space for your sleep. Sometimes, I have students so eager to communicate with their guides that they forget to turn off at night. Our natural state of being connects us with Creator. If we are One, we do not need to try so hard. Therefore, you can sit back; enjoy your life and your sleep! Your guides will get all the appropriate messages to you.

Say these prayers before going to bed, aloud if possible.

Sleeping Prayer

Father, Mother, God, Goddess, Creator, Source of All That Is; please help me sleep tonight. It is my intention to wake at ___ a.m. rested, rejuvenated and rejoicing! I allow my Self this time of conscious release and surrender. I invoke Christ Consciousness Light within and allow it to amplify through all my bodies, levels and areas of existence. I call forth the Almighty Presence of Creator to assist me in any way possible so that I may sleep soundly and comfortably on this night.

Thank you and Amen.

Safe Sleep Prayer

Father, Mother, God, Goddess, Creator, Source of All That Is; I call forth the original spark of love that is the highest form of truth. I allow this ultimate form of Light to be my guide. From this moment forward,

I will call this Light, in its most advanced form, Source. I allow this Light to continually advance and grow. I allow it to bless and teach me. As I learn about love, I will remember who I Am and know myself as the Divine spark that I Am.

I allow Source to show me Light. I allow Source to show me trust. I allow Source to show me faith. I am the ever-deserving witness and believer in the Divinity of Source and Oneness that warrant me love and protection.

Source, tonight show me a safe way to sleep. Show me peace and beauty in the form of a sacred garden. A garden surrounded by an impenetrable fence, secured with a gate only I can open. Within this garden, love and life bloom. I am safe in the high frequencies of Christ Consciousness Light that protect this garden. My garden resides in the dimensions of Light that no darkness can penetrate. When I close my eyes, I trust that Source, Creator of All Light will take me to my sacred garden and watch over my deep, restful sleep.

When I wake, I will be rested, rejuvenated and joyful. Let this prayer be my voice, my choice and my reality. From this moment forward, I command my own recognition of the Light Force that dwells within me. From that Light Force, I say, so it is.

Thank you and Amen.

Astral Travel at Night

Let's talk about astral travel. If you aren't familiar, astral travel is the idea that we can have an experience mentally or spiritually, without our physical bodies. It is similar to meditation, with the exception that you actually go somewhere when you travel astrally. I have to admit that I am leery. My first recommendation would be to do it while you are awake. That, my friends, is not a joke. Secondly, learn from someone experienced. Many times, I have seen clients with a strange porosity to one or more of their ethereal fields. My guides explain that this comes from exiting and re-entering. Whether taught or skilled many of us can leave our physical reality and "play" in the ethers. Sounds like fun, doesn't it? Why not go to another planet? Or visit a past life-time? The destinations are endless.

There's a better way. A safer way. My guides have taught me that I am not separate from anything; therefore I can bring all experiences to me; I don't have to go out to find them. This enables me to stay protected, and comfortable. Let me say that again, I can be protected while experiencing other times and places.

The first problem with astral travel is that the subconscious mind can be tricky. If you teach it to play, why would it stop playing at night? It is sort of like putting your two year-old to bed and leaving all the doors open. Why sleep when there's adventure waiting? The parental part of us must step in, as a form of protection, in the same way a child needs boundaries for safety.

A client came to see me with complaints of exhaustion. She would sleep during the night but wake feeling tired. After setting space and requesting the appropriate guides, I noticed a field of light around her that was full of holes. Our spiritual guides explained that she was exploring other realms at night. As an energetic form, she was leaving her body and fields of protection. She was astral traveling. Traveling who knows where and having a wonderful time, no doubt, but remembering nothing. She would wake exhausted.

The guides explained that we don't need to leave. Why would we, when we have a wonderful body to attend? There are other ways to see and know everything. One idea is to establish a plain room with one chair, all inside your *pillar of Light*. Ask for a screen so that you can see what you're searching for. I strongly encourage you to be specific. For instance, "Is there a past life causing me relationship problems? May I see it to resolve old issues?" This is not shamanic work, and not to be confused with that type of meditation.

I find that leaving any part of myself leads to trouble. In the beginning of my meditation practice, I admit, I wandered. Curiosity is strong in me, and I followed the little rabbit into the woods more than once. I left things behind and brought things back. Luckily, I met Rick and his group where there were healers and I found my way to clarity. While working with clients, I have seen many auric fields full of holes from hapless exit and entry. You may be skilled at astral travel, or remote viewing and defend the practice. I understand that, but for you own good, please be careful. Ask your guidance team to show you how to explore safely. My guides liken it to a house where one enters and exits through the walls and roof. A house of windows and doors is already full of holes to govern, it doesn't need more.

This prayer is to help you stay energetically safe and protected for sound, rejuvenating sleep.

Sleeping & Prevention of Negative Astral Travel

From this body and this mind, I state clearly it is my intention to sleep soundly tonight. I call forth Archangel Michael and Christ Consciousness Light to ask for assistance: Please repair any damage to the crystalline cord and structure that connect me to Source, please repair any damage to the grounding cord and structure that connect me to Earth.

It is my intention to sleep each night and wake rested and revived. I allow my cosmic physician to repair and heal all aspects of my being during my sleep. I allow and accept help from Beings that are the one-hundred percent pure unconditional love during my sleep state.

I ask for spiritual transcendence for my Soul and all aspects of my Soul at all levels, realities and positions.

I allow Spirit to guide me on my journey. It is my intention to allow healing, knowledge, wisdom and understanding to infiltrate my consciousness and bodies. I allow all that is guided by Source and surrender myself to Divine Will.

Thank You and Amen.

Hidden Trauma

Have you ever met anyone with a problem for which they cannot find a cause? A woman, let's all her Maria, came to see me about a personal issue. She yearned for love and attention from men. She was born from her biological father, adopted as an infant by her heart-father and when her adoptive parents divorced, she embraced a stepfather. She also had two brothers; men were everywhere. To have so much male attention into her life, and still desire more was a sign that something wanted to heal. Through our work together, I learned about past life issues hidden from Maria's current memory. She was trying to work out rejection from men—via multiple lifetimes. However, the opportunity to heal was present in this lifetime. Maria worked hard using many modalities to heal her subconscious need for extra attention from men. She bravely looked at her own behavior and actions, then took steps to healing. I was lucky to be part of her restoration.

Hidden trauma can show up through actions; watch for those that seem too aggressive for the situation. Much likes Alex's water theory, we need help when overwhelm begins to dictate our lives. Working as a psychic, channel or energy healer, you may attract clients that have not found relief with traditional resources. We, the Lightworkers, *are* the non-traditional resources. You may even attract these people as friends who do not realize your innate healing abilities.

The next prayer came through for someone experiencing trauma from their past life history. Whether it is this life or another, some events are too painful to go back and visit. Many of us have experiences that were violent or devastating. We may have seen death, violation, destruction or genocide. If you sense something difficult to see, for you or a client, begin by clearing as much energy as possible with prayer. Try the following words to release the burden of trauma from a violent past.

Release Violence from the Past

Father, Mother, God, Goddess, Creator, Source of All That Is; I ask, in this moment, to be cleared of any frequencies that resonate with violence from this life or any other life. I ask that I be cleared thru all levels of light, through all dimensions and all space. I ask for karma to be released, cleared or completed that has to do with violence, assault, aggression or anger. I ask that I be released and cleared of all grief concerning any experience with violence. I ask that peaceful messages come upon me and that I be gently guided to a form of release that is appropriate for me.

I ask that I be empowered to understand that I can release, that there is a place where these things are held and it is not within my physical body. I ask for help in knowing that there are guardians of these archives and they will help me to move through these changes peacefully, easily and comfortably.

In the gentleness that I create for myself, I ask that Source remind me, as long as it takes, over and over again, that I am in a peaceful existence. I release any energies of guilt or shame that cause me to deny myself a peaceful existence. I allow all violent frequencies to move past me without my notice and if possible, into the Light.

I ask that my Light attract Light and that my mind recognize that my dominant force is Light, that I am One with Source on this planet and I create peace, ease and comfort. I create love, healing, happiness. Even if I witness otherwise, I command that my mind recognize it is only something I see. Let it be known now that I do not have to experience everything to know it. As I learn through all experiences, I am more aware, I am more conscious, I am more awake.

My gratitude to all who help me on this journey.

Thank you and Amen.

Chapter Eight

Group Support

The first time I witnessed channeling was when I went to Rick Lewis's group. To be honest, I thought it was strange. What happened after, well, that was even stranger. Concisely: I went to a gathering, a person spoke, I judged and doubted... and then I began to heal. I can laugh at myself now, but the beginning was not funny. In fact, it was quite painful.

Part of the strangeness of Rick's channeling was that when he spoke, his voice altered; he even spoke with an accent. The new voice introduced himself as "Kathumi", whom I later learned is an Ascended Master. You probably already know that Ascended Masters are beings that have completed Earthly lives and have learned to clarify their energy fields. This allows them to ascend to pure Light. They are messengers between Source and humans and are known for their wisdom. We can reach Ascended Masters through meditation and fifth dimensional frequencies, or higher. But I didn't know much about Ascended Masters, back then, or Kathumi. What a strange name, I thought, and then I listened. The advice Kathumi gave is what brought me back to the group. My judgment of 'new agers' was harsh. I looked around at flowy clothing, crystals dangling from necks and thought these are not my people. I was wrong. Rick/Kathumi's information brought me into a new place of thinking, beyond my fear and confusion. Eventually, I surrendered, Rick's channeling was magical.

These were tough times for me. Emotionally I felt inside-out. My vulnerability was daunting, my *pillar of Light* was open to the unknown (certainly unknown for me) and I had no idea that I was in charge of my own energy. Imagine of the worst knot in your shoelace. I was that tight and twisted; I needed something to cut me open. Rick's group was the knife. I released so much in those early days of my spiritual opening, during my introduction to channeling. Even though I doubted (a lot), I healed. The changes were evident, so I continued seeing that strange person who channeled, the one who I questioned and judged in the beginning.

Our group bonded over common issues and energy healing. Many of those people are still in my life today. (In fact, several are *friendly editors*.) We spoke, asked questions and/or listened; but there was something else happening. Maybe it was some kind of spiritual drain-o that cleared the group. Then it gave us a new way to perceive, after we released old baggage or karma or burdens. Rick helped me open to my guides, for which I will be forever grateful. He taught me to discern Pure Light. I don't know what our Soul agreements were, but I do know that I resisted and made it messy. As a group we challenged each other, likely all in ego, but when I reflect on it now I see service. I see support.

Opening to Channel

Currently, I teach people to open to their guides, to channel their inner God/Goddess voice and live their Divine Truth. But in the past, in Rick's group, I was not in a teaching mode. It was all about learning. As negative energy released from my energy fields, my personal guidance of voices and visions became strong and intense.

Friendships formed in Rick's group, and we began to share our experiences more intimately, we began to trust each other. Picture me as the novice with my notebook full of notes and thoughts, ready to tell anyone that would listen about my experiences. I wanted badly to be in community and share the messages I was receiving. Spiritual communication felt strange, I wanted someone to understand and make the strangeness seem normal. I desired approval and wanted to be accurate, I wanted someone to notice me, to verify that I was worthy of something special. Most of the people in Rick's group were older than me and more experienced in spiritual matters. It was a passive aggressive move against myself to constantly need feedback. There was nothing in my history (at least in this life) to help me understand what was happening, so I gave my power away to anyone that would listen. It was a move that supported self-sabotage.

What I see now as Divine Order in perfect timing, was excruciating to live through. I wanted people to like the messages I heard, or at least be touched by them. Can you imagine? Picture yourself as a learned participant in a spiritual group. Someone new comes along who believes they are channeling, they even want you to verify their information. Annoying. I even annoyed myself. I hated the neediness; the questionability of it all. I felt like a victim while I was integrating the most magnificent gift.

To make matters worse, when good came I resisted. It's a funny thing, resistance. There is invariably a message under the ice of reluctance, but clarity was on vacation in Hawaii when I needed it. My saving grace was Rick Lewis. Without his faith in my work, I might have given up and collapsed under the hard work it would take to get clear and remain clear. He was my advocate and trained me by seeking counsel through me, but I get ahead of myself.

Now you can see why this part comes later in the book, it's too much pity-potty and not enough savoir. After reading the prayers, you have experienced the healing and clearing I had yet to know. You can step into the healing of my story, instead of the pain. More than fourteen years later, I can still feel what happened. I am a School of Hard Knocks alumni and not proud of it. However, I am the master teacher of my life, as are you of yours, and the teaching continues—with the exception that now I create peacefully, easily and comfortable. (Thank you and amen!)

For years, I heard voices in my head, which is not something one mentions to the general public. After working with Rick the voices were less chaotic, they became loving. When I began to hear Kuthumi outside of the group, as I mentioned, I thought it was normal, or at least normal for the people that assembled for spiritual counsel. Without experience in that environment, I assumed it was part of the deal. Didn't everyone hear that voice echo and speak?

My mind couldn't wrap around the idea that it was only me. My lack of confidence echoed out into Rick's group and among my friends. I experienced terrible loneliness. Because my ego was not clear, I felt confused, encumbered, attacked, wrong and unfortunately, suicidal. Living seemed to be something that caused more pain than I could handle. I loved my family, but even that wasn't satisfying. Hindsight offers that the energy trying to stop my Light from shining might have presented alternatives, like suffering or even death. But I didn't understand those forces then.

There were those who came like Angels to save me from myself. I am so grateful for their care and understanding. But there were also people who stood in judgment and pointed out my faults. It was appropriate for me to move along my path without some of them, but I resisted. My old friends, my trusted confidants stopped listening. I felt less love, probably my imagination, and more conflict, likely my projection. These beings were the way-showers. Some led gently; some pushed, shoved and forced. I take responsibility for this experience. Now, I actually love what happened. But I didn't then. Misery was my theme and I lived it.

I felt great amounts of pain and agony over the changing relationships in my life. My friendships shifted rapidly. Spiritually, I had no training and was not very well read. Everyone intimidated me. When I received information from Spirit, I would doubt it, worry about delivery, and interfere believing I would make it easier for everyone. Vast amounts of energy can be expended making life easier for everyone else.

And that was me, co-dependent as hell, wanting a rescue and at the same time I was conversing with Ascended Masters and learning about God/Goddess aspects of myself. I was a hurricane of energy that challenged itself and my outer world reflected it.

Gratefully, I realize now that each person I had trouble with was teaching me to love and forgive myself, to listen and speak without judgment. I learned to rely on Source instead of books, people or education. Then finally, I learned to stop looking to others for approval. Remember the old lesson from Cindy Fox, my teachers are ethereal. That sounds wonderful, but learning to rely on meditations instead of human contact took some time to integrate. I had to break thousands of habits and turn off aspects of my personality that no longer served.

During this time, I had a good friend I'll call Samantha. I knew her before my spiritual path became the most important thing in my life. She was what one might call a best friend. My new talents weren't sitting quite right with Samantha. When she asked me to check-in with my guides, her reaction was often challenging and argumentative. I would feel defensive and seek approval by offering information when it wasn't requested, or I would over-explain trying to help her understand what the guides meant. How extremely human of me. Unrequested information from ethereals, never a good idea. As you can imagine, it did not make Samantha happy. When she would complain or judge the message. I often felt hurt. And, predictably—everything felt like a personal affront.

By this time, I was taking appointments and doing readings. A business was forming via word-of-mouth and referrals. But friends were different. Many friends would seek advice, yet not value my offerings enough to pay or compensate for them with a heartfelt gesture. I related this to my worthlessness. If the messages were valuable, wouldn't friends want to pay me for my time, or offer something in exchange? Samantha was not the only one teaching me this lesson, but the energy between Samantha and me is necessary to understand. She was my closest friend and her rejection hurt me deeply, because it was personal, right? I was so self-absorbed that it never occurred to me that everyone else was processing and struggling as much as I was.

You may find that on your path of spiritual growth there is one person, someone close to you, that serves as a spiritual broom. They seem to hit you in the behind and push you into whatever it is you are resisting. With Samantha, I had to admit that if I chose spirituality as a job, which was the obvious choice because it took over my life, then I had to be okay with getting paid. I learned about clear exchange, gifting and letting go even when you feel slighted. Or unappreciated.

If you feel called to channel, know that it changes you. Opportunities open inside the subconscious that grow like oak trees. Or telephone poles, they aren't all pretty. If you can't see clearly, you will create a house of mirrors to get messages to yourself another way. I hated my house of mirrors, and mostly because I didn't know how to love my mistakes, errors, blunders and mishaps. My guides once told me that we don't yell at a one-year-old that falls down. We let them learn to get up and walk. On my spiritual path, I was one. Maybe two.

In the years since, I have healed my attitude. I try not to focus on what others are doing; instead I explore what I am creating, my own personal thoughts. My guides have explained more than once that we learn from our surroundings. If you have only one person in your life, he or she will be your teacher and student. Those closest to us will reflect and teach because we have Soul agreements. Are we unconsciously in service? I believe that we are, yet if we search for what we are teaching others, it becomes conscious—and that is typically a written invitation for ego. Our spiritual service and Soul agreements have a manager, Source, which makes life a lot easier.

I spent many years healing my interactions with Samantha. We distanced and healed without each other, but remained friends. There was no formal falling out for us, although I have had those heartbreaking separations with others. My favorite prayer in those days was *Discord Prayer* (in this chapter). During a lunch, seven years after I opened to channel, Samantha confessed to feeling jealous. Jealous?! My insecurities never even considered jealousy. Once again, in hindsight, I see it clearly.

Wouldn't I have been jealous of a friend with sudden knowing from beyond? My only concern back then was a vain perspective of struggle. I wanted help, understanding and love. I wanted support. I wanted compassion; which I didn't have for Samantha, and frankly, I didn't have for me. I could not see my Light; therefore I could not see the Divine Outworkings around me. It never occurred to me that so many changes might affect a friendship.

Our lunch reestablished how much we cared for each other. We were able to see an evolution of healing and growth. That is why I was surprised when, one morning much later, I meditated and felt Samantha's energy. I wrote this during the meditation:

> *(Edited for clarity.) After my opening prayers, I ask for protection in my sacred space, and then do a Light Raising. I feel the energy of Samantha. Why? I proceed cautiously. I remember being angry with her in the past for many reasons, but now I can see the truth. I felt abandoned. During all the changes, I felt afraid and I needed her. When I started channeling, I felt so alone. I struggled.*
>
> *Can I forgive her? Yes! But, will I trust her? And should I talk to her about this?*
>
> *I hear, "No. She will defend and apologize but the energy won't shift." I spend a moment in gratitude to the people that loved me through my changes.*
>
> *A guide comes. I check his lights and ask his name.*
>
> *"Mark, you have called me in the past."*
>
> *We go up my pillar of Light to a great Light. We go into the light where there is a room. Mark explains that there is a 'server', which is similar to what we use for our computers. It sends and receives. We sit in comfortable chairs, much like a theater.*
>
> *I start to speak, but he says, "Listen." So I do, and I hear a hum all*

around us, like a million quiet voices and then I see... information. It floats above us and all around in codes and equations. I think I can read them or grab them—but only in incomplete ways. Then I sense that through the server I can get complete information.

I ask where we are.

Mark explains, "We are inside the Universal Source." I am shown how I made this vision so that I could understand. I look again at all the information floating around. I wonder how I can get that information. Can I channel it?

Mark answers my thought, "Yes. At any time, you can channel any number of ideas. But they are not Divinely yours. Your attempts to make them into something will fail because of your contracts. Not all carry the steadfast energy of procurement you chose for this body. You only accept the purest and truest and therefore will stop anything else."

I believe Mark is telling me that I try, then give up because I feel lack. I ask, do you mean I sabotage myself?

"Yes, or forget, lose interest."

That makes sense. I wonder, is that a habit?

"No, beloved, not a habit merely a repeated experience or memory or archive."

Do I need to bypass some part of my mind to complete tasks?

"Yes and no. Diligence, discipline and decision are your key factors. Don't be afraid to share your vision. Others will help hold the frequency."

Is this why Samantha came up?

"Yes, you are upset, you feel she let you down when you thought she was support."

Was she?

"No and yes. Her support was inadequate; you wanted more. This taught you to be stronger, yes?"

Yes. Can I learn without heartache?

"You already are."

Is she not my friend?

"More of a teacher."

I flash back to my lessons with Samantha. She taught me about independence; to listen to my heart concerning needs, alliances and mentors.

"There's more."

Help, please!

"Beloved, she taught you what you want!"

Oh!

"She taught you about people who block love and accept only what their hands can hold. She expanded your concepts of resentment, hierarchy, desire and need."

I feel gratitude. I say a prayer of thanks to Samantha. I wonder, should I tell her?

"You could. But, why?"

The energy feels undone.

"Then heal it. You want to let her know she hurt you and make up for that by calling her teacher, yes?"

How does he know that? I reply yes.

"Why?"

I ponder for a moment. My ego flares up. I answer: To level the playing field. To heal my compromise—where I got hurt. I want to give myself the upper hand. Maybe she will wake up... I want to push back.

"Hmm," I feel awkward as Mark tells me, "Acknowledge the why and heal the how. Unless she asks, your communication is for you."

Yes, I see, thank you. My mind is registering quickly, I can see that I am still hurt and I can heal how I was hurt by understanding why.

"You will never allow yourself stagnancy. You will move yourself in creative and unusual ways. The stream of consciousness that comes in is consistent, you need only listen."

I see it all around me. I feel that I have a new clarity concerning this old situation. When I could not see myself as worthy consciously, I pulled people in to reflect my inner feelings. Samantha came to the plate and batted a homerun. She was not playing for the other team, she played for mine.

Mark spoke again, "Fair thee well, blessed one. We are never far."

We move back down the pillar of Light and I ground, present again in my physical body. Then I hear the words of a prayer:

Prayer to Disconnect From and Forgive the Past

Divine beloved Creator that I Am, my movements on this planet and in this life are completely understood through my High-Self.

I release now resentment of any plans, actions or happenings that brought about pain or discomfort at any time, via any experience.

From this moment forward, I create learning peacefully, easily and comfortably for my Divine self and my third-dimensional self.

I allow realization to happen. I release old habits of learning the hard way. I discontinue patterns of sabotage, abuse, neglect, abandonment, fear, loneliness, lack of confidence or failure.

I embrace friendship, love and safety in relationships. I am healed from all past happenings that resulted in hardship, suffering, sadness, misunderstanding, unhappiness, distress or any other discordant energy. I now welcome trust, faith and joy.

My heart, mind, body, Soul and Spirit forgive my creations of pain and those who participated, including my Self. I completely release any energetic obligation from any person or circumstance I have used to learn without love and acceptance. I accept full responsibility for my existence. I am loved, nurtured, cared for, and I welcome me as I am!

Thank you and Amen.

Affirmation: People love me; I love me... as I Am.

Many people have used *Prayer to Disconnect From and Forgive the Past* to free incidents from the past in a general way, and a few have changed the words to apply directly to their situation. Below is Mary's version, which I found to be particularly moving.

Prayer to Disconnect From and Forgive the Past—Mary's Version

Divine beloved Creator that I Am, my movements on this planet and in this life are completely understood through my High-Self.

I now release resentment of any actions, events or plans that brought about pain or discomfort at any time, via any experience.

From this moment forward, I create peaceful, easy and comfortable learning for my Divine Self and my third-dimensional self. I release old habits of learning the hard way.

I allow awareness and I discontinue patterns of judgment, victimization, fear, assumptions, expectations, unworthiness, struggle, sabotage, abuse, neglect, abandonment, rejection, betrayal, competition, jealousy, loneliness, fear of failure and lack of confidence. I chose to heal from anything in the past that resulted in any form of my suffering.

I now welcome acceptance, trust, faith and joy. I embrace love, nurturance and safety in relationships. I allow grace into all my relations and experiences.

My heart, mind, body, Soul and Spirit forgive my creations of pain and those who participated, including my Self. I completely release any energetic obligation that I have used to learn without love and acceptance. I accept full responsibility for my existence. I am loved, honored, valued and cared for—by myself and others. I welcome me as I Am!

Affirmation: I love me... as I Am; People love me... as I Am.

Thank you and Amen.

As the Responsible Party

The path to forgiveness is indeed a path of discovery. As Lightworkers, we are a pretty responsible bunch. We claim to understand our creations, we lean toward compassion, we judge less and love more, right? Well, at least we intend to.

Sometimes there seems to be a hitch. On occasion, we have difficulty rising above our emotions. Like me, blaming Samantha for not being supportive. Maybe it's a shred of ego hanging on, or an incomplete past life trying to surface. Regardless, there is one thing that we have: The power of prayer. You can actually say a prayer and let your guides do all the work. If you can allow yourself Divine Assistance, if you can release and relax, Light will work its magic.

There are times when we know we need to forgive, but we can't quite get there. Our minds feed us reasons for our discomfort and we look for someone to blame. I admit to these actions. I have projected and blamed. In addition, I have received projection and blame. The key to forgiveness is compassion. If you can unlock your compassion, understanding pours forth and healing can begin. For many years, I held Samantha in a position. She was my poster child for rejection, lack of support and other negative feelings. After the meditation I shared with you, I worked with *Prayer to Disconnect From and Forgive the Past.* I began to feel less triggered by my emotions and I was able to forgive Samantha, for whatever I thought she had done, and then myself for having those thoughts in the first place. I experienced an incredible healing. I felt compassion for Samantha, and her experience. Understanding flooded into my mind and I forgave her, myself, and the situation.

The healing continued. My personal journey had, as it often does, attracted others with similar problems. I noticed as I released blame, I became free of negativity in other areas. But some energies didn't clear, and I received the next phase of working with compassion, clearing and healing the past via *Forgiveness and Empowerment through Unconditional Love.*

Forgiveness and Empowerment through Unconditional Love

Fully, your heart open, know yourself to be a Divine Creation! Fully, your heart aware, see no separation.

Upon abandoning what you think is real, you have only Light to guide you back to the pure place of no description; forgiveness for your travels, your choices, forgiveness Divine.

Expect your enlightened neighbor; expect your masterful friends; believe the Law of Attraction; see your manifestation.

Remember, as a blessing you have earned through a thousand lifetimes, a million Soul agreements. Be your own witness. Let the critic die. Let evolution recreate and rebirth your own inner negativity into Divine Service, Divine Witness, Divine Love.

Be it known – the heart is open, love is welcome. Present ever, beyond the air you breathe and ground you traverse upon, Divine Unconditional Love reigns.

Call upon it, as if it were a butterfly to alight, a dream to visit, call upon it.

Thank you and Amen.

Stuck in the Muck

Sometimes we find that we can't surrender. The more we try, the more surrendering becomes an issue. It reminds me of trying to pull gum from a shoe. I pull, get frustrated and wonder who the heck dropped this gum! WHO!? Whom can I blame and what can I say about them?

There is a delicate line between talking about an issue for processing and providing information for allies (aka gossip). The more work I do with people and on myself, the more I understand that I talk hoping to get allies. I want people to see my side, to agree with me, to know how wrong the other person is! One day, long ago, I complained about someone. I wrote about how bad this person was and how I was *not* a victim and that my beliefs were fine. Then, when I paused for a breath... a prayer came through. Actually, it was the *first* prayer. These words launched my prayer writing and opened me to receive. These are what I consider the most healing words in this book!

Why is this prayer better or stronger or more healing than any other? Just read it; let me know what you feel. I find that it seeps into your subconscious mind. It quells the conscious and pets the ego. It nurtures while it clears. It is mama energy with papa's resolve. It is pure, essential and quietly radical. It's the *Discord Prayer*. Am I poking fun? Maybe, but only because I have seen this particular set of words work. If problems arise between two people, the *Discord Prayer* helps resolve stuck energy. This prayer is the first prayer I ever programmed into my subconscious mind. Yes, I said programmed into my subconscious mind! (I will explain that soon.) It has a definite St. Germain flavor. If you aren't familiar with St. Germain, he is an Ascended Master, like Kuthumi. When you research Ascended Beings, Angels or the like, you will learn that they have traits and if you study them, the traits will become recognizable.

Use *Discord Prayer* to help all situations. It is powerful for work relationships, addictions, family and many other situations. The first time I used it, I had a case of blame and projection, which healed. My attitude shifted, then my beliefs—and then my reality.

Discord Prayer

On this day, I feel discord with you. I release this discord. I release all negative energy concerning it. I sever all energy cords I have sent to you and all energy cords you have sent to me; completely, above, below and around. I withdraw all energy I have inflated in any situation, conversation, past life or current life occurrence with you.

I forgive you for everything. I forgive myself for everything.

As the God/Goddess that I Am, I turn all negative energy I have sent to you into love. As the God/Goddess that I Am, I turn all negative energy you have directed towards me into love.

I accept only love from you and offer only love to you. I send you blessings for all the lessons you represent and wholeheartedly accept them. I release you from any further obligation I have created that could bring negativity into my life, or yours. I allow myself to see the role we have both played in this learning and thank you for helping me see that I Am a whole being of loving Light, and that I choose to learn in a loving and caring way.

Thank you and Amen.

How to Program a Prayer

I shared *Discord Prayer* anytime I could. If someone mentioned a problem with a friend, I offered the prayer. Problem at work? Try this. There was something to it, something that was working. And in the beginning, it was the *only* prayer. I thought it was a gift, so I gave it to anyone who was interested. (I still do, it's on my website!) It received enthusiastic reviews. I was surprised, amazed and pleased that something I wrote helped people. When a few of my friends and I were talking about how *Discord Prayer* helped each of us. One of them, Lynn, a busy ski instructor, told us she did not have time to read the entire prayer, so she simply said, "Only love, only love." That can't work, I thought—you cannot shorten spiritual words into a nickname. Lynn, by the way, nicknames most everyone. She calls me "Berry". I should have expected her to dub the prayer, but I felt protective over words from my guidance. I decided to go into meditation and check with my guides; I found the energy of the prayer to be fully present with Lynn's shortcut! When I researched the idea, I learned that other people program prayers and create shortcuts.

In classes, I explain to people that prayer does not have to be ceremonial or elaborate. You can make it work for you, even if it requires a shortcut. I shared this information with another Lightworker, Ginger, who works in sales. She took the shortcut idea to another level by programming the *Discord Prayer* into the back of her top teeth. Yes, I said *top teeth.* She told me that anytime she feels distress with a client she touches her tongue to the back of her top teeth and thinks of *Discord Prayer.* She claims it works quite well. Can a person do that? Once again, I checked with my guides and yes! Another shortcut!

How do you program your subconscious mind? It's easy, let's shorten *Discord Prayer* to "only love" as an example. Take a few moments to get vertical, set space and call in your guides, Angels, Ascended Masters and Beings of Light. Next, state your intention, for instance, "I intend for my High-Self to remember *Discord Prayer*." Or you might say, "Guides, Angels and Beings of Light, please help me to remember the words of this prayer." Now you must read *Discord Prayer* aloud. Then add the shortcut, "I intend to remember every word of this prayer when I say 'only love'." Read the prayer a second time. Re-affirm your intention, "Every time I say 'only love' it means these words... " Read the prayer for the third time to continue programming your High-Self, subconscious and conscious memory. I program by repeating the prayer at least three times and dowse (use the pendulum) to see if I have it, muscle checking will work, too. You may need to reprogram every few months, depending on how often you use the prayer. It is also nice to read the words occasionally so that you can feel the entire impact.

Remember, one of the reasons this prayer works so well is that we are taking responsibility for *everything*. When we settle our blame and take responsibility for creating it, we heal. When we examine a problem, we can gain knowledge about our fears as well as how we operate in the world. Take time to analyze yourself if you feel discord with someone or something. This will help you unravel the reason you created the circumstances in the first place, and to see any energetic cords you have sent—or energy cords sent to you. Honoring our tendencies to cord someone energetically is part of understanding our humanness. We can learn to examine interactions carefully, so that we manifest with love. A full appreciation and expression of Light is our natural and original state of being. In order to be the Light we are, we must see Light in each other.

I Understand that I Don't Understand

Have you ever been stuck on something that you were positive was true and you found out later it was not true? How many times have you misunderstood someone and repeated the erroneous information? We have all had those moments of assuming something and professing our truth, only to find out later we were... wrong. When we feel incorrect, our minds engage with all types of negative emotions. In sessions, I have watched people release feelings of dishonesty, poor ethics, sin, immorality, shame and guilt—all stemming from an experience of being wrong. Sometimes these events are from this life, a current memory that haunts the mind; some are from past lives, a subconscious effort.

Do you remember seesaws? Those fun long boards at the playground with a seat at each end? Imagine yourself standing safely in the exact middle of a seesaw, finding balance. To one side you see a seat labeled "right", to the other, a seat labeled "wrong". This is a metaphor, whether you are hung up on being right or wrong, both take you out of balance. *Both* represent ego. The center is a place of surrender; when we stand there, we are in a place of no attachment. Finding that balance may not be easy. Honestly, how many people do you know that do not care if they are wrong? I will admit that I love being right! It feels wonderful; and my business depends on accuracy. To maintain balance, I pray for indifference and detachment from the desire to be right.

Several problems come into play when we monitor what is right or wrong. Let's say you are giving someone a spiritual reading and you speak about something that you see because you *think* they need to hear it. And let's say that you are *right*, they do *need* to hear it. You know that because they complained of an issue and this is what causes the issue. So you are going to help them. Right?

If your client walks across four lanes of traffic in the middle of the block and then comes to you and complains about angry drivers and honking. You might suggest using a crosswalk—because its common sense. And it would eliminate the complaint. Use a crosswalk; no honking, no angry drivers. Simple.

Can you see the problem? If you tell your client something before they are ready, then *you* are wrong. Later you are right, but first you are wrong. I am not talking about confrontation and whether or not you are strong enough for it, I am not talking about pushing to resolve something; I am talking about using your idea versus being in service and waiting for Divine Timing. Drivers honked at your client. He/she does not want angry drivers and honking.

Remember, when working with energy, we must be open to Divine Guidance, not our ideas of how one can change a situation, even if it is common sense. Be ready to ask your guides questions. For instance, "Should I mention a crosswalk?" If the answer is no, you can delve deeper. Likely, they will ask the client questions, versus making an obvious suggestion. Even if it is common sense.

Surrender means being open to unconditional love. Channeling is a position of power; people are listening to you. Source Light, no matter where I am emotionally, is perpetually gentle. If you are channeling and the energy is curt, acerbic or harsh, *stop*. Re-center, ground and say your opening prayers again, because it's not Christ Consciousness Light. Get Vertical. Clarity comes through a precise current of Pure Light, settle for nothing less.

If you offer advice that doesn't bring the expected result, people can get angry, which is generally a reaction to feeling hurt. This is where peace, ease and comfort have another facet. As a Lightworker, do you want to push, shove, suggest, point and direct? Or would you like to offer, suggest, teach and be of service? It's important that we use our *Pillars of Light* to maintain contact with our guides for information and timing. If you remain clear and work with en-*light*-ened information, you will find yourself involved in Divine Timing. Maybe the complaint about honking, angry drivers isn't addressed. This happens in sessions, so be prepared for yourself and others, sometimes we don't know the answer.

Our powerful mental bodies need protection from any and all judgment. That protection can come easily, through Divine Channels, in the perfect form for each one of us. The prayers in this book offer the verbiage for this protection. In addition, we must learn to use heart-centered energy to interact with ethereal beings and to receive messages. If we use the mental body or ego system, we are susceptible to shame and guilt because the mind likes to be right or correct or accurate.

One issue Lightworkers often struggle with is how to interpret a message. If there is one meaning, there is one way, right? We all know that isn't true. Consider what affects truth. Location, for one. Words have different meanings and colloquialisms. My Aunt Jackie, who hails from Tennessee, once told me that if you ask a local for a favor they might respond, "I don't care to", which means sure, okay or I don't mind. From my understanding it means, "No thank you, I don't want to." How would my mind know which interpretation is appropriate to deliver to a client? It's true that we are smart enough to interpret and offer valuable information. But there is a much better way to offer guidance. It's more of the same: surrender. However, with this type of surrender might feel strange at first. You might feel as if you are inventing words, or using them inaccurately.

On one occasion, I was doing a reading and the guides used the word "stupid" in reference to something. I was immediately aware of the word. It froze me, I stopped and apologized for using the word stupid during a session. It certainly didn't sound spiritual. After, I grabbed my old dictionary and looked up "stupid", it means *foolish* in older terms. I wouldn't stop a reading if the guides said something was foolish. It was a lesson in judgment and further surrender. I was grateful that I remembered to ask for help with interpretation and I prayed for clearer messages in terms each client could understand.

Ultimately, we keep definitions of words or phrases in a place much bigger than our minds. They are in that vast, ethereal library we call the Akashic Records. If you imagine Source as the main librarian and yourself as a student, it's easier to understand. Use *Interpretation Prayer* to open your heart to the possibility that you have access to Divine Understanding. This prayer is of particular use when you have interpretation problems with a person. It can be easily altered to suit your circumstances.

Interpretation Prayer

Father, Mother, God, Goddess, Creator, Source of All That Is; I call forth your assistance in understanding my interaction with ________. Please help me understand the meaning of all words and actions, from all participants in this situation including myself. Please help me see why I created this, and what I intend to learn. I allow all anger, jealousy, shame and resentment to evaporate with this understanding. I Am love. I Am Light.

Thank you and Amen.

Forgiving to Heal

As life proceeds in doling out lessons (as we continue creating lessons), we soldier on. Have you seen the bumper sticker that says, *Oh no! Not another learning experience*? I used that phrase as a subtitle in Chapter Five. It makes me snarl when I apply it to my own life, but it's sort of a theme in spiritual awakening, don't you think? Maybe that's why they call it light *work*. Working is good for us, but we must be aware of what we create and how.

Meditation is one of the best ways I have found to raise frequency so that life is gentler, hopefully eliminating awkward experiences. Here is another story from my meditation notes, edited for clarity:

I set sacred space, align vertically and call in my guides. I feel their presence. I sense a brooch in my hand. I look closely, turning it over;

one side is a fish, the other side a fishing pole. I wait for understanding. It's a metaphor, I can choose—do I want God to teach me to fish today? Or am I stuck, unable to learn? Is today the day I just need a fish? I remember the quote, "Give a man a fish, feed him for a day; teach a man to fish, feed him for a lifetime[29]."

Still in my Pillar, a guide takes me to a room of light and says, "Dream your perfect life."

That sounds simple enough. Yet, when I try, I am at a loss. I ask my guide, "What's the perfect dream?"

I hear, "Start with how you feel."

Ok, I am happy and loved. I love and feel expansive and limitless. I am calm, then active. I am cared for, and caring. I feel grateful, in surrender, guided, complete. I feel serene, balanced and healthy.

"What do you see?" he asks.

I reply, "I see gentle, loving hands coming to hold me. I see balanced monies, simple surroundings. I see learning; peace, ease and comfort. I see family, friends, laughter."

"What do you know?"

"I know that I am me. I know what I love, what I want. I know how to create, how to express and how to receive."

He speaks again, "Who are you?"

Slowly, I answer, "I'm not sure. I am me, but the atmosphere seems different. Ahh—I'm everyone."

"Yes! And what do you want?"

The energy is moving. I feel a current as I say, "I want happiness and peace for those who don't know it. I want economy and purity. I want love and Creator to abound!"

I feel excited, yet he remains calm, "Mmm. How do you feel now?"

With confidence, I reply, "Attuned."

The scenery is changing. I am in a garden. There are so many huge, bright, beautiful flowers. They are fantastic. I pick them and throw them in the air! I ask my guide about the flowers. He tells me they are my messages.

I pick more and throw them in the air! Such beauty, such joy! I hear this message, "Free yourself, Beloved. Be present with your presence. Live without regret. Use Light and forgiveness. Bless and consume with consciousness. Bless again."

I feel the words; one by one, they sink into my consciousness. Suddenly, I worry about my flowers. I picked them –consumed them.

I hear, "A flower blooms and dies on the vine. It is a great privilege to be loved so much that you are picked."

Oh! I relax.

"Know, Beloved, your wholeness is a matter of perspective. You are never less than whole and never seeking less than wholeness. Anytime you deny a neighbor, you deny yourself."

My mind's eyebrows rise, "What do you mean?"

My guide replies, "Honor self and others via heart frequencies. Urge your mind's assessment to see beyond to the core desire of each human. Forgive the ways of those lost. Acknowledge them and love them. Your truth shines on theirs."

Ah, yes, look inside! Take responsibility –we are all equal, there is no contest. I am only as great and powerful as I am, and as they are.

With laughter he smiles and says, "Oh, yes, great and powerful one, bow before the mirror, kneel before poverty, serve your peers. Then you will know oneness."

Ohhhhh—ONENESS!

I laugh at the "great and powerful" statement, because it sounds like ego, but I realize that he is only showing me how I assess others and that if we are all one then it is ultimately me. I consider the other words. Bow before the mirror. I tend to put others on a pedestal, bowing before what I admire or aspire to. Bow before myself. Is he reminding me to feel equality, to stop diminishing myself? How can I understand being 'one' if I separate myself from others so quickly? I need to work on that. Kneel before poverty, serve your peers. These are important statements that I will study later. But I can see there is a leveling being suggested, and the theme is oneness.

I recall a friend and wonder, why do I judge her so? My guide replies, "Because she cries for a cookie, but takes not one from your plate. Even as you offer."

"Why?" I ask.

"Again, beloved, history can orient your life. Pain, unrequited love, mistakes –they can leave you confused."

I wonder, "She is confused?"

"Ah, yes."

"How can I help?"

"Bow before your peers," he replies.

"Ask her how I can be of service?"

"Yes, she will show you how, and then you can use her parameters to bring the love, buckets of love!"

"OH! Oh!" I see opportunity for service, for my learning. But I also see I have to be aware of what people can accept, how they open to love or service. It may be that I have to listen. It isn't always action and healing. I reflect on how much love and gratitude I have for my guides and Angels. They have reminded me once again to be in heart.

As I released from this meditation, my heart felt full of love. I heard an echo from the beautiful words my guidance spoke. I began writing and *Be Present With Your Presence Prayer* was formed:

Be Present With Your Presence Prayer

Divine Creator in this moment I ask that my mind be balanced so that I may see my service. Show me how to be present with the presence within. I welcome gentle reminders to love my neighbor, to forgive my judgments, to remember my service.

As I bow before the mirror, please help me to remember Oneness. As I kneel before poverty, help me to know my abundance starts within and I am free from restraints. I am limitless.

As I recognize wholeness, I see that I am whole. As I seek wholeness, I know that I am whole.

Divine Creator of all that is, I welcome assistance. Help me to know my heart, to forgive the ways of the lost, even if they are my ways. I am in truth, I am truth. I shine truth from the Oneness that I Am.

Blessed are those who reflect the truth, for they are me and I am them. We are one. Divine Truth reigns free, upon my heart burdens are lifted and I Am free.

In gratitude for the abundant blessings that make up my life, Amen.

Healer, Love Thyself Enough to Want to Heal Thyself

This chapter could have come with warning label. Something akin to, "Your Surgeon General has determined that reading prayers and processing through healing may be dangerous to your ego's controlling health."

When we are out of balance, our ego/mental bodies love to snatch up the reigns and take over our lives. This is not the time to hate. Love that enormous ego to pieces. Love it; appreciate it; tell it that it's smart and resourceful. Because it is. Tell your ego that you won't live without it, but that you crave balance. Make up jobs for your ego, like choosing healthy foods or balancing your checkbook. Your mental body is an innate part of your being: a blessed, beautiful part of you.

Now is the time to bow down before the proverbial mirror. Ask yourself if you can allow frequencies of self-love and understanding to be the guardians of your judgment. Even though it's not easy to control the negative voice inside, have patience and faith. You may have issues to process. Through our DNA; we are genetically connected to all past relations. We also work through archetypal influences, which are our past lives, and guess where that information is held? In our DNA. That means you are not only connected to your blood relations, you are scientifically encoded to everyone. You were born with genetic and archetypal connections waiting for a high enough frequency to begin healing. These are known as *codes of light*. I read a great book called *The Lineage of the Codes of Light*[30] that helped me understand what I can do to heal my lineage.

Processing, clearing and healing can be done regardless of dimension or time. That is why Lightworkers find such difficulty working through their issues. Imagine your guides saying, "You are dealing with rejection in your life right now. Do you mind if we add rejection from a few past lives and have a thread of it carried through from your mother's family?" Face it, if you are clearing and doing your own personal Lightwork, you are working hard. At the spiritual buffet, two distant relatives just gave you their helping of say... misogyny, and now you're the healer everyone relies on to get the job done. (Women can carry misogyny, it's in the DNA.) Similar to when you need three items from the store and you come home with two full bags; some jobs grow as we attempt them. But guess what? You can do it, I know you can.

Even at your clearest, most centered moment, you will probably have flashes of judgment; and sometimes that is good. We use judgment every day, however, it can be helpful when done with love. Don't you judge when to involve yourself in a conversation? Or when you decide which road to take on your way to work? I refer to this type of judgment as *assessment*; a talent we want to keep. The berating, belittling voice is what needs to be stifled. It's time for all of us to be free of negative judgment, especially self-judgment. This is a helpful analogy, which came through for a client, "Pretend you have an Angel on one shoulder and a devil on the other. They are both talking to you. Knock the little devil off."

To whom would you rather listen—your inner hater or your inner lover? Pick love! We are on an astounding, wonderful, guided, spiritual path. And each of us, through our personal trials and tribulations, has covered some ground. However, until it's all about love, we will keep learning how to honor and appreciate ourselves until we wake up one morning, bow before the mirror, kneel before poverty and serve our peers; which, don't forget, are us. We are One.

Imagine a world of self-love. Could you be an example of perfection in every evolving moment? Our next prayer is part of the evolution of self-love, heart-centeredness and Divine knowing. Use it often.

Appreciate Self Prayer

Father, Mother, God, Goddess, Creator, Source of All That Is; show me the way to self-appreciation. I ask for assistance in seeing and understanding my value. As I walk this path of learning that I Am, please help me to release anything in the way. Please show me where I shine and how I Am an aspect of the Divine Force that holds all. As I Am in service to the Light, help me to feel forgiveness when I am harsh to others or myself. Please assist this release on all levels, through all time and space.

Thank you and Amen.

Chapter Nine

You as a Divine Creator

You can awaken to the reality that you are a Divine Creator by remembering. It's sort of like un-understanding or un-learning. As Divine Creators, we have chosen to shield ourselves from our immense Lights, limiting our abilities and creative powers. As human incarnates we are trying to learn and create, to know our ability to manifest. The funny thing is, we don't have to learn anything; we already know.

Understanding you are a Divine Creator can be challenging; it does not mean that you create everything with your mind. For instance, if I stub my toe I did not create the circumstance of stubbing my toe by having this thought, "I believe I will stub my toe. Here goes!" But I may be able to find out why I stubbed my toe by asking myself what I was thinking before it happened. Was I present in my body; conscious, awake and aware? Did I feel angry, bitter or resentful? Many times, we can discover a particular mindset right before an incident, like stubbing a toe, which belies a negative emotion or feeling. This negative emotion, or feeling, may be the memory of an incident trying to get our attention for healing. I do want to mention that many a toe is stubbed at night, which is usually a sign one is not grounded. You can help yourself by sitting on the bed for a moment and saying, "I am awake and aware of my physical body; I am going to the bathroom and I will resume sleep in five minutes. Thank you and Amen."

Carefully step into your Divine Creator shoes, with caution and awareness. Our ego's idea of taking on this creative process is akin to standing on the front porch and screaming, "I demand all my abilities right now." We do want it all; we want to create ways to make our lives easier, but we must learn to wield the heavy sword of responsibility carefully to avoid getting hurt. Luckily, we are created in perfection; we incarnate with a system already in place. When you hear people talk about ascension or having a light body experience, they are speaking of becoming the true Light that is the Oneness of All. When I began working in the ethereal realms, I so desperately wanted to be better, to be my Divine Lighted Self. I would spend hours in meditation trying to find the secret. The answers were consistent; I will paraphrase what I have heard many times in many different ways:

> *You are Divine Light; you cannot be separate from it because it is in every cell of your being. You have cloaked your origins, veiled your abilities and joined humanity for an incarnation. Step wildly into your happiness, but cautiously into what you may think or believe to be enlightenment. Your truth and essence come from no less than Creator. Your love and life are no less Light than your Creator, God, Goddess, I Am. You are from the Divine Light, of the Divine Light and never separate. Can you understand that? Rather than search for what you want, we suggest you awaken, because that is where the Light exists, within you.*

So here we are, human and incarnated, looking around for Divinity. All the while, it is in the mirror. Stop trying to find and repair what is wrong with you; because as long as you look, you will find. Change your thinking. Use the good, grand and special parts of you to amplify Light. Honor who you are, where you truly came from and ponder *that* Light. Dwell on it. Amplify your radiance to perceive clearly, with positivity.

Think of yourself in your *pillar of Light*. Above you visualize your High-Self, or Oversoul; this is your personal archive for information. Imagine it similar to the Library of Congress. It is your personal access to the Akashic Records, a place for every bit of knowledge and information available. As incarnates, we gave up information. We moved into fetuses without memories to learn as if we were never here before, step-by-step. You made the choice to be a Soul, in surrender, occupying a new body so that energy, education and experience can expand on Earth. This is incarnation, your initial manifestation. If your Soul was Divinely guided to your body, and your Spirit created for this incarnation, one might assume that manifesting is part of our innate talent. You already know how to do it.

We are, as a by-product of being human, Divine Creators. We are creating and manifesting everything, either directly and on-purpose or indirectly, unconsciously. In order to create with consciousness we must awaken the Divine aspects of our selves.

Lightworkers can be unconscious and unaware of their connection to Source. They can create, love and live happy lives without ever giving Divinity a thought. Yet you are not one of those beings, are you? This book has landed in your hands; you are experiencing this as a creation of your own accord. In a sense, you are the Divine Creator of these words, this moment and all that comes next.

Does this sounds a little like a “who’s on first” skit? Maybe we sound like this:

Self says, “I want money.”

High-Self, “Okay, manifest it.”

Self, “I don’t know how.”

High-Self, “How did you know about it?”

Self, “I don’t know.”

High-Self, “Don’t know what?”

Self, “How I know about money.”

High-Self, "Why are you talking about money?"

Self, "Because I want to manifest it."

High-Self, "Okay, manifest it."

My guides have told me, since the beginning of my spiritual journey, that I am creating and manifesting everything. Therefore, as the impressive, intelligent, incredible Light that I Am—I am manifesting every problem that I have! Why on Earth would I do that? (Pun intended!) What the h-e-double toothpicks was I thinking?

The awareness that we are Divine Creators, responsible for everything in our lives, can be overwhelming. While you are rediscovering your all-powerful, omnipotent self, please do not get mental about how you create agony and pain. There are interfering energies we strive to be free of so that we may live in peace with love and compassion as our primary resources. Until life appears to be peaceful, we must focus on our connection and surrender to God/Goddess/Creator. *Manifestation Prayer* and *Understand Manifestation Prayer* assist us in freely surrendering into an alignment of higher wisdom while embracing life.

When you read these prayers, consider your dedication to the Light of the I Am and your resolve to be peaceful and conscious. Focus on the intention we all have to make our positive aspects of self stronger. The best way to fight negative energy is to deny it. Water the flowers. Feed the Light.

Manifestation Prayer

Father, Mother, God, Goddess, Creator, Source of All That Is; I follow my heart's desire. I allow my inner vision to be the map that brings my desire to a clear and present reality. I allow lesser frequencies to rest without my attention. I see Light, and I only react to what is appropriate for my growth and desires. In this, I see that Divine

Order is simple, gratifying. In this, I see that Light will lead me to comfort and possibility.

I allow my manifestation ability to be guided by God, Divine Will and my desire to be one with all. I allow comfort and nurturing, trust and conscientiousness to be mine. As this manifests and grows, I release judgment about how it arrives. I smile, I feel warm, I am loved. I am nurtured, I am trusted, I am well. My process, my lessons, arrive and are experienced peacefully, easily and comfortably. Therefore, as I Am that I Am, I accept my developing abilities of manifestation as the Divine Will of God/Goddess/Creator. Thank you and Amen.

Understand Manifestation Prayer

Father, Mother, God, Goddess, Creator, Source of All That Is; please assist me in understanding my creations.

My full awareness is opening. I am able to see how and why I create the life I live. Angels and guides from Source are assisting me in this understanding. I am currently experiencing the Divine Order of my creative talents.

As my opportunities to learn unfold peacefully, easily and comfortably, I embrace each one with an open heart. I am supported in witnessing the current situation I call 'my life.' I am supported in all ideas of change and improvement. These ideas and implementations will be for my highest good, or they will be forgotten.

Therefore, what I forget, I release. What I remember, I embrace. In the Divine Light that I Am, I allow Source Light to express unconditional love, forgiveness and spiritual empowerment through me.

Thank you and Amen.

Divine Thoughts as Divine Creations

As master creators, it is necessary that we manifest with clarity and focus. Try to organize your thoughts by writing what is most important on a piece of paper. Put your paper in a special designation: envelope, altar, mirror, etc. This focus will let your guides know which thoughts are priority to you; apparently recognizing our most significant thoughts isn't as easy as it sounds.

I wanted a new car, well new to me. After raising three kids I was ready to downsize my beloved Toyota SUV that bragged two-hundred and four thousand miles. I knew exactly what I wanted: a VW Passat. It was my dream car, a sporty blue sedan. But I had trouble focusing on my own needs. It was obvious with thoughts like, "I want a new pair of jeans, right after I make sure the kids have what they need." My thinking was habitual, forever putting myself last. However, I had no idea that my thoughts weren't precise enough to manifest, I felt I was quite efficient in that respect.

My full attention was on this new but used car. I did Internet searches for what year I could afford; I test drove one to be absolutely sure. I knew exactly how it would look: a dark blue beauty with tan leather interior. But, I thought, I would be flexible if the price was right. My heart felt pure and clear, but my car did not arrive. There were other options, those with too many miles, or too expensive. Many nearly right cars, but not 'the one'.

Why wasn't my car coming? I was focused, dedicated and ready. I was following all the rules, doing the manifestation suggestions I had read about. Still, no car. So one morning I woke up and decided that I would meditate on this; not the want—but the frustration of searching to no avail. I set *sacred space*, got vertical and called in my guides. I asked them why my car was not here. What was I doing wrong? They told me that they could not tell the difference between the small material items I wanted and the vehicle I was thinking about. They claimed my thoughts were difficult to understand, and that until I was more focused, the energy would be reluctant to flow. It was for my own good.

What? That made no sense! I was concentrating so hard! I was focused, specific and putting attention into my little dream car. Wasn't I?

They showed me a scene. I saw me, sitting in a restaurant, affirming with intensity, "I want a car with leather seats, mechanically sound, dark blue, great price—oh my, those are cute shoes I wonder where she got them—power windows and door locks, automatic shift..."

I had to laugh; my mind does work like that. I can concentrate deeply, get interrupted, and then resume my previous thought. It must be that feminine multi-tasking energy in me. It's a great talent for rearing children and tending to a family, wonderful for organizing, running a business, driving, cooking... but not so much for communicating mentally with spiritual guides.

My guides asked me how they were to know which thought was my priority. Was it the car or the cute shoes? Immediately I pieced this together; realizing how much I interrupt my own thinking. During prayers, I make grocery lists; I remind myself to put the clothes in the dryer, send an e-mail, call a client back, check on a friend. Get carrots.

How can I amend this? What would override my management skills, quiet my mind and let my guides know my heart's desire? They told me to prioritize. Yes! I would make a list by priority! They told me that the written word showed them my focus, among a myriad of thoughts. The guides reminded me that my thoughts are like grains of sand on the beach. My focus is their focus; they are my guidance team, after all. They are the higher residual essence of me; the extended mind of my mind, the ether connection to my expansive God-self. Therefore, if I am scattered, energy dissipates into the pancake of life. And I create nothing.

Right after that meditation, following their suggestions, I wrote a descriptive list about my car including that it come to me easily and within my budget. On another piece of paper, I wrote 'blender' so that I could make smoothies for breakfast, and on a third: 'desk'. The desk needed to be two-sided, for my office and unique, maybe antique, and affordable. I tucked the papers into an envelope from my recycling bin and stuck it on the fridge with a magnet. The action felt so good that I decided to relax my hunt for my new car, to surrender. (This is a great time to create a manifesting page in your *SRB*!)

Within a month, my car showed up! Although it was different than I imagined, it was perfect for me, under budget and the best part was that my husband found it and brought it home; so it was easy. My surrender allowed me to sit back and receive. What a blessing. I have since learned that lists should include, "This or something better." My car ended up being black, not blue and a wagon instead of a sedan. Otherwise, it was perfect and after my initial objection, I loved it. My husband never understood why I didn't want a wagon; my SUV was often hauling some artistic project or salvaged supply. He was right; the wagon suited me. It was my little artist's car.

About three months later, I remembered the envelope! I emptied the contents onto my kitchen table; three little pieces of paper reminded me that I had given focus and intention by writing. My wonderful car was in the garage. During a visit to my daughter's home, I noticed a blender in her cabinet. I asked, "Is this your blender?"

"Yes," she replied, "but I never use it, do you want it?"

Bingo. And the desk, it came as well. Everything I listed came easily and perfectly. I learned an important lesson about cluttered thoughts, focus and priority. What we assume we are communicating may be different from what our guides are receiving. As I mentioned, to them our thoughts look like *grains of sand on a beach*. We must pick up a tiny grain and show it to our spiritual guides, "*This* one is the one I want to have in my life today, *this one*!" (Or, proverbial great High-Self, something better.)

The next prayer, *Clear Mind Consciousness*, offers assistance by helping to release mind and open to our higher power. It is a compelling prayer of surrender and alignment; best said in *sacred space*. So get vertical!

Clear Mind Consciousness

Father, Mother, God, Goddess, Creator, Source of All That I; I call forth the highest frequencies of Light to release all burdens, encumbrances, entities and parasitical influences.

Please send forth all things appropriate for me to reach clear mind consciousness. I am a willing servant to the Light. I banish all frequencies less than one-hundred percent unconditional Christ Consciousness Light.

I release my mind's idea of clarity and protection and receive my Creator's. I accept in place of all mental body ideas and influences Divine Intention, Divine Knowledge, Wisdom and Understanding, Divine Love.

My love is the conduit from which I receive. As I am, my existence explains my ability, probability and capability of receiving Creator's love. I am a living, breathing example of the perfection of Divine Love. I heal myself through the presence of the eternal heart flame that I Am. I balance all bodies and existences through all times and places, I allow peace to be my emission, love to be my example and Light to be my existence. I Am.

By the power of creation, I now decree my life as guided, guarded and protected by the love of God/Goddess/Creator. I am guided by Divine Will and those directed by Divine Will. I am guarded by the vertical energy known as my pillar of Light extending between Source and the core of Earth. I am protected by Light, as is my right according to Universal Law.

Thank you and Amen.

Surrendering to the Universe

Speaking of manifesting a desk... I thought a two-sided desk would be perfect for my office. Clients could sit on one side, me on the other. It could not be too modern, expensive, big or heavy. I looked at local stores, but nothing suited me. Then I remembered a chart my friend told me about. I wish I could offer credit to someone, but I don't know the originator. The chart is easy to create; you simply make three columns on a piece of paper. At the top of the first column, you write 'Me' for everything you plan to do yourself. Label the second column 'Help', for what you need help with; and at the top of the third column write 'Universe', which is where you put your complete surrender items, everything you want to happen without your help. This chart needs to be in everyone's *SRB*. I love it, and again, wish I could give credit to the author.

I made one of these charts. It took a bit of consideration for me to decide where to put 'desk'. After searching for a few more months, I had nothing. Maybe, if I looked a little longer the desk would show up, especially if I had help. I tried it. I put 'desk' in the 'Help' column and then I mentioned to people that I was looking for a desk, I looked on-line and after more time passed, I gave up. My desk needed to switch columns. Something was going on; the desk was not with me; it must be out of my reach. I surrendered to the 'Universe' section of my chart. It was time to let go. This was when I created the manifestation envelope, perfect timing to release my desk-hunt and let the Universe take over.

About two weeks later, I was at my sister's house, listening to her talk of cleaning up, purging and redecorating. We were sitting in a room she uses as an office and creative space. I realized I was sitting next to a *cute wooden desk*. A *two-sided, smallish, wooden desk*. My heart picked up pace. "Are you releasing this?" I asked.

Surprised I would be interested, she said, "You want it? Great! Take it out of here!"

I gave her forty dollars for the desk and we put it in my car. (I still had the SUV then. Such a smart Universe!) It fit in my office wonderfully; it is beyond perfect and I still use it. The funny thing is that the desk was at my sister's house the whole time.

She lives close by; she knew I was looking for a desk, yet neither of us saw the prospect until I released my want to the Universe.

However, even though the Universe/Creator helped me find a desk after I removed my mind from the situation, I am still responsible for the event. A few things had to rearrange to allow the arrival of my new item, one being my ego. Sometimes we have blocks to receiving that we cannot understand. It may be complicated. A fear of prosperity could have impaired my ability to manifest; this desk would be where my work happened, where I received money. We could spend time and energy on a deep psychological evaluation of my fear and resistance, but why? Why not surrender to the Universe?

Are you ready to surrender to the Universal Higher Power of Creator/Source? Surrender might mean that you heal; our guides are resourceful. Somehow, I was able to skirt around my blocks so that I could create my vision of the perfect desk, but it didn't manifest until I surrendered. And I did it on paper, no confusing or identical grains of sand in the way.

The following prayer, *Witness yourSelf as a Creator*, is another way to open your manifesting abilities and align with Creator. Use this prayer to join these forces within yourself. Create with Divine Will. Align with your truth, your High-Self. Be the Divine Creator that you are. While you're at it, agree to remember!

Witness yourSelf as a Creator

Father, Mother, God, Goddess, Creator, Source of All That Is; I allow Light to bless all those I love, including mySelf! I am willingly in surrender and service to my original Source of Light. I allow blessings and reminders of this Light to be abundant in my life. I allow all things blocking my memory of Source to leave now; I choose to remember. I allow my existence to be the only example I need that I am one with

God/Goddess/Creator. I easily move into a peaceful experience and allow Christ Consciousness energy to envelop me, nurture me and help me see who I Am.

As I continue to experience love and release fear in this physical expression I allow mySelf to be the forward expression of Light.

Thank you and Amen.

Divine Order/Whatever

Have you ever felt like you are not in on the secret? I bet I looked for that desk for six months. Was the desk waiting for me to clear something before it could live with me? Maybe I was waiting until my sister was ready to release it? I have often wondered if I am intuiting something or creating it. Have you ever had a thought of someone you have not seen for a long time and then randomly run into them? I tend to question if I thought of that person, thereby creating a destiny type of meeting; or, did I sense he or she was going to be at my destination?

It's a chicken or egg situation. We could hash this out all day. We could get riled up, have a debate, ignore our intuition, question destiny/destination and doubt. On the other hand, here's an idea: We could (once again)... surrender.

When Brook came to see me for a reading, she was introverted. Brook's communication skills were strong, but her confidence was underdeveloped. I was surprised when I learned that her job was to give tours at a popular beer brewing company. She talked to strangers, explaining how the company brewed and bottled their products. Why, I wondered, would a shy girl take a public speaking job? During our sessions, I noticed that she had potential to be comfortable in front of people. In fact, she carried an exceptional Light with intuitive gifts concerning communication. We worked together on releasing energetic blocks and eventually, Brook found her confidence in giving tours and communicating with strangers.

As Brook gained strength, she had a significant realization: she wanted a different job. I asked her, "What is your ideal job?" She didn't know. Brook liked the brewery and wanted to stay there. Yet she did not feel fulfilled by her position giving tours. I asked the question that would seem obvious even to Brook, were she outside looking in, "What do you want?"

During our sessions, the guides helped Brook open to the idea that she could create her world. Once this complex issue opened, Brook excitedly created a vision, her perfect job. She got in touch with her wants, needs and desires. Ideas poured forth; she thought of her skills, education and how they could benefit the company. We made a detailed list; Brook's confidence grew.

Although Brook had experienced great personal growth through our sessions, she wasn't quite the empowered being I sensed she would be in the future. It was not my place to press Brook; I waited for spiritual guidance to show us where to focus our work. It was easy to grow fond of this remarkable young woman. It is not easy to watch someone move slowly toward happiness. However, I felt my patience was important, Brook needed support as she felt her way into confidence and self-esteem. But the brewery was not proving to be a good fit. Finally, when Brook was frustrated enough to quit her job, an idea came through. Brook's guidance gave us the message, "Create the job you want, create a new position at the brewery."

Brook thought this was pushing the envelope. How do you create a place for yourself in a company that is already established? She studied her qualifications and abilities, and then thought carefully about where she could best be of service to the brewery. She thought of efficiency, support and structure. She found it! Brook saw a place where her skills could make the business run better by adding another position in that department.

Brook presented the idea to her boss. It was incredible; without any interference Brook's vision manifested! Her idea became a new position in the company, and she got the job! The one she imagined and created.

Do you see how close she was from the beginning? The brewing company was perfect, once Brook opened to her innate knowledge, addressed her fears and focused on happiness, the Universe responded. It was beautiful.

Brook's experience is an example of learning about empowerment through spiritual work. She used (and still uses) the prayers in this book to free herself from limitations.

In the midst of chaos, when we are unhappy, it can be difficult to seek help. The first step is to ask: What's easy? What is available? You can add prayers and ideas to your *SRB*, especially the one about listing your skills and education. Don't forget your wants, needs and desires. *Lists*, I promise you, they are important. However, there are times when reaching out to a counselor, therapist or intuitive is necessary. You can struggle alone, but you don't need to have a lonely struggle. Pray for the perfect person to come into your life to help you with a problem. Put your request in the 'Universe' column and expect Divine Intervention.

Lastly, remember that Divine Order may be what is in the way.

Making Source Do What You Want

The secret of running the Universe is... you are already running it! Brook's experience is a perfect example. From the perspective of Brook's High-Self, and even via hindsight, everything that happened to Brook was in *Divine Timing*: A perfectly orchestrated set of circumstances arriving on time and naturally unfolding for the highest good of all involved. I was privy to Brook's frustration and sadness during her self-development. The challenges were real. We, as humans, seem to be addicted to creating with drama, suffering and bumpy learning curves. You are on Chapter Nine of this book, now is the time to change everything. Now is the time to claim your right as a Divine Creator and engage your higher mind, heart, and Soul while saying, "I learn peacefully, easily and comfortably." You can say that to the Universe. I am formally giving you permission to be your empowered, radiant, beautiful self and claim a peaceful existence.

We manifest primarily from our subconscious minds. Therefore, our (yours and mine) controlling interests are not conscious. Consider this: You have a sovereign leader, which is the subconscious; and subjects, which are conscious. No matter how much the subjects vote or yell and scream, the sovereign leader is in charge. The trick is to get in harmony with your ruling power and your day-to-day consciousness. You may not know exactly what your Soul has planned, but if you use meditation and prayer to synchronize yourself in body, mind, Soul and spirit, you can create harmony. With practice, you can adapt an on-going sense of balance.

Do you remember when I talked about using red traffic lights as a messenger? If I hit too many, I am alert. It is my conscious choice to flow in traffic, which means lots of green lights. If I hit a red, no problem. Two, I perk up. Three —all hands on deck! I start praying for clearing, healing, alignment or anything to bring me back into balance. I check my energy. Where I have been? What I have said? Do I do this because red lights are bad? Absolutely not; they are simply where I invested an agreement with the Universe. When my energy synchronizes with pure Light, I flow; people greet me with a smile, doors open. I use everything around me to gauge my frequency because I create from inside, from my subconscious, and the easiest way to know what is going on inside is to open my eyes.

Knowledge, Wisdom and Understanding Prayer is an extraordinary approach to get what you want in any situation. Remember, *all* creation energy (positive and negative) is working toward to your Divine Plan. Did you say, "Drats!"? I did... I mean, knowing that I have a Divine Plan is incredible. However, it can interfere with what my ego/mind/mental body wants. When this happens, I have to talk myself down, "It's okay if my plans don't work out, because something better is coming."

Luckily, our guides are free of ego-system judgment; they love and help us regardless of our disappointment or attempts to steer the ship-of-life to diamond caves and martini resorts.

I try to remember that the fulfillment of a request could interfere with my Divine Plan. Have you heard of the phrase "thank God for unanswered prayers"? If Brook had found her ideal job before she worked as a brewery tour guide, would it have worked out? Look at the education we create through suffering. Brook learned how to present her best qualities, in all their grandness, to be considered for a new position.

As a side, I want to mention that learning the hard way is what we are trying not to do. However, when it happens I encourage you to embrace it. Love it like you would a child who scribbles all over a paper and says, "It's you!" We are learning to love the messy, jumbly, energetic-mish-mash that we are. When we love ourselves truly, we begin to create in a new way.

I would love to write about how I have manifestation under control, but my subconscious mind is still healing. After helping people (after helping myself) I am still learning to let go and let God. I will compliment myself; after all this hard road rubbish, I am significantly better at releasing criticism. Mine and others. There's more work to do, though, and when I fail to remember that Divinity is within, I turn to these prayers. Divinity is within me and it is within you. Bow down to your reflection and then stand, smile and carry on.

Try this prayer when you want to focus energy on understanding something. JFill in the blank with what you desire to learn about. Just keep in mind, you are praying for Divine Understanding.

Knowledge, Wisdom and Understanding Prayer

Father, Mother, God, Goddess, Creator, Source of All That Is; I request assistance in filling my heart's need. I request knowledge, wisdom and understanding concerning ________. Please assist me in locating, discovering, acknowledging all wisdom and learning concerning ________ in my life and around me.

Source, help me understand this knowledge and wisdom so that my mind can release and my connection to Divinity can strengthen. I allow all this as further truth that we are all One.

I allow my mind, body and Spirit to integrate knowledge, wisdom and understanding from all sources of one-hundred percent pure Christ Consciousness Light and unconditional love.

I am guided, guarded and protected on my journey.

Thank you and Amen.

The funny thing about the struggle of surrendering mind and ego, is that when the hard labor is complete, we are usually happy. You can use *Knowledge, Wisdom and Understanding Prayer* to ask for what you want. Just beware; your request may change. If the diamond cave doesn't show up, you might find yourself wondering what you would do with all those diamonds anyway. What a responsibility. There would be so many duties and obligations to organize and broker. You could give them away, but then why have the cave in the first place? Why not pray for someone else to find the cave and give *you* diamonds!

This type of thinking is indicative of growth. Your desire may morph. If you find yourself in that space of change, you might ask why you thought of your desire in the first place. For example, why a diamond cave? You might answer, "Diamonds are a sign of prosperity, and they are beautiful." Hmm, is it prosperity and beauty you want, or a diamond cave? Praying for understanding unveils the reasons for your intentions and desires.

It is easy to place responsibility upon something that you *think* will make you happy. Mentally we may grasp an image; for instance: big house equals wealth. Yet we know that within a mansion, a destitute person may live. With understanding and surrender, our guides can teach us about the root of the mind's desire. I have learned to be wary of using the word *abundance*. As my guidance has pointed out, we have an abundance of many things: t-shirts, shoes, dishes, bills, chores. Simply asking for a great and grand amount of something does not make sense to our ethereal guides. It is important to understand what fulfillment we yearn for, what exactly will make you happier. Ask many questions. Endless questions. Don't forget that your team of ethereals responds to what you ask. If you want a swimming pool, say it. Then explain, because maybe you want exercise, sun, grounding or a party place for all your friends. Search for the deeper desire and put everything on the table. Or grab your *SRB* and start making a list. What I want, why I want it and how I will settle for Divine Blessings for this or something better. Thank you and amen.

I often ask my guides to assist me in creating money for my savings and checking accounts, simply for my comfort. When I realized that not worrying about money helped me focus on my work, I created new thoughts. Use *Prosperity Prayer* to open your energy fields to all possible types of prosperity, including money. You, as an incarnate, are a creative force worthy of your heart's desire; remember to be open to learning exactly what that is.

Prosperity Prayer

Father, Mother, God, Goddess, Creator, Source of All That Is; I ask for assistance with prosperity. From this moment on, I allow my prosperity to be in the hands of the Divine. I ask that any form of attachment to my ability to manifest that is not in Divine Accordance be immediately severed. I ask that all forms of manifestation that I have in any way participated in, be either removed from my being or returned to my being, whichever is for my highest good.*

I allow myself to experience all forms of prosperity, but particularly money. I allow cash flow and welcome disposable income without judgment of where it comes from, how it arrives or how I will spend it.

If any form of my energy is stalled, trapped or stagnant concerning prosperity, I ask that Beings of one-hundred percent pure Christ Consciousness Light assist me in releasing, disconnecting, claiming, motivating or taking most appropriate action so that I may experience continued prosperity and abundance.

Creator, Source, as I grow and expand, as I raise my frequency I ask that this work, or more appropriate work following Divine Accordance, be done to increase my ability to prosper financially with integrity and responsibility. I welcome new aspects of abundance; I welcome all forms of love and Light, including the form of money.*

Thank you and Amen.

**This refers to Divine Accordance Prayer.*

Manifest then Manage

When we ask for more, Source will supply us with appropriate energy to meet our requests. Luckily, we have all kinds of protection put in place to stop us from making our lives a train wreck. Our ideas, goals and desires can lead to the manifestation of too much incoming energy. Whether we are creating the exact desire or tools and lessons to make room for what we desire.

On the other hand, to get what you want, you might need to make room—whether it's physically, mentally, emotionally or spiritually. During big changes in our lives, we could all use a little help with *Juggling Frequencies* so that times of release and integration can emerge more easily, peacefully and comfortably.

We need this type of help. Our genetic history reflects too much struggle and suffering for us to ignore this prayer. When we clear, we not only release something from our physical bodies, we release its foothold and its ability to affect the future, and that future extends to all of humanity. From a spiritual perspective, clearing can happen now, in the future and in the past simultaneously. By doing your Lightwork you are healing your *genetic connections*, as well as your *relationship to all of humanity*. It may sound like a tall order, but you can do it. In fact, I suspect you have been doing it since you were born.

Juggling Frequencies

Father, Mother, God, Goddess, Creator, Source of All That Is; it is my intention to move forward in my chosen third-dimensional expression as an example of unconditional love. I allow any pattern, thought form, frequency or interference that can be changed to accommodate and accept unconditional love to be changed now.

For myself, I allow further understanding and compassion so that my journey on Earth is a walk of peace. I ask for protection for all bodies, levels, planes and aspects that make me who I Am.

Let this protection come in the highest, most advanced form of Light. Let it begin within me and move out to others in the form of unconditional love. I allow myself to be an example of Light, good health and joy. I release any programs, thoughts, ideas, past lives, occurrences or influences that restrict my connection to God/Creator/Source. As Light fills my expanse, replacing what I have released, I remember that I Am the very spark that began all of creation.

By the power of all that I Am, I declare myself free of negative influences, free of negative interference, free of energies carrying less than one-hundred percent pure Christ Consciousness Frequency. I proceed guided by Divine Will as an example of Light, unconditional love, balance, good health and joy.

Thank you and Amen.

How do you feel about the person responsible for your bumpy road? Whom do you blame for your pain, frustration, hard knocks and dark nights? If you project your responsibility onto others, please forgive yourself; we all do it. Who doesn't look around for their car keys and wonder who took them? I found it difficult when my kids moved out to take responsibility for happenings like missing pens, chipped drinking glasses and spots on the carpet. (I was absolutely positive my kids were responsible for missing socks!)

When there is nowhere else to look, we invariably have the mirror. And don't forget to compliment yourself. Try, "You are magnificent! And beautiful!" Remember the *mirror work* from Chapter Five? Try it; give yourself the compliments you crave from others. One person I worked with had trouble making eye contact, *with her own eyes!* Imagine being so shy that you can't even present yourself in the mirror—to yourself.

Here is one of my lessons:

Years ago, before I knew about my spiritual gifts, two friends and I decided to dress up like Goddesses for Halloween. We each chose a theme; my costume was a Spiritual Goddess. (Are you laughing?) I bought an authentic looking eye at a costume shop where they showed me how to apply it to my forehead with theater make-up. It was the exact brown of my eyes; I even put false eyelashes on it. (People were a little freaked out, I will admit!) One friend chose to be an Art Goddess, the other a Fairy Goddess. During the month of October, we talked on the phone about our costumes and plans. When the Fairy Goddess friend called she would say, "Hello Goddess!" For some reason I would cringe.

My first response was, "Don't say that."

She replied, "Why not, aren't you a Goddess?"

My reaction troubled me; why couldn't someone call me a Goddess? What was my problem? I took it to the mirror. I followed Louise Hay's advice and talked to myself until I could handle the word 'Goddess'. Each time I visited the bathroom I would say, "Hello, Goddess." With a forced smile I accepted the responsibility, the word and finally... the energy. Who knows why I couldn't handle my friend calling me a Goddess. Past life, memories, worship issues, inverted ego, whatever! I am now very comfortable with my Goddess-ness, thanks to the mirror.

Expressing love to ourselves can be challenging; after all, being spiritually centered does not mean that we are *right*. There will be mistakes, or at least the assessment that a mistake happened. My Ethereal Teacher taught me that being right is the polarity of being wrong; as long as we have attachment to either, we remain imbalanced. Remember the seesaw? My Ethereal Teacher gave me another image. Try this: stick your right hand out to the side, now your left. One hand is right, the other wrong.

One hand is an extreme, the other a counterbalance. We want neither. Now, place both hands over your heart. This, I am told is where we feel balance, in our hearts.

Neutrality is the key to creating the equilibrium we need to feel balanced. At first I didn't understand how being right could possibly be a polarity. As I mentioned, my business reputation *relies* on accuracy. Let's face it, being right feels pretty darn good. That was my clue, feeling right feels good. So good that I might *try* to be right, or attempt to continually be right, then crave being right and ultimately experience disappointment. With that amount of intention toward being right, how can I remain a clear channel for Divine Light?

When balance alludes you, and you feel that you are to blame, try *Embrace Self Prayer*. It will remind you that we are still learning; embracing self is a continuous effort. We are constantly releasing negative thoughts and aligning with Source for Divine thinking and integration of Light. *Receive Light Prayer*, following, offers further assistance for healing and integration as you open to Light and receive all that is pure. As we give, we receive; as we release, we integrate; as we love, we heal.

Embrace Self Prayer

I am clearing and releasing and I love it! I love my cleansed body; my youthful, healthy self! I embrace the ease and comfort from which I think, live and breathe.

My comforts are many. My friends are many. My beloved SELF exemplifies worth, love and empowerment.

Through all that I AM I seek TRUTH, LOVE, LIGHT.

I embrace unconditional love and all aspects of Light that I Am.

Thank you and Amen.

Receive Light Prayer

Father, Mother, God, Goddess, Creator, Source of All That Is;

-I allow Light to bless all those I love, including mySELF!

-I am willingly in surrender and service to my original Source of Light.

-I allow blessings and reminders of this Light to be abundant in my life.

-I allow everything blocking my memory of Source to leave now; I choose to remember.

-I allow my existence to be the only example I need that I am one with God/Goddess/Creator.

I easily move into a peaceful experience and allow Christ Consciousness energy to envelop me, nurture me and help me see who I Am. As I continue to experience love and release fear in this physical expression, I allow mySelf to be the forward expression of Light.

Thank you and Amen.

As the mystical magical beings that we are, how do we manage to get ourselves into situations of strife? Juggling our desires and our higher-mind knowledge can be challenging. If you feel like you are throwing knives in the air, I have only one recommendation...*run*! Get out of the way. Let the knives clatter to the floor, then sit beside them and give up. Move all your thoughts, desires, needs, complaints, agonies and hopes out of the way. Take one moment to surrender. Breathe. Have you heard of the four-part breathe? You might want to add this to your *SRB*; it is simple. One: Breathe in on a count to six (or any number you choose). Two: Hold that in-breathe for six seconds. Three: Exhale for six seconds. Four: Hold for six seconds. Breathe, hold, exhale, hold, begin again. I find it wonderful for calming and centering.

During a breathing exercise, our bodies can rest a moment. Meanwhile, oxygen is doing its magic, toxins are releasing and you, ever so minutely, can heal. Look for that healing, lock onto it and say, "THAT! That is what I want! Healing, more and more, all over!" Express gratitude. After this (maybe five minute) experience, talk to Creator. Get centered, surrender and *then* ask for what you believe you want. Occasionally, you may feel your energy is just plain stuck. In that case, try *Receive Blessings Prayer* to open your heart for Universal flow.

Receive Blessings Prayer

Father, Mother, God, Goddess, Creator, Source of All That Is; I call forth my Highest Source of Light for this prayer. Please help me to receive blessings that are for my highest and best good. I surrender my will, ideas, ego and personality to the Divine Will of God/Goddess/Creator. I allow anything no longer serving me to be released into the Light.

I ask for assistance so that I may receive blessings, including: abundance, good health, happiness, prosperity, self-confidence, JOY, balance, deep rewarding sleep, smiles, LIGHT, love, friends, fun, etc. (I allow God to use "etcetera" as appropriate!)

I initiate blessings in this moment. I welcome blessings from all aspects of Light. I bless myself and all those I love. I bless the planet, its people and dimensions of expression. I bless the Light of God, so that it may expand and create an avenue for blessings into my being. I welcome the Light of God; I welcome all that is mine. Within this frequency, I embrace Light and I openly allow it to flow from me as an expression of the God Force that I Am.

Thank you and Amen

Where the Light Takes Me

I have heard people say that their guides told them to do something. For instance, "My guides told me to move." This is a delicate topic. I certainly don't want to downplay guidance, connection or intuition. Yet on the other hand, my truth meter can go off like a fire alarm when people mention being "told" to do something. Does that mean people are lying? Certainly not. In most cases, it means that their interpretation may have interference. When Nicole, an intuitive woman, came to me and said her guides told her to move, I felt my inner truth meter lifting and starting to ding-ding-ding.

After her relationship ended, Nicole felt alone and unhappy. She craved her family and wanted to be near water. Nicole was doing her personal work; she was proactive, taking responsibility and clearing negative energy. In fact, she was using the prayers in this book. I was impressed with Nicole's connection to her spiritual guides and the meditations she shared with me. However, when she announced that her guides told her to move, I was leery.

> *There have been times when I have had a strong desire to have something; but I have no idea what that something is. A few years before I became conscious of my guides, I had a strange awareness that fulfillment and happiness were waiting for me somewhere new and different. I felt something from inside me, I had no idea what it was. The only thing I knew was that I had to move.*
>
> *So I put my house on the market. I cleaned out closets and storage, I released and gave away, I organized and polished. I prepared for what was coming, for I could feel it was near. My passion was so pure that it affected my husband; he agreed that it was time to move. We listed our home with a local real estate agent. We decided change would be good. Many people viewed and loved our house; a unique old farm property with a barn and other outbuildings. Three times, we*

found buyers; three times, the purchase fell through. I couldn't understand. I had received a clear message that I was moving! How could I move if I didn't sell the house? After almost two years of showing our home spring, summer and fall, aggravation and disappointment, we decided to stay.

More than fifteen years later, I am still in the same home with a barn, which is where I work. So what was the 'moving' message all about? Was I getting bad guidance? Hindsight being what it is, I can say that the message was accurate, I was moving. It was my interpretation that lacked consideration. I sensed 'moving' and I thought my home needed to change.

Changes did come about, and they were significant movements: I began to channel. The movement I sensed was about me. My free will could have chosen another home. However, I believe now that Creator best served me by holding onto my home and interfering with every contract, buyer and sale. Did I misunderstand the message? Possibly, but maybe I needed a distraction, and everything was in Divine Order. Maybe I took the energy of spiritual movement and launched it into the third dimension, creating a big drama as a distraction.

When Nicole mentioned moving, I could not see any contracts supporting the idea. Yet, she said her guides told her to move. I did not want to challenge the information; I know how easy it is to misinterpret a message, as I mentioned above. During our sessions, I felt strongly that my job was to align with Creator, stay vertical and to do my best to be of service; even though my mental alarms were going off.

One thing I have learned in spiritual business (more than once, sigh) is that one must get out of the way. People are creating learning experiences! Whether her message was accurate, or not, was not for me to decide. In fact, it wasn't even important.

My place was to support Nicole by being a channel with clear spiritual messages. Nicole was searching for a place where her life and heart could open and be free. Whether my assessment of her interpretation was off, or not, simply did not matter.

If you sense the urge to move and then you meditate on a question, be careful. For instance, "Guides, I love it here, I feel incredible. What will happen if I move here?" Your guides will give you something that answers your energy. You may see that your presence/Light will improve the land, even heal it. When communicating with your guides, be thorough. Do not let your hopes steer the questions. Remember to ask about your happiness. Ask about timing. Would it be better to wait? Is there an easier way to create my lessons? Will I be disappointed?

What happened with Nicole? She moved, had a fabulous time, and then came back. Nicole did sufficient grounding and Lightwork at her new location, but the area did not support her financially as she thought it would. There are two lessons here. One, it is rare that we are 'told' what to do by our guides; and two, we are evolving. Being involved in a spiritual evolution means you will change. You will grow and shift. Your belief systems will change. Please, do not confuse answers from your Guides with what you want to hear. Our free will, by its very nature creates direction for our satisfaction. This is the *Law of Attraction*. Nicole's free will found the place best for her to learn something, but what? Did she learn that she is strong enough to move from state to state if she wants? Did she learn that she is powerful and amazing? I hope so; and I am optimistic that Nicole learned to expand her connection to her guides, through prayer and meditation, for additional information. The move was not in vain; we are useful as Lightworkers no matter where we are. Nicole's physical presence joined with other Lightworkers for frequency alignments that brought much needed Light to our planet.

Through this interaction, a prayer came. I am grateful for the energy that brought forth *Relocation Prayer,* our next prayer. It applies to anyone who feels a call, listens to a call, or wants a call from Spirit. When we match the vibration of Christ Consciousness Light, everything is possible. When you read *Relocation Prayer*, think about all the places where you could be vibrating your Light, singing your song, dancing your rhythm. Then ask Source to bless those places, and remember when it comes to any big decision, be thorough. Ask questions!

Close to the same time that Nicole decided to move, Brenda felt called to return to her home state, one she left in frustration. She was experiencing financial challenges and desired a home near her elderly parents. While Nicole's move did not look prosperous to me, Brenda's move was the opposite. I could see financial gains, respect in the community and support. What did these women have in common? Relocation. They both desired something and saw possibilities somewhere else. What were they both to do, in service to the Divine? Anchor energy.

When several different clients show up with similar problems, I know that I am holding that issue myself. That is one reason prayers are significant; we can heal together when we work together, surrendering our separation. Now you too are part of the conspiracy to heal. Our Light has aligned! As you read *Relocation Prayer*, you will receive energy from a residual pool of thought that offers healing to all of us, one word at a time.

Light is prevailing! Or should I say, Light prevails! I almost projected that energy into the future, when it belongs right here, with you and me. If appropriate, take the following words to your heart; apply them to your transition, whether you are moving physically, spiritually or otherwise. Integrate these words and you will shine out truth and comfort. Who can resist that? Be the unconditional love that you are!

Relocation Prayer

(For those who listen to the call of Gaia and move or travel to anchor Light.)

Father, Mother, God, Goddess, Creator, Source of All That Is; through the kindness of my own true heart I call forth the release of judgment. In my heart, I unify all belief systems. This I call 'Oneness'. I command an echo of the Oneness for my mind and Soul.

I am now familiar with enlightened thinking and I now portray consciousness. My love for the Divine is my love for humanity and every living thing.

My understanding of religion and belief is now returned to the seed of origination. In the beginning, there was only love. That is all I remember.

I am compassionate and open to my fellow children of Light. As they heal, I heal. As I heal, they heal.

Oneness prevails; I judge not. I am free from separation; I embrace truth and unconditional love.

I am prepared for God's work as I am now. Any mistakes are forgiven and forgotten, all wounds healed. I am compassionate and forgiving. I love and I am loved. I forgive and I am forgiven.

I embrace my ethereal brothers and sisters. I lead them to the Light, to understanding, joy and peace.

My awakened heart speaks of love. I am a beacon, a Pillar, a sun. Light anchors through me and I am healed.

In my wholeness, I hear the call. I follow my heart, my knowing and I arrive to do my work.

I remember! I remember that not every step is measured; I am not judged. My choices are guided, expressed and guided some more.

I am loved! I gather support around me. I shower upon those legions of help my love, adoration, appreciation, gratitude: my Light.

My awakened heart speaks of Love. Under any label, religion, race or gender, I love you. Under any façade, lies, corruption, crime, judgment or hate, I forgive.

I am a Lightworker. In whatever language, location or vocation, I am in surrender to the Divine Creator. I will show you and be shown. I will teach you and learn. I will talk and listen. I will be active and rest. I will move; I will live; I will love.

As I visit and experience different places, my Light grounds into Earth. Seeds of love from my heart are planted. When I am gone, these seeds grow; they flower and reseed.

Many lifetimes, here and away, I have given of myself in this way. It is my way. I am the love and peace I seek, even in my pain, even when I can't remember…

I AM LOVE!

My truth vibrates out when I forget to speak it.

My integrity echoes forth when I forget to honor it.

My love is visible when I forget who I am.

I AM nurtured, held and loved. I AM fed, sheltered and provided for.

I AM guided, guarded and protected.

By the Light that I AM, through my Divine Service, with my free will:

-I AM a directionless feather that floats upon the wind extracted from an ethereal wing.

-I AM a directional beam of Light, focused and true.

-I AM a channel of Light, a voice of Divinity

-I AM at peace in my travels and always home.

-I AM one with my surroundings.

-I AM grounded.

-I AM connected with the I AM Presence.

-I AM expansive; I am serving; I AM served.

Through the Light of Creation... I AM. My heart beats true with the current of Light that runs like a river through each of us. One. We are One.

Thank you and Amen.

Chapter Ten

Life Lessons & Getting Familiar with Death

Since childhood, I have known about death. My earliest memories include dressing up, which I detested, and going to a large family gathering where one person lay motionless in a casket. Both my parents came from big families. I was raised knowing that people died and relatives mourned. Then they ate; there was without exception a celebration after the funeral. Cook, eat and then talk about memories. As a child, I knew only that I had to be uncomfortable for a while and then I could run around, eat desserts and enjoy a family gathering. Because someone died every year or so, we didn't schedule family reunions. My maternal grandmother's funeral was the worst. I was nineteen and felt her death in an adult way. My grandfather went to pieces and I was at a loss.

Because I grew up with funerals, caskets, burials, urns, graveyards and gatherings to honor the deceased, life and death seemed natural to me. It wasn't until I was an adult that I learned there are people who have never been to a funeral. Unlike me, they are not familiar with death, funeral preparations, burial and grief. However, even with many funerals and my awareness of death, I had no idea what happened afterward.

Between society's portrayal of the afterlife in movies and a bit of imagination, well, it's not surprising that we might have a confusing idea of what happens after life.

My childhood experiences with death gave me a strong foundation for what I experienced in my twenties. I learned about the other side of life in slow increments, with some difficultly. This was another part of my resistance and encompassed some tough learning experiences. I hope you can use these circumstances to create gentler situations for yourself, or possibly, to maintain spiritual alignment through an occurrence of death.

In my twenties, I lost two close friends. The following sections explain the circumstances of death and my reactions. It is now clear to me that I created this path of learning. From each incident I gained insight, education and strength. I share them so that you can see how the prayers in this section can help when someone is terminally ill, or gone. To survive in a world of suffering, it is imperative that we gain control of our emotional bodies. I am not asking you to stifle emotions, or speed through a process. Please don't negate your feelings; remember, they are *feelings*. Naturally, they rise and recede. They were never meant to become Pillars in our lives; emotions are simply the decorations.

Nancy

Did you ever meet someone so sweet and beautiful that you loved him or her instantly? That was my friend Nancy. We were fast friends and my grade-school-aged children enjoyed, A.J., her son five-year-old son. Nancy was a single mom so I invited her to dinners; we loved to go out dancing and had fun together. On her fortieth birthday, I threw her a surprise party; she had never had one before. A few years into our friendship, Nancy's ex-boyfriend came into town. She welcomed him back into her life because he seemed kind and she felt it was time to let go of old grudges. "Let bygones be bygones," she told me. At first, he appeared to be perfect. He acted lovingly to A.J.;

he was supportive and generous. However, the day before she died, Nancy whispered to me on the phone, "I remember why I broke up with him; I will explain later." The next day, he shot Nancy seven times as she was running out her front door. A friend found her lying outside, on the concrete. She was wearing her robe; her hair was wet. After he shot Nancy, the ex-boyfriend committed suicide.

She left her son. She left me. Murder is jarring, like being hit with something unexpectedly. I felt like life had grabbed my shoulders and was shaking me so hard all I could do was cry. The day after I found out, I ran a hot bath so I could cry into the water. As I relaxed into the heat, Nancy came to me. I could hear her, as if she were standing in the room, she was crying, I said, "Wait, wait!", while I hurried out of the water. It was heart wrenching to hear Nancy cry and I wanted to help so desperately. I felt scared and vulnerable. I wanted to be clothed, centered and sitting by a lighted candle or something completely spiritual. By the time I grabbed my robe and centered, the moment had passed. Nancy was gone.

It had not occurred to me that God/Goddess/Creator does not care if you are naked or vulnerable. This was my first clear-as-day clairaudient visitation, and I was not prepared. My ego got involved, which made clarity impossible. I was still learning about psychic communication then. In fact, I had often said I would *never* talk to dead people. Nancy's visit launched a search. I was determined to find out where she was. My anger and pain were inconsolable; I replaced our friendship with determination. And I cursed God. I *really* cursed. I searched for psychics and asked questions. Even though I could not hear Nancy, I could feel her anxiety. I felt that something had to be done.

I learned the first three days could be confusing for those that pass, especially if it is unexpected. Their emotions may still be present, yet without the body. In the beginning, they experience loss and frustration because they cannot communicate. I learned that sometimes the deceased re-live their dying experience. Other times, they feel obligated to take care of something and try to communicate with someone for assistance.

Through books and conversations, I became educated about the conductivity of water and how it assists psychic communication. My bath opened something that I had to learn about, if I wanted to do the unthinkable: talk to dead people. When I finally found an intuitive who knew about crossing over, she said that Nancy found her way into the Light, and I was relieved.

My education on death was beginning. I thought I had experience with losing people, funerals and being dead. It wasn't enough. While trying to contact Nancy, I knew nothing about protection, my *pillar of Light* or entities. My abilities opened doors to the astral field, and this led to a big mess. There was a lot of psychic and/or negative interference, which made my lessons harder. I was like a four-year-old with a sledgehammer. When I could lift it, I invariably hit the wrong thing. Everything that came in was something that should have stayed out. Imagine my guides looking at this mess. Maybe they were thinking, "She will have to find displeasure with this activity to teach herself about protection and responsibility." (Couldn't I have just read a book?)

Nancy, bless her Soul, taught me about ethereal doors; if we open them, we must close them as well. We create these openings inadvertently, via curiosity or intention. This experience taught me that I could remain in chaos, or ask for help, which I eventually did. Then prayers came through so I could write this book. I believe Nancy chose to exit, and that it was a choice made by her Soul. I have never been happy about it, but I respect her decision. I miss her very much and I am so grateful for the moments she gave me.

Tami

Five years later, a long-time friend died. Tami lived in my home state, Missouri. I met her when I was nineteen and we became close friends instantly. We traveled together and we knew each other's friends and family. Tami went through my divorce with me; she nurtured me when I moved to Arizona—oh the long distance bills in the eighties! Tami was there when I went home. She loved my daughter and, when I remarried, my new husband and stepsons. Tami was a friend to many. She would see people she knew all over the place. One time it happened in Las Vegas! Have you ever known anyone like that? Charismatic, appealing, charming and smart; Tami was intelligent and her memory was indelible. I was devastated when I received a phone call that Tami fell and was in a coma. She passed out, and they were unsure why. She died seven days later due to complications from an aneurism. While Tami slept, I believe she came to terms with her death and left peacefully, maybe those were seven days of negotiation.

A few years before Tami died, she began collecting Angels. Well known for her collections, Tami found wonderful items and displayed them in her home. In the past, she had collected memorabilia, old items; now it was Angels. When I first heard about the Angel obsession, I admit that I worried that tastelessness had finally gotten to her. Our country roots had possibly gone awry and Tami had succumbed to tackiness. Imagine my surprise when I walked into Tami's house and found gold-leafed frames around magnificent oil paintings. Her collection was elegant and sophisticated. It was incredible, like you were visiting heaven.

At that time, Tami and I were both fascinated with metaphysics. My search for answers after Nancy died had pointed me to new age studies. I was dabbling in psychic awareness, which I admit usually resulted in frustration due to the learning curve and my stuck-in-resistance-ego. When I look back, it is not surprising that Tami fell in love with Angels—she had one foot on the other side. It's as if she was reaching up and playing with the Angelic kingdom; maybe they conversed in her dreams, and she knew how to die. First, embrace the other side and display it prominently for all to see. Next, die quietly over seven days so that your friends and family can say good-bye.

Going home for the funeral was a blur; there were so many people from my past, all grieving one incredible woman. Afterward, life changed for me. I had lost a friend, hated God, liked God again, and then lost another friend... I was teetering. Who was this immense Source energy that kept stealing my friends? AND, he/she/it better not mess with my children! I became angry, arrogant and then defeated, pleading, "Please, let this be the end of it, please don't harm my kids." Grief is a hard way to learn. Yet there are experiences only grief can teach us.

Since Nancy's death, I had learned more about psychic ability. I was able to center, sometimes, and focus, sometimes. I meditated with the intention of contacting Tami. I couldn't believe it, she was right there as if she were waiting for me. She felt light, she told me about a 'bubbliness' and 'buoyancy' on the other side. She was joyful and told me about heaven from sheer happiness. Still, I was not mature enough in my spirituality to put aside my grief and ask the right questions. I could tell she was with her beloved Grandmother, and another relative. However, I didn't ask about ascension, or any of the other questions I would ask now. I missed her too much. She was part of my support system here. My abandonment kept asking, "Why did she leave me?"

Tami taught me that I have a capacity that exceeds my human life. She pulled me toward higher dimensions by being in them; I would look for her and find myself at peace. She taught me that life after death is full of joy, that you can love everything. You can love your enemies, your exes, your fears. Tami demonstrated with energy, but not blatantly. She guided, like a true Angel, and drew me into spiritual opening and clearing. It is our choice, you know. We decide when to be born and when to exit. Like a great play, it's down to each act and each actor.

Tami's fall and hospitalization were devastating to her mother. What Soul agreement did they share to have that experience? I have learned to do my best to be in the moment with death, to lean into my emotion and be there while it is available. This is much better than storing emotions for later when they tend to get rigid and challenging. When my heart is open, I can see my dead friends, they are laughing—we are laughing.

I miss Tami greatly; especially her humor. However, having an Angel on your side is incredible, not quite like talking to a friend for two hours, but equally fulfilling. Tami may not be available for a phone call or vacation, but she resides in my heart and our Souls are friends for eternity.

On Memorial Day, I remember these names: My Father (Jim), Grandmothers (Frankie and Barbara), Grandfathers (Winifred, Dan and Larry), Aunts (Linda, Rona, Pauline, Ethel, Kay and Ella), Uncles (Leslie, Grim, Max, Putter, Hadley, Ray and Tony), In-Laws (Shirley, Dick and Jim), Brian, Dennis, Mark, Tralene, Billy, Kenny, Judy, Aaron, Paul, Tami, Nancy, Tisha, Angela, Eric, Meredith, Wally and Rick. People lost to suicide, murder, accidents and natural causes. Regardless of circumstances, when it comes to life or death, we create the opportunity to live and the occasion to die. I do not enjoy loss or grief, but I respect choice.

Again

The year after Tami died, my husband's ex-wife, the mother of my stepsons, succumbed to cancer. She fought a strong battle and denied every doctor's prognosis, lasting two and a half years. She joined my other Angels to watch over us, while I managed the grief of yet another death. This one closer to home.

Tyler and Scott

While working with Sharon she mentioned that her thirty-something son, Tyler, suffered greatly from the loss of his best friend Scott, who had died two years earlier. Tyler and Scott met as teenagers. I heard stories about how much trouble they caused, you know the type; and how much fun they had getting into that trouble! They were brothers from different mothers; what I call true-heart friends. In tribute to their friendship, Scott named his son Skyler, a combination of Scott and Tyler.

When Sharon asked about Tyler during a session, she explained that he suffered from anxiety and felt haunted by Scott's death. I immediately began to see an astral energy, which I assumed was Scott. After telling Sharon what I saw (heard/felt), we decided to share the vision with Tyler. He wanted help and asked for a session. Tyler, who I imagined with tattoos and motorcycles (perhaps he thought of me with heavy eyeliner, shawls and a crystal ball) was actually nearly that, although the motorcycles were four-wheel-drive vehicles; he was not my average client. Beyond his tough exterior, he was a sweet, dear Soul experiencing drama and trauma from the death of his beloved friend. Repeatedly. He needed help.

When I worked with Tyler, after *getting vertical* and creating *sacred space*, my guides verified that he was experiencing visitations by Scott's Spirit. They explained that this it's not unusual. What was strange was that Scott's Spirit came to Tyler repeatedly with the same emotion. Trapped in a repeating cycle; Scott was experiencing his suicide over and over. Each time Scott experienced the moments of his death, he came to Tyler. In emotional distress, he was searching out his best friend for comfort. Tyler reacted with anxiety. How do you abandon a loved one when they come asking for help? This happened quickly and on an emotional level that Tyler did not understand. In order to heal, Tyler had to do what would hurt even more: he had to let go of Scott.

Scott was stuck in the astral field; he did not go into the crossover Light brought to him at his time of death. I learned from my guides that Scott was in a cycle of three stages, pre-death, death and shock. Tyler's cycle, also three-fold, made him feel like he needed to help, followed by pain he could not understand and then apathy. Tyler lived with the feelings of exasperation, hopelessness and fear, while Scott's Spirit repeated a cycle of overwhelming struggles with life, release through suicide and anxiety.

I experienced two intensities during this reading. First came a deep understanding, with detailed perspective and knowledge of how the situation could heal. Following that, I felt something surprising, *all out fear*. It sounded like this: "You don't know what you are doing; you can't possibly know what you are doing; you hear voices; how could this be?" Luckily, I knew enough to identify that I was getting involved emotionally. Not only was my emotional body struggling, I was dealing with Scott, who was in the astral field. The door was open and everyone wanted in! An entity is not beyond using your own self-doubt to influence you. I asked my guides and Angels for help (through prayer), my insecurities became misty, and my vision cleared. I refocused and followed my pure Christ Consciousness Light guides.

Without my guides, I would not do this work. I say this for significant reasons. If you are meant to do this type of work, you will know. It *chooses* you; the work absolutely chooses you. Some might say it is a calling, regardless; the answers that we hold inside of us are unlocked on a level that is outside of our conscious understanding. If it were conscious, this book would read like a car manual. If you are doing anything on an ethereal level, you need an ethereal guide. Please do not take matters into your own hands. If I were to go in and start releasing trapped Souls without a new destination, they would likely get stuck with me. Do you remember reading about that in the clearing chapter? I hope so. It can be captivating, we are all curious about the other side, but having gone through these types of attachments many times, I can say I do not recommend poking around in the astral field.

As my guides showed me Scott's last moments, I shared everything with Tyler. I listened carefully, checking with Tyler often to verify that I was on the right track. We talked about the circumstances of Scott's death, the frustration of his life and the agony of suicide. From Source Light, as directed by my guides, I requested help for Scott to cross over, or make a decision that suited his highest and best good. I asked for Scott's personal Light Beings to assist, only working with Christ Consciousness Light. Thankfully, he went into the Light. If you find yourself in a circumstance like this, you might use words or phrases like these:

How can I be of service to this one?
Please show me how to help this one.

If it is for their highest and best good, please assist this one.

With permission from all involved.

I call forth to Archangel Michael; please help this one find his/her appropriate place.

I call Source Light to send someone that this one recognizes to help him/her find his or her way to the Light, working only with the highest regard.

Please bring Light to help this being.

You can see that each phrase requests something from my guides and/or Source. I did not tell Scott to go to the Light, nor did I recommend anything to him. I asked for the guides, Christ Consciousness Light Beings, to come forth for Scott's highest and best good. Scott may have other plans that I don't know about. Please, don't doubt your ability to alter energy and create issues that may harm you. You can do this; it does happen. People get themselves into spiritual trouble by leading instead of following. We are in service to higher resources, which makes it easy to be conscious channels, and Lightworkers. Our job is to listen and hold the frequency for healing.

After our prayers and requests, Scott went into the Divine Light of Christ Consciousness. Although it had been two years since Scott's death, Tyler began another, more healing, process of grief. When I checked in with Tyler months later, he told me that his anxiety around Scott's death disappeared after our session.

Kelsey

Before Kelsey arrived for a session, I sat in my office with the intention of preparing for our work together. The lights flickered several times; common sense told me that the electricity had surged. However, I sensed a presence and I felt a little spooked. It was before I had set space, and certainly before I had invited anyone from the ethers to visit! I called for guides, truly for every Light Being I could remember, and waited. The presence left, so I continued meditating and preparing for the reading.

Kelsey showed up nervous. I used prayer to create *scared space*, invited our Christ Consciousness guides forth and went to work. I knew that Kelsey's fiancé, Zack, was deceased; she explained that he committed suicide six months earlier. From the beginning of our reading, I felt that something wasn't right. Kelsey was anxious, scattered and ungrounded. Then the lights began to flash again and she said, "He's here, that always happens when he comes." She seemed indifferent, as if she were used to it.

My guides immediately showed me a perforated ethereal field around Kelsey, which was allowing negative energy to enter. The field needed to heal for Kelsey's protection and comfort before we went any further with our reading. I called Archangel Michael and all appropriate Light Beings to assist; asking for them to do what was best for Kelsey. (See *Release Protocol*, Chapter Three.) I watched as Kelsey received healing. Her energy stabilized and the frequency of our session increased. As per her request, I looked for Zack. My first impression was his desperate attempt to communicate. He had thoughts and could not figure out how to speak. His temper was flashing the lights and other electronics.

> *This, I knew from experience, could be costly. My history is full of weird electrical problems, which can be expensive! Electrical conduits and waterways are easy hosts to lost spirits. In their excitement, or anger, the collected energy can 'blow' an electrical appliance. For instance, many years ago I realized what a grounding force my husband is for me when he went out of town for a month-long job. The refrigerator stopped working (reparable) and so did our clothes washer (irreparable); our hot water heater wouldn't heat and light bulbs were burning out all over the house, especially at the front door. The cherry on this dessert was my car breaking down more than an hour from*

> *home, which turned out to be an electrical problem. My energy was not grounding properly. I could feel something was wrong, but had no idea how to stop currents of energy from causing all types of trouble.*
>
> *The easiest way to deal with this type of problem is to stay grounded. My guides say that we are never adequately grounded, they explain that as soon as we stabilize... we ask for more Light.*

Back to Kelsey. I asked Source for help and Zack calmed. The first thing I learned was that Zack's death was an *accidental* suicide. The intent and the tools needed to take one's life, in Zack's case it was drugs mixed with alcohol, were present; but he did not make the conscious decision to take his own life. He was depressed, addicted and reckless. When he lost control, his body did not survive and he died by his own actions. His energy eased when we spoke of this, but not enough. He was greatly agitated about something else. I asked questions. That was when I learned that Kelsey was pregnant when Zack passed and the stress of his death had led to a miscarriage. Zack needed to communicate his sorrow and grieve with Kelsey.

As I relayed messages from Zack, upset, shame, grief and sorrow released to the Light for transmutation. It is not in my full understanding how these heal, only that when Light shines upon the truth, people begin to restore. After communicating with Zack, Kelsey began a new journey. She was finally able to begin a grieving period that led to healing, instead of more frustration. Zack moved into a position of Light, where he could begin his journey and assist Kelsey from the other side.

Kelsey had a full recovery from grief and stress. Eventually, she met a man and began co-recreating a new life. She has thanked me over the years since that session. In my line of work, clearing energy is like teaching little birds to fly. They go on with their lives, busy with wonderful new experiences. When someone remembers and feels gratitude, it is powerful. Kelsey's gratitude was a reminder that I do this work for a reason, a good reason.

James and his Family

I should have known that dead people were trying to contact me in my early twenties when my sister's boyfriend, Brian, died in an auto accident. Afterward, I saw him everywhere. I would see him at the grocery store, chase after him, only to see someone completely different. Now, I know that the subliminal mind can super-impose a face upon someone. We simply identify the frequency/signature of someone and 'see' him or her. If we are not paying careful attention, the brain slips into receiving information from the subconscious and merges it with what the eyes see. Perhaps Brian knew that I had the psychic ability to see him and was visiting me. I don't know. It happened many times, for years. Unfortunately, back then I had no idea I was clairvoyant.

Tall and handsome, James came for a session when he was twenty-four. I had worked with both his mother, Shelly, and brother, Thomas. I do not know what they told James, but he came reluctantly to my lair which was full of shrunken skulls, bones and dead animal debris. I had him sit next to my caldron, smoking full of frogs and beetle legs. Sounds inviting, yes? Actually, at the time I worked in a cute little office behind a metaphysical store in Fort Collins, Colorado. We sat for a reading in comfy chairs and I lit a white candle. Low drama, I know.

Even with my apparent normalness, James seemed nervous and slightly suspicious. People often are in the beginning; even booking a reading can cause a surge of energy. It's as if one signs on the dotted line, "I agree to work with Source. Signed: John Doe." That is why I was amazed when I set *sacred space* and took a peak at James' energy. He had an incredible amount of Light around him! On behalf of the guides, I spoke of his potential. It was astonishing, seeming to be so much more that his spiritual mother and brother; in fact, I thought he was nearly the brightest human I had ever seen. I tape recorded the session, or I at least *I tried.* (Cassette tapes, if you can imagine.) After talking for some time, I peeked at the recorder and it was off. No! All these wonderful words describing his beautiful Light were not recorded. But alas, this happens every so often and I try to trust that Source guides me and maybe there doesn't need to be a recording. I kept talking and taping as of that moment. One thing I remember clearly is that there was something indescribable all around us; something great and glorious and beautiful. The guides told James, "You will surprise everyone, especially your mother and Thomas, you are going to do something in great service to the Light and it will truly amaze them."

The Light that shone from James' being was bright because it was closer to the Divine than anyone I had ever read energy for. I had never seen anything so magnanimous. It was incredible, even a bit exhilarating. After the session, I felt elated, touched by this wondrous radiance.

How could I have known that his ultimate service would be surrender? James died a few months later in a car accident. He was twenty-four years young, and loved by so many. With her spiritual foundation already in place, Shelly was able to feel and occasionally hear James from the other side. Over the next year, I donated my time to the family as they grieved. I gave them messages from James, which helped me understand more about my gifts while Shelly's abilities to be in contact grew stronger. James taught me more about the other side and for that, I am so grateful. One of the most important gifts James gave, was preparing me for Angela.

Angela

To honor the privacy of Angela's family, names, places and details in this story are changed.

Occasionally, clients bring their (adult) children to see me, and that was how I met Angela. Her mother, Madison, gifted her an appointment. Angela arrived glowing. She radiated natural beauty; her eyes an astonishing blue, the kind you look into and are reminded that these are the windows of the Soul. She had such bright Light around her and, had I been a bit more experienced, I might have guessed what that meant. She passed away several months later.

Angela was not fortunate; she did not die quickly or easily. Why didn't I recognize that Light around her? Why didn't I warn her? What was that Light? Was it a piece of heaven; an Angelic presence? A foot on the other side? I didn't know, then. But I remember relaying that her potential was immense, exactly what I told James.

Angela was kidnapped, brutalized and murdered; like James, she was 24-years-old. During the time she was missing, I organized a worldwide Lightworkers network for prayers and psychic help. We had chain of command for all psychic information and I was the funnel tip. I did this for her Madison and family. My part was hard work physically and emotionally, but spiritually it was treacherous. My experience did not provide me any education concerning this type of energy. One of my most valued teachers was out of the country and could not be contacted; I dove into the situation with a flimsy light/life jacket and I swam with the energy sharks.

I organized a local meditation group comprised of Lightworkers who knew each other and Angela's mother, Madison. Our intention was to send support and Light to Angela, her family and all those searching. By this time, we knew that a man driving a brown SUV had abducted Angela. Although it was our intention to work through the Divine Light of the I Am Presence, it was nearly impossible to avoid involvement with the highly negative energy (one might say evil) around the perpetrator. We asked that mercy be blessed upon him, for Light to heal him, and that he release her.

Our full focus was to work with Divine Light, to ask Creator to do the work. However, it was as if we were yelling at our neighbors about rabid dogs. The dogs knew that we knew; we could not hide. I tell you this for a specific reason: it is never safe to engage with an energy strong enough to create horrific crime. If you look, it will know and it will use the connection created by that one simple contact. Unfortunately, we did just that. We opened to something so negative and so dark that I was sick to my stomach. However, there was a chance Angela was alive and we held strongly to our goals. After the meditation, we focused on releasing any energy connection we had to the kidnapper and asked for connection to his High-Self through the I Am Presence, not via the entity-laden, compromised human.

The man released Angela that night, only not the way we intended. The same evening that we met for meditation and prayer, Angela left her physical body permanently. Much to my disappointment, after three days of searching, law enforcement officers found evidence of Angela's death. The worst had happened.

Angela's murder would not be confirmed for three more days. Meanwhile, our meditation group worked to disconnect from the perpetrator's energy; it was unwieldy, aggressive and invasive. We all hoped to help find our dear friend's daughter, regrettably connecting to an energy that opened a door to the fourth dimension or astral field, leaving us open to various types of interference. Take heed; only use your guides for eyes and ears on the other side, stay in your *pillar of Light*. The repercussions can be debilitating; I have learned this the hard way. We are curious beings. After doing a clearing *my* way, instead of in service and by following instructions from my guides, I have suffered mental, emotional and physical anguish and ailments. Knowing this, I explained to each person at our meditation group: do not look! Use your guides and Angels, listen and request. However, the negative connection still happened.

We were Madison's friends and we formed an alliance. We prayed and we held Madison energetically; when she came home, we held her physically. At Angela's memorial service, we sat behind Madison and her husband, a group of eleven.

After all that happened, my words can scarcely convey the event and its impact. When the energy settled somewhat, I meditated and saw a bright, content Spirit; it was Angela. Angela visited often and I watched her go through the phases of death. I donated sessions to Madison for one year, during which I was able to see Angela in her glory, free of pain, harm and fear. Although her absence is felt, so is her presence. The dark shadows that plagued Angela's mind before her death do not live in her memory, they were transmuted. Madison and her family hold strong to the radiant Light that I was privileged to see, because they feel it, too. They serve Angela's memory by living and remembering her as the beautiful, loving young woman that she was. God/Goddess bless all who have lost a child and remain to remember.

I wrote the following for Madison, Angela and myself. Remember, these are writings for a moment in time, please alter them to suit your needs and desires. The first is an exercise.

Protocol Exercise – When Someone Is Lost or In Harm's Way

Use Vertical Alignment Prayer (ground and connect), Prayer for Setting Sacred Space, Prayer for Protection and Release Protocol. State that you intend to be in service, even if you have already proclaimed this via prayer; it is imperative for your safety. Ask your question and/or set your intention. (i.e.: I am in Divine Service, is there a way to find _______?)

Wait. Your request will be fulfilled to the appropriate degree, as decided by the Divine. Once a dispatch is made, you must create time and space to receive your answer.

Utilize fairies, Angels, Ascended Masters and Earth creatures to help you. Make a clarion call to them. (i.e.: I call to the Angels, please send help for this situation. Please help release pain, give me clear thinking and please help ______. Thank you and Amen.)

Maintain patience. (This is not easy.) Divine Order is at hand. Ask for understanding, peace and calming.

Through your guides, call to the High-Self of the person you seek to help, ask for permission to work with him/her via an Oversoul (Soul to Soul) connection. Ask all guides to help him/her to recognize any manipulation. (Please keep in mind, there may be no manipulation; a situation, no matter how painful, may be karmic.)

Again, wait.

Journal everything –clues can be overlooked.

Consider that you many have the wrong agenda. Know that you may be led somewhere for reasons you do not understand, remain in service and surrender. There may be higher outworkings, something Soul related.

Remember, all things in Divine Service.

Close with Release Protocol, Prayer for Protection and Closing Prayer. It is essential that you do not connect with any energy concerning this situation unless you are in sacred space.

As you can imagine, Angela's death was extremely difficult for her family and friends. Family distress is not only hard for those left behind, but for the deceased as well. *Transition Prayer* offers a bit of tenderness for those crossed over and their beloveds. Angela is used in place of someone's name, please adjust according to your situation.

Transition Prayer

In me, there is a guide, one aware of journeys. I invoke that guide now.

Father, Mother, God, Goddess, Creator, Source of All That Is, safely show my beloved Angela the Light of Transition. Help her know that I am fine.

My heart aches with loss; my mind is reckless with fear, yet I know she is only taking her place among Angels. I will hold her memory, hear her laugh and remember her Light. As I heal, I am comforted in two ways. One, she is with God. Two, she was with me.

My privilege and honor to know Angela will be exemplified by my graceful healing. I am able to feel her always. Through God's grace, she never leaves my heart.

My memory may fade, my body weaken, but my heart will never release the love I have for Angela.

With God, she is. With God, I Am. We are never apart, eternally connected through the Divine Oneness that we are.

Thank you and Amen.

After loss, grieving can manifest in many ways. When one of my clients has a death in the immediate family, I usually offer my services as a gift. (After I check in with my guides for appropriateness.) Much of this gift is simply holding space for unconditional love and listening. Loss is like an eraser, it makes us feel like we are empty. If you get vertical and set *sacred space*, you can feel love from Creator and even from the deceased. It's a matter of frequency and showing up to receive.

I encourage grief counseling. We feel supported when people that have similar issues speak about them. It takes courage to talk about grief, especially in front of others. However, getting grief help is often difficult. Motivation vanishes; we tend to wallow. Grief can turn a person inside out; one can start living backwards, feeling before seeing. If one 'feels' the deceased psychically, sometimes they can become stuck in that area of consciousness, attempting to follow their love. This can lead to loneliness, anxiety and confusion. When someone dies, remember they go through transition. Locating them does not mean they will be in that place the next time contact is made. As in all Lightwork, ask your guides to locate your beloved, or someone you wish to speak with on behalf of a client.

Mourning prayer is for Madison, for those long days of sadness following death. There are blanks for someone's name.

Mourning

Beloved, I miss you. Your body gone, your Spirit alive. I hold on to this physical expression, the one you choose as _______. I revel in your memories. I listen to stories; I stare at pictures; I miss you.

I miss myself. The way I was with you. How I felt, what we said, when we touched.

Once more if I could caress your cheek, touch your hand, hear your voice. Would not I give anything?

Beloved, my heart aches today, yet I heal. I only offer these words to inform all, I intend to heal. You would not want me to cry, so I see. I watch a blooming world continue. I watch myself continue.

You would not want my guilt. Therefore, I honor your chosen path, your release, your choice. I extend forgiveness to all. To all.

God's will is helping me heal. I am healing. Oh, how I miss you, oh how I heal.

My beloved, my transitional one.

Thank you and Amen.

Many therapists and writers encourage people to journal their thoughts and emotions. I am a big proponent of writing out your anger, *but not sending it*. I like to type, as an exercise to release on paper or through a keyboard. Afterward, I work with my guides to remove what came from my ego. This usually means that seven or eight pages become a paragraph. I have also taken the writing and made a clearing list. A list for me, not others.

Once, I saw my friend Cindy cry for someone. Cindy held a suffering friend and said, "I feel like you need to cry and you can't." The person nodded, and Cindy cried real tears to help her release emotion. I wrote *Grief* for the same reason, it is a release or purging of misery. How can someone write or cry enough to release when they have lost a beloved?

Grief

I swim through grief like thick mucus. It slows me, clogs me, fogs me. I am unable to get anywhere. My thoughts are incomplete and hang in the air as if birds stuck in flight.

In the moments when the mucus clears and the bird thoughts fly, I complete tasks, eat, organize and then I am, out of nowhere, under an avalanche of guilt. Why am I alive when you, my beloved, are gone?

My nerves are like old guitar strings, no longer pliant. I snap easily and do not care why. I see love in the world, hands help, smiles exchanged. I hear people laughing.

What are they so happy about? I have aching places that have no name.

How am I bonded to you? And why have you left me? Why is every face yours, every moment yours? I am lost in a sea of memories. One that will empty eventually as I forget.

Then I will sit in a forsaken hole of vacant dirt, fertile with potential I can't imagine. I am alone without you, devastated with grief.

Grief is dirty and gritty and painful. It bucks and yells and screams, then it lies dormant until you forget then rises again. Sometimes we need words of comfort, other times we need understanding and silence. My dead people, Tami, Nancy and the others, have taught me that we don't truly recover from loss. We continue to hurt and regret. But as life goes on, we grow and we love again; and as we love, our capacity to hold grief increases. While human death and pain remain with us, we become larger.

Death isn't smaller. We, the incarnate Souls of Earth, are infinite. When we experience death, we have the opportunity to learn a bit more about our expansion.

From Dust to Dust

Do you have an opinion on cremation or burial? I like cremation because it seems more permanent. If I am done with my vehicle, I am done with it. However, some prefer burial. Before Cameron's father, Bob, passed, he requested a Catholic funeral and burial. When I offered my services after he died unexpectedly, Cameron asked me to 'clear' the burial plot. That was a new one! After many homes, businesses and old buildings, I had yet to clear a burial plot. It was the first time I thought of clearing land at a cemetery, it sounded interesting but dangerous. Have you walked in a cemetery lately? Imagine a playground for ethereal energy, much of it fourth dimensional. Nevertheless, I wanted to help Cameron.

I prepared to do the work by setting intentions and *sacred space*, then proceeded to ask my guides for the land to be cleared, but I was stopped. My guides told me: *"No words or actions will move out what belongs there. Rather than clearing, you may entrust a blessing of safe travel and passage. The human heart yearns for its lost love, desires healing for loneliness, and requests support. Clear the way for memories and laughter."*

I became aware that Cameron wanted a safe place for her father to rest; however, the message from my guides reminded me that we could trust the Divine for that. I wanted to please and help a grieving friend; but once again I was reminded to surrender my ideas and trust.

The following, *Prayer for Finding the Arms of God*, came for Cameron.

Prayer for Finding the Arms of God

Father, Mother, God, Goddess, Creator, Source of All That Is, today we entrust the body of _______ to Earth. Please assist us by providing a safe place for this body here on Earth. Please bless this gravesite with peace and loving reflection upon a life well lived.

Please help _______ on his/her journey to the Light. Please assist his/her family and friends as they release the body of _______ and embrace the memories, love and happiness he/she has left them.

As God sends Angels of Mercy, we pray _______ accepts them and sees his/her family's own Angels so that he/she may embrace the beacon of Light sent to him/her. God, please help _______ remember his/her oneness, his/her true origin. As he/she releases, we request a line of communication for all who desire.

The Light is ever present and awaits us all.

Thank you and Amen.

The Truth

I wrote, and you read, an entire chapter on human death and its effect on us. Us, the humans, brothers and sisters of incarnation. But it's not a true story, it is fiction.

During the grief and pain of death and loss is not a good time to study esoteric conjecture, or what one person believes is truth. If you are there now, skip this part. Otherwise, open yourself to the truest form of alignment. Use all these prayers and your connection to Creator to expand your *pillar of Light*. Try a meditation, or whatever you can to raise your frequency to the highest level possible. Then take in the experience. Witness it. After all of our grounding and connecting, the only thing you'll ever find is that Creator, Source and The Light is within you. It's all inside. We aren't separate, we are not lonely aspects of human bodies sent here to suffer. Every time you reach God/Goddess/Source, the energy will come back to you. You are the embodiment of it.

So when people leave, they are not really leaving you. They are changing into their next version of themselves. And we, the mourners and grievers, change into new versions of ourselves. Only now, we have beloveds in pure Light. We have more guides to help us. Another ethereal to make this incarnation easier.

We are emanations of the Divine Light of Creator. We come from, and exist as, no less than Christ Consciousness Light. We are not wounded; we are not victims and we are not lost. We are one with every beloved being, living or otherwise. In the kingdom of Heaven, the fifth dimension, we reunite in mind and Spirit with our Soul family.

I wish that I could say that living without my loved ones is easy because we are all one and will unite again, but I cannot. I have chosen a third-dimensional feeling and emotional life. I made that choice, and for all those who feel as much as I do, I wrote about our illusion of death.

Chapter Eleven

Can I truly live this?

After years of learning how to release and clear; after education, experience and healing, I have learned one thing that has never shifted: end with gratitude. Pile your complaints to the ceiling, have a fit, break glass, pound a pillow with your fists; then sit down and write a list of things for which you are grateful. Gratitude is a tricky little friend. Don't forget it. If you fall and scrape you knee, that's a good thing to complain about. Afterward, be grateful you didn't break your leg or scrape both knees. Make your gratitude longer, clearer, wider, grander, louder and better than your complaint. And please, by all means, complain. Don't squeeze anger into your little human body. Let your fear and resentment flow out, and then use gratitude to neutralize all the energy you purged.

Gratitude is easily expressed. Thank you, thanks, a physical nod or even a wink. These prayers offer a formal approach to giving thanks. They also open the door so that we can consciously take responsibility for creating the ability to receive. When you offer gratitude, it is like blowing a wish, or the brush of a butterfly's wing—our Universe answers everything. So watch as you open the door to giving thanks and receiving through Divine Light.

We are a polite society, but sometimes we do get so busy that we forget to act grateful. And every so often, we thank out of habit therefore forgetting to embody the essence of gratitude. Not to worry, in gratitude there is hindsight. If you find yourself feeling gratitude for a gift from the past try asking Source to bless the person you want to thank with *Prayer for Gratitude.*

We have so much for which to be grateful. *Prayer for Gratitude* uses the example of a gift, but you may think of other circumstances to be thankful for, like sun, rain, family, friends, smiles, apples, memories, vision, awareness, honor, integrity, paper, pens, books, etc.!

Prayer for Gratitude

Father, Mother, God, Goddess, Creator, Source of All That Is, I am so grateful for this gift! I whole-heartedly receive this amazing present. Please bless the giver with the highest frequencies of Love, Light and appreciation on my behalf. I am so grateful for this example of abundance in my life. I am so grateful for the giver, her/his inspiration and action. Through this blessing, I acknowledge my part in this creation. Therefore, as we create together we receive together. As we receive together, we give together.

Thank you and Amen.

As you remember to stay vertical, ask for cords to be cut and then send blessings everywhere, add one more thing to your toolbox (*SRB*). *Try not to 'send' anyone anything.* What? No offerings of love and peace and good luck? No. This may sound strange, consider the idea that everything you think of is exactly that, what you *thought*. Even a heartfelt thought is still a thought. What if someone is having an illness to learn something and you use your super power prayer to heal them? You could interrupt their Divine Experience! That is why I am following my guide's advice and *asking Source* to bless each of you with bountiful blessings and buckets of joy! I send you, *through the Divine Light of God/Goddess, Creator Source of All That Is*, my gratitude for participating in this journey. We aren't bulletproof, yet. This book isn't perfect. In fact, it's full of contradictions and challenges; but, that's okay. Together, we learn and open and expand. We explore, evolve and become. You and I, creating in separate bodies, but ultimately, as One. For participating, for making your way, for your personal evolution I say, thank you. Thank you. Thank you and Amen.

Thanks Giving

Divinely guided voice within, I am listening. Open to me and for me. Show me how to speak truth from my heart. Show me how to expand the Oneness that I Am and how to stay in balance with my surroundings.

My life, my service—they are Divine, an example of true Oneness. I am not a random result of coupling. I have not grown in question. I am not a lie.

I have choice. I am allowing. I am voice! My life is an education; I am an example. I am loved and I love. I am grateful.

My Light shines from within, because my Divine Source exists within. Beyond all time, all measure, I am Light. Never have I been separate.

My gratitude expands now. My love brought me here for this experience. My doubt brought education. My loneliness brought love. My questions, answers. My pain, healing. I am so grateful.

Each time, I learn I am young, born again as a spark of yearning, a craving, a hunger to become part of something glorious.

I speak now. I listen now. I give and receive now. I am open. I am a vessel for original love, and I am grateful. I am so very grateful.

Thanks giving. Gratitude in the giving. I have given up my former existence to be here, now. I changed myself to be here now. Yet, I am one with my previous. I am one with my future. I am one with my parallel. I am one with you.

Peace abounds in my heart and I send it out. Let the wind carry it like a seed today to be shared and, if possible, rooted.

If I am responsible for love, peace, forgiveness or Light, I am grateful. If my seed roots, grows and finds its way back to me, I am grateful.

We are not different, you and I. We are one. Thank you for your example, your teaching, your love.

I am grateful. I am grateful. I am grateful. Amen.

Acknowledgements

Thank you for reading this book. I am in great appreciation of you, the energy you put forth in Lightwork and the love you represent. I ask that each reader be blessed through the Divine Light of the I Am Presence. I ask for blessings of peace, ease and comfort for you and those you hold sacred. I ask for love and light to bless each being involved in the creation of this book. Thank you and Amen.

After completing an early draft manuscript for *Divine Accordance*, I asked ten friends for their feedback. I call them *friendly editors*. They are friends who are not professional editors (except one), but review and edit when you ask nicely. It was perhaps a daring move on my part, asking friends to read a poorly written first draft. But I needed help. I wanted opinions from people that I trusted. Unbeknownst to me, I needed to ground energy to make this book real. You may reason that choosing friends to edit is not the best idea, and I admit there were times that I worried. But who better to make sure my book was speaking for me, and ultimately, for my beautiful team of guides and Light Beings?

I begin my gratitude with Cindy Fox. Cindy is a close friend and consistent influence on my spiritual education. Cindy taught me to meditate properly, to ground and to listen to my guides when I thought education was elsewhere. Her honesty and integrity are exceptional. I trust her implicitly in spiritual matters. Her input on my writing is important to me and I was relieved when her feedback was positive. Cindy has continuously been a level-headed influence and encouraging voice for my evolution and growth. Thank you, Cyd, for being there, for saving me when I thought I was too crazy to be here and for being the Divine Light that you are.

Michelle LeJeune is a published author and a professional editor. We have been friends since 1990, scouring over each other's writings through the years. She told me that she could not return the manuscript without talking to me. Oh, a talking-to, I could hardly wait! I trusted Michelle to give me the no-holds-barred editorial truth. I was not surprised that she was appalled by my grammar and unusual capitalizations. I didn't mind when she said that my sentence structure was confusing and nearly impossible to follow. After picking up the book, then putting it down a few times, Michelle told me she was able to finish all (then) nine chapters full of content in which she had no interest whatsoever. She told me that the beginning was weak, which it was, and that she didn't get most of it. (Did I mention Michelle is not familiar with the metaphysical world?) However, she felt changes in her life (I smile), positive changes (I smile again). When I realized that *Divine Accordance* affected Michelle, I knew that the prayers within were potent and they work whether you believe or not. You can credit Michelle for correct grammar and proper usage of the colon. I would like to thank her for being a writing and editing influence for many years but, above all, my friend.

One significant influence in the development of *Divine Accordance* is Becky Robbins. As a client she is meticulous; Becky has a remarkable ability to interpret spiritual messages. She listens intently then works diligently to understand and utilize guidance. I attribute some of this to her years with the Tony Robbins Organization, but predominately to her beautiful heart and expansive points of view. She has called me many times after working together to thank me when a particular message expands into a realization or epiphany. Through her gratitude, I have been able to learn more from my own channelings. When she explains what she heard, I actually receive the message again from another perspective. It has been my great pleasure and honor to work with Becky, and to call her my friend. She is remarkably clear and concise when it comes to energy, bringing my attention to the exact frequency needed, furthering my points of reference. Becky has bought many copies of the *Pocket Prayer Book: Excerpts from Divine Accordance* for friends and family, each time declaring, "It's not enough, I want more!" Thank you, Becky, for your belief in me and my work and for years of treasured friendship.

My least effective friendly editor was Bobby Burger. I am afraid my husband is too much of a fan to critically review my work, for which I am grateful. He did read the entire manuscript (I spied on him), but his input was only complimentary. Thank you Bobby; you have put up with all types of nonsense during my psychic opening and writing. In addition, you have listened to a stream of unsolicited spiritual suggestions for your own personal development. (Yes, I see that I may need to work on that.) Bobby, I love you dearly and treasure you as a true supporter of my life's work and primary grounding engineer.

Alli Brook was my student for many years, blessing me with so many lessons that I have a hard time thinking of myself as her teacher. More accurately, I would say we traveled a road of learning together. Her questions were like bait, fishing in the great sea of ethereal wisdom. What a blessing it is to meet someone like Alli; she has an exceptional mind. She is a wonderful, heart-centered, genuine person who is a healer in her own right. Experiencing this book as it was written, her on-going editorial help was integral in the forming of the bones of this book. What is a body without a spine? I value Alli as a friend, virtual assistant and Lightworker. She is a main ingredient in my life, a gift and blessing.

Another dear friend, Sharon Owings, wrote, "This gift should be on everybody's bedside table for reference on a daily/nightly basis!" When I read her input, I had to decide something. Does my faith in Sharon reign, or will my insecurities prevail? I trust

Sharon; she is extremely well-read. Her metaphysical knowledge expands from Buckminster Fuller to Ramtha and beyond. I find I am able to discuss anything with Sharon; her extensive study of new age topics has helped me many times in my search for information. She is a radiant and beautiful person whom I treasure. Her faith in this book motivated me to hold the vision of a finished, published book filled with love and light. Thank you, Sharon, for your friendship and insight.

I gave a copy of the manuscript to Barbara Vaelli, ND, LAc. She is my friend, something that is evident by the fact she wrote "gorgeous" on the first page. Barb pointed out that the wording in my original introduction "sounded like the readers are doing you a favor instead of vice versa". That hit home. I was reminded: Bloated ego and inverted ego are polarities. They work against us and the only way to find balance is to stay away from both. Don't over sell, don't doubt. Because of Barb's faith, I dragged a fine-tooth inverted-ego comb through the entire manuscript. I am grateful for her friendship and that reminder. I needed to bridge the channeled information, but not with my insecurities.

My astrological sign is Sagittarius; when I was born the sun was in Sagittarius and the moon in Aquarius. What does that mean? I don't know exactly, but my friend and astrologer Carola Eastwood does. Carola reminded me that I had not mentioned how "one's life can be affected by connectivity with Source—connectivity without guides." Wow, how could I have omitted that? In my work I have seen many positive changes in people after spiritual clearings and healings, why didn't I offer examples? For instance, released addictions. I have found that addictions block many of our desires from coming to fruition; and that those addictions can be rooted in the subconscious mind. My guides have helped many people expand into healed relationships, new careers, release of past fears and Soul healing. I had mentioned none of that.

After clearing negative energy I have been privileged to witness my clients create new lives without pain and suffering. Space clearing helps homes sell or rent, insomnia, arguing and strange pet activity. I have seen energy clearing help women heal from abortion and fertility issues. My work assists Soul healing, entity release, exorcism and more. Precious hearts have healed in my presence. I've witnessed Souls enter, re-enter, exit, heal and merge. People have walked away restored, relieved, joyful, confident, and united with themselves in a new way. Clairvoyance has presented me with colors, symbols, visions. I have seen indescribable Lightwork, chakra alignments, healings and integrations, and heard voices of ancient wisdom cross lifetimes to speak. Carola reminded me that this work is not simple; it only seems that way when it is done. Thank you, Carola, for reminding me to look back once in a while and to understand the impact of Lightwork.

Diana Saunders offered her wisdom, which I trust inherently. She is a licensed counselor, life coach, dream interpreter and special friend. Over the years, Diana has helped me tremendously. When I began doing sessions, I couldn't believe a woman like her—refined, beautiful, educated, tall, would come to someone like me—inexperienced, working in a barn/art studio, self-doubting, short. Not only did she come back time and time again, but she recommended me to her colleagues, friends, family and clients. This influenced my business dramatically. I was able to get experience, which helped me gain confidence in the unique work of channeling. Diana and I have discussed many spiritual concepts, books, authors and types of healings. She helped me see myself in a new way. I credit Diana with much of the confidence I have in my work, the prayers and this writing. I am deeply grateful for her wisdom and exemplification of spiritual living.

One friend, Lesly Black, didn't return the manuscript. Lessy was around in the beginning, when I met Rick and Cindy, and her influence does not escape these pages. She offered something special to me that I can hardly explain. During this writing Les began a new life journey and became busy with travel and love. A new love, later in life after death and loss. The unreturned manuscript isn't important. What is crucial is when someone becomes part of your foundation. When they witness inexplicable energy releases and hold you until you can stand alone. Lessy, like Cindy, saved me. She sat or listened or corrected. She kept me on track when my life was scrambled. Thank you, Lessy, my heart to yours. My love, gratitude and appreciation will have to echo in heaven to be enough to thank Lesly Black and Cindy Fox for their service to me and to humanity.

Lastly, I would like to express one more heartfelt thanks and I hope this one echoes in heaven as well: thank you, Rick Lewis. My God/Goddess. We battled, cried, healed and learned. What a roller coaster. Thanks for everything. May the Divine Light of Our Creator/Source of All That Is bless you eternally.

Each of my *friendly editors* is a precious, appreciated and highly valued gift. My heart fills when I reflect on the time and energy it takes to read a manuscript, correct spelling errors, restyle sentences, figure out flow and offer general opinions without wounding the good intentioned, soft-hearted, eager and sensitive author. They each worked in their own particular way, proving to be essential in the creation of this book, and I am extremely grateful; every one of you is truly a Divine Gift.

Endnotes

[1] Anne LaMott, *Bird by Bird: Some Instructions on Writing and Life*, Pantheon Books, 1994.

[2] Vianna Stibel, *ThetaHealing*, Hay House, 2011. You might run across *Go Up and Seek God* or *Go Up and Work with God*, Stibel's original books on ThetaHealing, self-published.

[3] *Medicine Cards: The Discovery of Power Through the Ways of Animals*, Jamie Sams & David Carson, Bear & Company Publishing, 1988.

[4] Author, speaker and beautiful Lightworker, check out Patricia Cota-Robles and her many books at: www.eraofpeace.org.

[5] Emily Post (1872-1960) is an incredible American author known for her writing on etiquette. Great quote: "Manners are a sensitive awareness of the feelings of others. If you have that awareness, you have good manners, no matter what fork you use."

[6] One of my absolute favorites; a spiritual bible: *Animal-Speak: The Spiritual & Magical Powers of Creatures Great & Small* by Ted Andrews; Llewellyn Publications, September 2002

[7] Crazy long title, excellent book: *Animal Spirit Guides: An Easy-to-Use Handbook for Identifying and Understanding Your Power Animals and Animal Spirit Helpers*; Steven Farmer, Hay House 2006.

[8] An oldie, but goodie. Excellent words on nurturing and loving your inner artist. *The Artist's Way*, Julia Cameron, Tarcher, 1992.

[9] Amazing and comprehensive collection of mineral qualities. (Does not include pictures.) *Love is in the Earth: A Kaleidoscope of Crystals*; Earth Love Publishing House, 1995.

[10] Groundbreaker of its time: *Out on a Limb* by Shirley MacLaine; Bantam, November 1986.

[11] If you aren't familiar with this term, Grasshopper, check out *Kung Fu*, a television series from the 1970's. Warner Bros. Television.

[12] *Archangels & Ascended Masters* by Doreen Virtue; Hay House, 2004. A great reference for every clair-person working with ethereals.

[13] Excellent informational resource: *The Light Shall Set You Free* by Dr. Norma Milanovich & Dr. Shirley McCune; Athena Publishing, 1996.

[14] *Relativity: The Special and General Theory*, 1920. Albert Einstein (1879–1955).

[15] Words from the American theologian Reinhold Niebuhr, 1892-1971. Adopted and made famous by Alcoholics Anonymous and other twelve-step programs.

[16] *The Grapevine*, The International Journal of Alcoholics Anonymous, January 1950.

[17] Must haves by Louise Hay: *You Can Heal Your Life* (1984) & *Heal Your Body* (1984), Hay House.

[18] See endnote #3.

[19] RIP, Rick. He died April, 2012. Thanks for everything, Rick, I am sorry I never got to tell you.

[20] The crazy soap opera my mom watches, she calls them her "stories", *Days of Our Lives* ©NBC Universal Media, LLC.

[21] *Eat, Pray, Love: One Woman's Search for Everything Across Italy, India and Indonesia* by Elizabeth Gilbert, Viking 2006.

[22] *Terms of Endearment*, tearjerker movie with Shirley MacLaine (love her!), Paramount Pictures, 1983.

[23] *Gone With the Wind*, nice long, dramatic, tear-jerker, Selznick International Pictures & Metro-Goldwyn-Mayer, 1939.

[24] Sonia Choquette is a forerunner in spiritual practices and author of *Trust Your Vibes: Secret Tools for Six Sensory Living*, Hay House, 2005.

[25] *Power vs. Force: The Hidden Determinants of Human Behavior* by David R. Hawkins, Veritas Publishing, 1995.

[26] Hanna Kroeger (1915-1998) was a German herbalist that lived and taught in Boulder, Colorado. If you can find it, *The Pendulum Book*, self-published 1973, is a gem.

[27] Chetan Parkyn, author of one of my favorite books, *Human Design: Discover the Person You Were Born to Be*; Harper Collins-UK 2009, New World Library-USA 2010.

[28] Jekyll/Hyde refers to dramatic changing of personality. Made famous by Robert Louis Stevenson (1850-1894) in his book, *Strange Case of Dr. Jekyll and Mr. Hyde*, 1886.

[2929] Lao Tzu, usually credited for this quote, is the founder of Taoism and the author of *Tao Te Ching*, perfect for anyone on a spiritual path.

[30] Jessie Ayani writes incredible books about Light. *The Lineage of the Codes of Light*, Heart of the Sun, 1998. Also recommended, *Brotherhood of the Magi*, Heart of the Sun, 2002.

94090549R00159

Made in the USA
Columbia, SC
22 April 2018